Deena

Thanks for

Your support a

encouragement.

Also by the Author

So You Think You Can Teach: A Guide for the New College Professor in Teaching Adult Learners

DIVERSITY MANAGERS:
ANGELS OF MERCY
or
BARBARIANS AT THE GATE

An Evidence-Based Assessment of the Relationship between
Diversity Management and Organizational Effectiveness

Dr. Shelton J. Goode

iUniverse LLC
Bloomington

DIVERSITY MANAGERS: ANGELS OF MERCY OR BARBARIANS AT THE GATE
AN EVIDENCE-BASED ASSESSMENT OF THE RELATIONSHIP BETWEEN DIVERSITY MANAGEMENT AND ORGANIZATIONAL EFFECTIVENESS

iUniverse books may be ordered through booksellers or by contacting:

iUniverse LLC
1663 Liberty Drive
Bloomington, IN 47403
www.iuniverse.com
1-800-Authors (1-800-288-4677)

Because of the dynamic nature of the Internet, any web addresses or links contained in this book may have changed since publication and may no longer be valid. The views expressed in this work are solely those of the author and do not necessarily reflect the views of the publisher, and the publisher hereby disclaims any responsibility for them.

Any people depicted in stock imagery provided by Thinkstock are models, and such images are being used for illustrative purposes only.
Certain stock imagery © Thinkstock.

ISBN: 978-1-4917-2091-2 (sc)
ISBN: 978-1-4917-2090-5 (hc)
ISBN: 978-1-4917-2089-9 (e)

Library of Congress Control Number: 2014900594

Printed in the United States of America.

iUniverse rev. date: 01/27/2014

Praise for *Diversity Management: Angels of Mercy or Barbarians at the Gate*

In *Diversity Managers: Angels of Mercy or Barbarians at the Gate,* Shelton Goode provides a comprehensive and authoritative examination of the relevant research, theoretical arguments, and current best practices in diversity management. The book provides diversity practitioners with proven methods for developing diversity-management strategies and discusses the classic mistakes made when implementing conventional diversity-management initiatives.

—Steve Olson, PhD, director of Center for Ethics and Corporate Responsibility, J. Mack Robinson School of Business, Georgia State University

Dr. Shelton Goode has written a thoughtful and scholarly book. *Diversity Managers: Angels of Mercy or Barbarians at the Gate* critically examines the potential benefits of conventional and contemporary diversity-management initiatives and identifies practical applications for business leaders attempting to effectively manage diverse work teams and create inclusive work environments.

—Richard Smith, managing partner of Benton&Bradford Consulting, LLC

Dr. Shelton Goode knows from firsthand experience what to do and what not to do in executing diversity management as a strategy. In *Diversity Managers: Angels of Mercy or Barbarians at the Gate*, he provides a comprehensive and authoritative examination of the relevant research, theoretical arguments, and current best practices in diversity management. More importantly, he adds his unique insights and shares his practical experience from working in the field. This book provides diversity professionals with proven methods for advancing diversity management as a strategy and avoiding the classic mistakes made when implementing diversity initiatives.

—Jim Rodgers, CMC, FIMC, The Diversity Coach,
author of *Managing Differently: Getting 100%*
from 100% of Your People 100% of the Time

Dr. Goode has pulled together findings from several disciplines and presents the best research available on diversity management in an effort to examine the impact of diversity management on organizational performance. *Diversity Managers: Angels of Mercy or Barbarians at the Gate* emphasizes the necessity for research-based diversity-management initiatives that contribute to the strategic goals of the organization.

—Dr. Felix Verdigets, PhD, advisory senior manager of KPMG

Diversity Managers: Angels of Mercy or Barbarians at the Gate helps both business leaders and diversity practitioners come to grips with diversity management by helping them understand varied perspectives in a scholarly manner that is both contemporary and insightful.

—Pauline Streete, diversity leader of SASK Power

Dr. Goode uses an array of research and theoretical frameworks to help readers understand some of diversity management's challenges. Although a departure from the more traditional and functional perspectives on diversity, *Diversity Managers: Angels of Mercy or Barbarians at the Gate* is beneficial to both business leaders and diversity practitioners who are struggling to link diversity management to the bottom line.

—Jill Green, director of human resources of Darden Restaurants

Diversity Managers: Angels of Mercy or Barbarians at the Gate provides diversity practitioners and business leaders valuable insights that will help them pinpoint diversity strengths and opportunities in their organizations. Dr. Goode's work provides us keen insights into actions that will further our organizations' goals by leveraging diversity management.

—Tippi Hall, director and regional diversity
manager of The Boeing Company

To

JR and Marcus,
my sons,

for their lives in a better world

and

Dr. R. Roosevelt Thomas Jr.,

who is widely considered as the founder of the field
of diversity management. The thought leadership he
provided launched the careers of an entire generation of
diversity-management practitioners, including mine.

CONTENTS

FOREWORD

J. R. Hipple, president of the Albright Group

I have read many books and papers on diversity and have been part of many discussions on the subject as the founder and president of the Albright Group, a reputation-management company. However, *Diversity Managers: Angels of Mercy or Barbarians at the Gate* is the first book that I have read that makes sense to me as a business leader trying to leverage diversity to enhance business success. Job number one for a CEO is to serve as spokesperson in chief, as the behavior and tone from the top set expectations for employees and tell customers what they should expect from the company. This book is an invaluable resource for business leaders like myself.

As the title suggests, Dr. Goode seeks to spark and refresh the dialogue on diversity management. His book asks us to consider two decades of research and provides a conceptual framework for organizations that are embarking on or renewing their diversity efforts. He chronicles the empirical research on diversity management and shares his views on the potential performance benefits and problems of implementing diversity management initiatives. Dr. Goode's aim is to provide diversity practitioners and scholars alike with a road map for designing and implementing diversity-management initiatives based on research instead of rhetoric.

Diversity Managers: Angels of Mercy or Barbarians at the Gate examines diversity-management initiatives that have become popular among organizations despite the absence of hard evidence that they enhance organizational performance. Organizations have often implemented these initiatives to defend themselves in court, inoculate themselves against liability, improve employee engagement, increase market share, increase workforce diversity, or enhance brand and organizational image. In the final analysis, however, the measure of these initiatives should be whether they do anything to improve organizational performance.

After examining twenty years of diversity-management literature, Dr. Goode discovered that there is a rich tradition of diversity-management theory and research; however, he contends that this work may not always hold clear implications for organizational performance. Broadly speaking, his research suggests that although the underrepresentation and social isolation of nonwhites and females still exist in organizations, the best hope for addressing these organizational issues may lie in assigning organizational responsibility for change to the chief diversity officer. Dr. Goode bases his theory on classical organizational behavior rather than social justice. His research found that organizations that embed diversity-management accountability and authority with the CDO are the most effective in increasing the number and percentage of nonwhites and females. Moreover, these organizations achieved increases even when faced with intense competition for top talent. Dr. Goode also found that the presence of an energetic CDO catalyzes other diversity-management initiatives, rendering each initiative a bit more effective.

Dr. Goode is practical in suggesting that some diversity-management initiatives also prove more effective among publicly traded companies and government organizations, likely because legal requirements encourage these organizations to assign responsibility for oversight. Diversity-management initiatives that target employee beliefs and behavior, such as diversity training, show virtually no effect in the aggregate on long-term measurable and sustainable organizational performance. They show modest positive effects when linked with senior-management compensation. But they sometimes show negative effects otherwise. Dr. Goode found evidence in the research that suggests interactive diversity-training workshops often generate backlash among white employees.

I was personally enlightened by the fact that diversity-management initiatives designed to counter the social isolation of women and nonwhites, such as mentoring, affinity groups, and employee network groups, actually work. Dr. Goode's research found mentoring to be particularly effective in increasing the engagement level and subsequent performance of women. The modest performance of diversity-management initiatives that address the social-psychological and social-relational dynamics of organizational performance should not be taken as evidence that these forces always produce measurable results. While the preponderance of empirical research shows that employee networks are correlated to organizational performance, more research is needed to determine exactly how and why these diversity-management initiatives live up to their promise.

Dr. Goode challenges the speculation that the best diversity training is designed to shape the values and behaviors of managers. He argues that this belief is rooted in some mystical approach to diversity that is not supported by research or practice. In fact, when it comes to diversity training, Dr. Goode finds that the strategies designed to change the hearts and minds of individuals are less effective than the conventional solution of providing managers with leadership development and holding them accountable for applying these skills to achieve business results.

Dr. Goode found that the three most effective diversity-management initiatives operate in somewhat different ways. For example, whereas an enlightened and competent CDO exercises authority over and accountability for diversity-management strategy, employee resource groups involve employees at the front line of the organization, taking part in diversity efforts that will result in long-term sustainable and measurable results for the organization.

Diversity Managers: Angels of Mercy or Barbarians at the Gate is a book business leaders can understand! Diversity practitioners will also discover what initiatives help advance diversity and successfully shape a culture of inclusion in organizations. I found information and recommendations that I can personally use. I intend to also share them with my colleagues and clients.

PREFACE

For over twenty-five years, diversity-management practitioners have espoused the business case for diversity, which asserts the view that a more diverse workforce will increase organizational performance. Diversity management is defined as "an intentional process designed to create and maintain a positive work environment where the similarities and differences of individuals are valued, so that all can reach their potential and maximize their contributions to an organization's strategic goals and objectives" (Thomas, 1991, p. 46). Dr. R. Roosevelt Thomas Jr., widely considered the founder of the field of diversity management, suggests in his seminal book *Beyond Race and Gender: Unleashing the Power of Your Total Workforce by Managing Diversity* (1991), that a high-performance organization relies on a dynamic workforce with the requisite talents, multidisciplinary knowledge, and contemporary skills to help the organization achieve its organizational goals. Moreover, he asserts that such organizations must foster a work environment in which people are enabled and motivated to contribute to the organization's success and must provide both accountability and fairness for all employees. Other diversity-management scholars (O'Reilly, Caldwell, & Barnett, 1989; O'Reilly, Williams, & Barsade, 1997; Pelled, 1996; Pelled, Eisenhardt, & Xin, 1999; Avery & Thomas, 2004) echo Dr. Thomas and assert that in order to accomplish business goals, organizations must have a disciplined approach like diversity management in order to draw on the talents of employees at all levels and from all backgrounds.

Diversity practitioners were asked to what extent their organization's diversity practices accomplished desired objectives, and more than half (52 percent) reported that their organizations' diversity-management practices had created a work environment or culture that allowed employees to contribute to the organization's long-term sustainable success. In addition, they cited their organizations' diversity-management efforts for helping to increase nonwhite and female representation, enhancing the ability of people from different backgrounds to work effectively together, leveraging differences and similarities in the workforce for the strategic advantage of the organization, eliminating or minimizing managers' personal biases, and capitalizing on differences and similarities among customers and markets for the long-term benefit of the organization (Lasch-Quinne, 2001; Thiederman, 2003; Delong, 2004; Bacharach, Bamberger & Vashdi, 2005).

Realizing that they lacked clear evidence to support this view even within their own organizations, a number of business leaders called for empirical research to assess the connection between diversity management and organizational performance. Previous diversity-management research focused primarily on the impact of diversity management on certain employee groups (Dwyer, Richard, & Shepherd, 1998; O'Reilly, Caldwell, & Barnett, 1989; O'Reilly, Williams, & Barsade, 1997; Pelled, 1996; Pelled, Eisenhardt, & Xin, 1999; Thomas, 1993; Tsui, Egan, & O'Reilly, 1992; Tsui & O'Reilly, 1989).

Diversity Managers: Angels of Mercy or Barbarians at the Gate departs from previous research because it examines the impact of diversity management on performance at the organization level. Until now, this linkage has not been empirically investigated because most organizations were not collecting the data needed to assess the effects of their diversity-management practices on organizational performance. *Diversity Managers: Angels of Mercy or Barbarians at the Gate* addresses this gap in the literature by providing an analytical foundation and theoretical framework for understanding whether diversity management within the proper organizational context relates positively or negatively to organizational performance.

Moreover, *Diversity Manager: Angels of Mercy or Barbarians at the Gate* examines the previous research of the influence of diversity-management initiatives and provides diversity practitioners and business leaders alike with a road map for designing and implementing diversity-management initiatives that achieve results.

The book examines over a hundred studies published between 1990 and 2010 in an effort to answer the following questions:

1. Which diversity-management initiatives have researchers studied in the last twenty years?
2. What has been learned about impacts of specific diversity-management efforts?
3. What has been learned about the role of organizational culture in shaping the effects of diversity-management initiatives?
4. What practical implications, if any, does the research provide for diversity practitioners and business leaders as they address the multilevel complexities inherent in strategic diversity management?

To answer these questions, the strength and weakness of the business case supporting each diversity-management initiative is discussed in detail in each chapter of the book. The theory and rationale of each initiative is also closely examined. Lastly, in each chapter the empirical research supporting or challenging each diversity-management initiative is reviewed, and practical applications are offered based on the evidence or lack thereof.

Chapter one discusses the evolution of the field diversity management starting with equal employment opportunity and concluding with diversity management. In a number of ways, this chapter provides a baseline or foundation for understanding organizational efforts to manage diversity. Additional insight into the chronology of organizational performance is provided through further analysis of carefully selected studies designed to describe the development of diversity management and the extent to which organizations have approached the issue of diversity. Two additional important findings emerged from this chronology. First, research shows that some organizations have simply repackaged their traditional equal employment opportunity and affirmative action programs. These organizations have not, it would seem, fully embraced the broader concept of diversity management as reflected in the literature. Second, some organizations do not address some of the most basic and traditional dimensions of diversity such as race, ethnicity or gender. This raises a number of fundamental and intriguing questions about the content and purpose of diversity management programs within those organizations

Chapter two covers the business case for diversity management which includes the overall concept and approaches to diversity management, including the articulation of the proposed value of diversity management, the requirements of managing diversity management, and how diversity management is related to the culture of organizations.

Chapter three examines the heated debate taking place between those diversity researchers who think organizations should be more diverse because it is the right thing to do and those who think organizations should be more diverse because it actually enhances shareholder value. This chapter analyzes the empirical research to determine if there is a solid business case for diversity management as a bottom line organizational strategy. Based on the research, the chapter answers the question whether there is a positive and significant relationship between diversity management and long-term organizational performance.

Chapter four provides a model for evaluating the relationship between specific diversity management efforts and organizational performance outcomes. This chapter presents a model of the impact of diversity initiatives on organizational performance based on the research. The model identifies barriers that may inhibit the employment, development, retention, and promotion of non-whites and females in the workplace and suggests other significant factors that may influence diversity initiatives. It identifies the primary reasons and desired outcomes for managing diversity: improve productivity, remain competitive, form better work relationships among employees, enhance social responsibility, and to address legal concerns. This chapter presents a model as well as the best strategies for managing diversity. It also discusses components of an effective diversity management strategy.

Chapter five covers representation. It describes how organizations attempt to increase female and non-white representation. It also gauges the efficacy of such efforts and the degree to which these efforts support selection, retention and advancement of talent.

Chapter six covers affinity groups, employee resource groups and business resource groups. It describes the efforts of organizations to engage and invest in their employees. It explores the way employee networks are organized and evaluates whether the organization benefits from the efforts of these networks. Lastly, it gauges the programs and benefits provided to resource groups to meet the specific needs and concerns of their members.

Chapter seven covers diversity management training and education. It explores how organizations conduct diversity management awareness education and skill-building training, and the integration of such training into the overall training and development of employees in their organizations. The chapter takes a close look at the extent to which diversity management training are provided equitably to enable all to enhance both employees individual performance and organizational performance.

Chapter eight discusses recruitment, development, and advancement. It describes how organizations attempt to ensure diversity in their hiring and selection processes, and whether these efforts help create an organizational culture that increases diversity and enhances performance excellence.

Chapter nine explores diversity management strategy implementation. It covers the way that organizations structure or organize the diversity management function so that that it effectively executes the organizations diversity management goals. The role of the Chief Diversity Officer is specifically examined to look at the way they measure diversity management initiatives and whether they use research to support diversity management strategies.

Chapter ten discusses leadership and accountability. It covers the responsibilities of the organizations' leadership in shaping, guiding and leveraging diversity management. It also covers accountability methods for the CEO and other senior leaders in organizations.

Chapter eleven covers supplier diversity. It surveys the process organizations use to select, contract, and interact with the organization's small vendors and disadvantaged suppliers in a manner that supports and enhances economic inclusion along the supply chain. It gauges organizations' recognition of the diversity of its potential supplier base and its sensitivity to the nuances of languages and strategies used to attract and recruit prospective vendors.

Chapter twelve summarizes the research on several of the most widely used diversity management initiatives and whether there is any link to organizational performance.

Chapter thirteen concludes the book by discussing the challenges ahead for the field of diversity management. It assesses the current state of diversity management in organizations, describes realistic short-term and long-term goals, and challenges diversity practioners to set and stretch standards in order to achieve the desired state for the field of diversity management.

Diversity Managers: Angels of Mercy or Barbarians at the Gate is important to the field of diversity management for a number of reasons. First, it is vital to diversity practitioners because it scientifically investigates the link between diversity management and organizational performance by conducting an in-depth exploration of the empirical research that studied whether diversity management contributes to the success of organizations. Kochan, 2003; Barrick et.al. 1998) suggests that a book like *Diversity Managers: Angels of Mercy or Barbarians at the Gate* is needed to help diversity practitioners better understand the link between diversity management and organizational performance. This book answers that challenge by providing diversity practitioners and business leaders alike with a diversity GPS that will help them pinpoint areas that may be strengths and opportunities in their organizations. Chief diversity officers, in particular, will gain insights into actions needed to further their organizations' diversity strategy.

Secondly, this book examines some of the conventional wisdom on diversity management as it has changed over time. The book candidly points out the outdated paradigms and misguided diversity-management initiatives that have often prevented organizations from capitalizing upon the rich diversity embedded in their workforces. Diversity scholars will find the book valuable given their increasing interest in whether organizations have been able to maximize their workforce diversity and tap the strength of their people to achieve better business results.

Diversity Managers: Angels of Mercy or Barbarians at the Gate provides practical solutions to contemporary diversity issues. Based on a comprehensive and critical examination of the previous empirical research, the book points out that any organization's attempt at diversity management must begin and end with the company's top leadership because essentially, adoption of diversity management involves organizational cultural change. This type of change is most effective when it occurs from the top down, starting with the chief executive officer (CEO), who serves as a role model and helps integrate organizational values into the fabric of the culture. Leadership sets the tone for diversity management and helps create an organization that is more attuned to its employees, more aligned with its customers, and more competitive in its market. Moreover, CEOs should incorporate employees' perspectives into diversity-management strategy, which may include rethinking primary tasks, redefining markets, and reengineering business practices.

The book's most important contribution to the field of diversity management is that it distinguishes effective diversity-management initiatives from those that have failed. As a result, diversity-management practitioners can judge where their past initiatives have yielded success and what future efforts demand new approaches. Business leaders will also benefit from reading *Diversity Managers: Angels of Mercy or Barbarians at the Gate* because it will help them recognize the ways in which the workplace is changing, evolving, and diversifying. As a result, business leaders will discover where their efforts can help advance diversity management and what actions other business leaders have taken to successfully shape diversity-management efforts in their organizations. Leaders at all levels in the organization will find recommendations that they can personally use or offer to colleagues and fellow managers.

Since diversity management remains a significant challenge, business leaders must learn the skills needed in a multicultural work environment. They must be prepared to teach themselves and others within their organizations to value multicultural differences both inside and outside of the organization. Based on the empirical research, *Diversity Managers: Angels of Mercy or Barbarians at the Gate* suggests the need for business leaders to challenge diversity-management professionals to move beyond the business-case argument for advancing the field of diversity management and to develop and implement initiatives that unleash the potential of diversity to increase organizational performance.

ACKNOWLEDGMENTS

From the length of these acknowledgments, it may read more like an academy award acceptance speech than a simple thank you. I know my editor is rolling her eyes because she is always counseling me to be brief. But it is important that I thank the many people who helped me bring this vision to reality. Whether it was emotional support, interviews, editorial help, research, or supplying the thousands of pieces of information that make a book like this possible, I could not have accomplished it without the people listed here.

While the responsibility for the final product is clearly my own, I am indebted to numerous scholars and diversity-management practitioners for their helpful comments and critical suggestions on various aspects of the book. The journey to this final product has been informed mainly by the empirical research presented here, along with emerging leaders on the practical implementation of diversity-management initiatives. Because so much of the material for this book is rooted in previously published research, I owe a great deal of thanks to scholars such as Chris Argyris, Thomas Cox, Lee Gardenswartz, Katherine Naff, Chris Metzler, and Roosevelt Thomas Jr., to name just a few.

There would be no book, of course, if not for those diversity practitioners who were generous and brave enough to share with me their views on the current and future state of the diversity-management field. This kind of candor and courage is a lot to ask. Their practical insights helped me write chapters 9 and 13. In no particular order, these include the following contributors: Trevor Wilson, Richard Smith, Pamela Arnold, Jim Rogers, Deborah Williams, Bob Davis, Al Vivian, and Tippi Hall. A special thanks goes out to Frank McCloskey, who inspired me to write this book and offered important insights and encouragement.

I presented an earlier version of the *Diversity Management— Organizational Effectiveness Model* to several of my fellow diversity-management practitioners on the Conference Board's Diversity and Inclusion Leadership Council. Their critique and feedback helped shape my methodological approach.

As an adjunct professor at Troy University, I have had the privilege of interacting with some of the brightest and most energetic students I have encountered in my twenty years of teaching. They forced me to rethink several ideas, and they constantly challenged my basic assumptions about diversity management.

I am especially indebted to many of my friends and colleagues that I have had the privilege of working with, such as Dr. Conrado Marion-Landais, Cherryl Harris, Karen Ashley, Jeanie Vickers, Maureen Darcey, Moanica Caston, Ave Bowman, Michelle Dean, Robin Gerald, Barbara Nedoff, Dr. Gerald Durley, Frank Belati, William Stanley, Janice Mathis, Bertram Sears, Maritza Soto-Keen, Lindsey Vincent, Chris McCray, and Pollie Massey. Over the years, these individuals have helped me hone my ideas and improve my research on diversity management. Thanks to Paula Frederick, general counsel to the Georgia State Bar, who nominated me for the Georgia State Ethics Investigative Panel. While serving on the panel, I had the opportunity to explore more deeply the dynamic relationship of ethics and diversity management. A special thanks to Dr. Steve Olson, the director for the Center for Ethics and Corporate Social Responsibility at Georgia State University, whose vision to develop a new generation of ethical leaders constantly inspires me.

Every author needs practical help in addition to inspiration and encouragement. I am blessed to have had so many friends and colleagues who graciously donated many hours of their time to help with this project. Betty Bell deserves special mention for her meticulous reading of the manuscript and critical feedback throughout the preparation of the final draft. The final stages of permissions, copyediting, and meeting the publisher's deadlines would have been impossible without her help. A special shout-out goes to Anne Barcelona, who was my critical liaison with the publisher during the hectic process of finalizing the book for publication. I would also like to thank J. R. Hipple and Dr. Felix Verdigets for their critical comments on sections of this book and on related research work. I especially would like to thank two of my former graduate students, Keith Gray and Philce Gray, for helping me gather research and conduct interviews.

Many thanks to Denise Bennefield at iUniverse for her guidance and professional expertise. I was thrilled to work with Denise, who called on her considerable humor, warmth, and expertise to guide me through the often stressful and confusing process of publishing my second book. Special appreciation goes to Eddie Right, another member of the iUniverse publishing team, whose expert and sensitive advice clearly enhanced both the readability and value of the book.

Finally, I would like to thank my family: Shelton J. Goode III and Marcus A. Goode, my sons, who are my pride and my joy, and to whom this book is dedicated; my sisters Arvalee Wallace and Cecilia Goode; my brother Maurice Goode; my brother from another mother Ralph Armor, and nieces and nephews Arlene Williams, Mike "Blade" Wallace, Theodore "Man" Wallace, Angelia Charles, Maurice "MJ" Goode Jr., Markida Brown, and Alexis Goode.

CHAPTER 1

THE EVOLUTION OF DIVERSITY MANAGEMENT

In a number of ways, this chapter work provides a baseline or foundation for understanding organizational efforts to manage diversity. Additional insight into the chronology of organizational is provided through further analysis of carefully selected studies designed to describe the development of diversity management and the extent to which organizations have approached the issue of diversity. Two additional important findings emerged from this chronology. First, research shows that some organizations have simply repackaged their traditional equal employment opportunity and affirmative action programs. These organizations have not, it would seem, fully embraced the broader concept of diversity management as reflected in the literature. Second, some organizations do not address some of the most basic and traditional dimensions of diversity such as race, ethnicity or gender. This raises a number of fundamental and intriguing questions about the content and purpose of diversity management programs within those organizations.

Equal-Employment Opportunity

Following the days of segregation, workplaces were faced with a new business challenge—albeit one that was viewed not so much as a challenge, but rather a mandate—of complying with the proliferation of legislation and regulations that required organizations to increase racial and gender variation in order to meet federal equal-employment opportunity requirements. The first legislation of its kind in the early 1960s, Title VII of the Civil Rights Act of 1964, was landmark legislation that made it illegal for employers with more than fifteen employees to discriminate in hiring, termination, promotion, compensation, job training, or any other term or condition of employment based on race, color, religion, sex, or national origin. Since then, Title VII has been supplemented with legislation prohibiting pregnancy, age, and disability discrimination and sexual harassment. The Equal Employment Opportunity Commission (EEOC) is charged with enforcing Title VII.

In 1961, President John F. Kennedy signed Executive Order 10925 into law, thereby setting affirmative-action policies in motion. In the beginning, affirmative action was considered a positive weapon to combat racial discrimination. The language of the order stated that it was the "policy of the United States to encourage by affirmative action the elimination of discrimination" (Katznelson, 2005, p. 145).

In 1965, President Lyndon B. Johnson signed Executive Order 11246, which went one step further. The order prohibited federal contractors and federally assisted construction contractors and subcontractors that did more than $10,000 in government business in one year from discriminating in employment decisions on the basis of race, color, religion, sex, or national origin. Contractors were also required to "take affirmative action to ensure that applicants are employed and that employees are treated during employment without regard to their race, color, religion, sex, or national origin" (Katznelson, 2005, p. 145). Affirmative-action programs required employers to set goals to increase the utilization of underrepresented groups to achieve parity based on their labor-force availability. The Department of Labor's Office of Federal Contract Compliance Programs (OFCCP) was charged with enforcement of Executive Order 11246.

Because the legislation focused on "protected class" employees (i.e., discrimination was illegal based on race, ethnicity, sex, or religion initially; protection for other groups, such as people with disabilities, came later), nonmembers of these groups often resented their exclusion and believed that affirmative action led to the hiring of unqualified candidates and to preferential treatment for the targeted groups.

Affirmative-action policies were enacted during the Kennedy and Johnson administrations, but they grew under President Richard M. Nixon. Employers and educators were required to take race into account in order to redress the disparate treatment and impact against people in protected classes. Organizations were held liable for discrimination if their policies and procedures effectively excluded people in protected classes or diminished their opportunity—even if that was not the intent of the policy or procedure. This effectively shifted the burden of proof of discrimination from the employee to the organization.

Affirmative action has been deemed the single most important factor accounting for the growth and sustainment of the African American middle class (Katznelson, 2005; Patterson, 1997). A public policy, it has proven to be one of the most effective tools to advance the nation's commitment to the ideals of equality and fairness. Yet despite all of the gains in access and equality for racial minorities and women attributed to affirmative action, the policies have been challenged politically and legally. Consequently, affirmative action has reached an impasse and has come under increasing scrutiny. Efforts to circumscribe affirmative action began in the late 1970s and gained the support of President Ronald W. Reagan when he was elected in 1980. During his administration, Reagan appointed Cabinet members—and Supreme Court Justice Clarence Thomas, an African American man—who were opponents of affirmative action (Goode & Baldwin, 2005; Barry & Bateman, 1996).

One of the reasons affirmative action has come under scrutiny is because of its focus on race. The focus on women's gains through affirmative action has been all but eliminated from the current discussion on the policies. Instead, the discussion has been on racial preferences and benefits for African Americans and on the supposed reverse discrimination against whites. Ironically, women—particularly white women—have joined the ranks of those wanting to dismantle affirmative-action policies. Several scholars (Wise, 1997; Beckhard, 1969) argue that white women perceive that affirmative action prevents their husbands and sons from getting jobs.

Another reason for the opposition mounting against affirmative action is a belief by opponents that race-based considerations run counter to the ideal of color-blind equality. Consequently, most nonwhites believe they have experienced a backlash due to affirmative action, including having their qualifications questioned. African American men have failed to enjoy the same protections under Title VII and affirmative-action policies as African American women (Lacy, 2008; Beynon, 1973). Some believe that African American men have benefited the least from affirmative action.

Initially, affirmative action enabled African American men to gain roles in corporations that had been off-limits to them or roles that were created to focus on affirmative action or racial issues (Collins, 1997; Boje & Winsor, 1993). However, those racialized roles created dead-end jobs for many African American men as affirmative-action policies were scaled back. After the early 1970s, companies attempting to conform more expediently to affirmative-action goals began increasing their hiring of African American women because of the ability to double-count women (Lacy, 2008; Boyce, 1995). Lacy argues that this practice demonstrates that overlapping race and gender categories reduces African American women's attributes to commodities and virtually eliminates the affirmative-action consideration accorded African Americans. According to Lacy, African American men do not benefit in employment from privilege by gender; rather, they are totally separated from white men when blackness, a traditionally disenfranchised category, is combined with maleness, normally considered a privileged one.

Stewart (2007) also addresses the need for race and gender considerations in hiring, but extends that same consideration in examining the hiring of African American men. Stewart argues that companies with entrenched racism must go further than proclaiming they are equal-opportunity employers. Rather, their affirmative-action plans must include a race-plus-gender (e.g., African American males) provision.

In the late 1970s, the Supreme Court, in *Regents of the University of California v. Bakke,* held in a closely divided decision that race could be one of the factors considered in choosing a diverse student body in university-admissions decisions. The court also held, however, that the use of quotas in such affirmative-action programs was not permissible; thus, the University of California Davis Medical School had, by maintaining a 16 percent nonwhite quota, discriminated against Allan Bakke.

Glass Ceiling

The glass ceiling remains a pervasive fixture in the corporate workplace. While some acknowledge that women and nonwhites have begun to break the so-called glass ceiling (Hill & Fox 1973;Cobbs & Turnock, 2003, p. 215), others agree that the ceiling may be higher on the ladder to power than it once was (Rosenkranz, 2007; Cao, Clarke & Lahaney, 2003). Evidence that the ceiling continues to exist in corporate America is well-represented in the literature (Barrett, 2000; Palmer, 2005; Phelps & Constantine, 2001). Johnson-Bailey and Tisdell (1998) found the ceiling still has different meanings for different groups. Bell and Nkomo (2001) used the metaphor of a *concrete wall* to distinguish between the organizational experiences of white and African American women managers, finding African American women experience a concrete wall—a structure that is not only more difficult to penetrate, but one that cuts them off from the mainstream of organizational life and makes them invisible to decision makers on the other side.

African American men have a similar characterization of the glass ceiling. They call the barrier to upward mobility a *brick wall*. In a 1995 report by the Federal Glass Ceiling Commission, African American male executives voiced a concern that the rise and acceptance of other nonwhites had created a stalemate in their career development. They noted that their talents, education, and experience were devalued in corporate America, and they feared they were on the losing side of a zero-sum game, where the progress of one nonwhite group was achieved at the expense of another nonwhite group.

A 1997 US Department of Labor report acknowledged that the glass ceiling did appear to be lower for nonwhites than it was for women. This conclusion may support earlier contentions that race is a determining factor of inequity in the United States, but that when race and gender are at play in employment hiring and promotion, the ceiling seems to be lower for nonwhite men than it is for women (Ladson-Billings & Tate, 2006; Charmaz, 2000).

Diversity Management

The Hudson Institute has often been credited with sending a wake-up call to employers across the country by documenting the increasing diversity of the American labor force. In their report *Workforce 2000*, the institute warned that existing HR policies and practices that were developed when the workforce was hugely young, white, and male would become ineffective as the workforce became increasingly older, less white, and composed of more women (Johnston & Packer, 1997; Chatman & O'Reilly, 2004). To recruit and retain needed employees in such a diverse labor market, Johnston and Packer argued that it would be necessary for organizations to take intentional actions to ensure that their work environments were open to people from varied backgrounds. Eventually, significant literature emerged urging employers to adopt diversity-management strategies that would allow them to achieve that end and warning them of dire consequences if they did not.

The Hudson Institute study also predicted that in addition to an aging workforce and greater racial diversification in the labor market, rapid technological change and globalization would require diverse skills and education that would forever change the employment landscape. The Hudson report introduced a paradigm that shifted the discussion from how to comply with legal mandates to how to assimilate large numbers of women and nonwhites into existing homogeneous, mostly white organizational cultures. The assimilation approach, which focused on promoting equal opportunity, sought to increase conformity to the dominant homogeneous culture's ways of thinking and behaving.

Nonwhite employees resented and even challenged the notion that they were neither recognized nor appreciated for their individual differences. They rejected the melting-pot view that emerged in the early 1980s because it minimized unique individual differences rather than appreciating them. As a result, the term *diversity* was introduced into mainstream business language and management literature. Initially, many organizations defined diversity according to legally protected attributes such as race, gender, and age. As the concept evolved, organizations began to use a much broader definition, which included the entire spectrum of human differences.

One of the earliest contributors to the literature on diversity management was Roosevelt Thomas Jr., who argued that as the labor force became increasingly diverse, it would be necessary to move "from affirmative action to affirming diversity" (Thomas, 1990, p. 112). Dr. Thomas suggested that the goal should be to promote productivity within organizations by enhancing the ability of all employees to achieve as much as their potential would allow and to do it without artificial programs, standards, or barriers. Moreover, Thomas described diversity as being not just about race, ethnicity, and gender. Rather, it included other ways in which people differed from one another, including age, background, education, work role, and personality. Other advocates for diversity management who followed

Thomas also attempted to distance themselves from traditional equal-employment opportunity and affirmative-action programs.

Affirmative action, in particular, is a controversial concept, with vocal opponents who argue that it violates a deeply ingrained American value that advancement should be based solely on merit. As a result, a number of organizations have gone to great lengths to make explicit the distinction between equal-employment opportunity, affirmative action, and diversity management. This may be attributed to the transitional years when the corporate world had already begun to experience difficulty in achieving its affirmative-action goals.

While recruiting underrepresented groups posed a significant challenge, retaining women and nonwhites was (and continues to be) an even greater problem. Because of the revolving-door syndrome, significantly higher voluntary and involuntary attrition among women and nonwhites was a common phenomenon. Concerned about this disparity, companies began to conduct interviews with women and nonwhites still on the payroll to develop better retention strategies. Early efforts, which centered on achieving a numerically representative workforce with respect to race, gender, and ethnicity, most likely contributed to diversity management being seen as synonymous with affirmative action. These perceptions also resulted in the Civil Rights milestones being seen as the origin of diversity and efforts to achieve representation being referred to as diversity management. As expected, race-relations training and other efforts were also seen as diversity management. Overlapping aspirations and work efforts created confusion and blurred the distinction between the different approaches.

Diversity management as a business strategy attempts to embrace and leverage all employee differences to benefit the organization. As a result, managing all workers well has become the focus of many corporate diversity-management initiatives. Figure 1 shows the stages that diversity management has gone through as the field has evolved over the years. It also illustrates how diversity management as a strategy differs from policies and programs such as equal-employment opportunity and affirmative action.

Equal-employment opportunity ensures that employment decisions (e.g., hiring, promotion, pay) are made without regard to legally protected attributes such as an employee's race, color, religion, sex, or national origin. Affirmative-action programs, on the other hand, seek to remedy past discrimination and prevent current or future discrimination by taking proactive steps based on race or gender. Both focus on legally protected attributes, but diversity management aims to broaden the scope beyond legally protected attributes to include a much larger and wider pool of individual differences. Some scholars were concerned that as organizations moved toward diversity management, they would place less emphasis on affirmative-action programs, which opened corporate doors for nonwhites and females in the 1990s (Hansen, 2003). Whether these previous concerns have become a current reality is the subject of ongoing debate.

Figure 1. Stages of Diversity Management

Stage 1	Stage 2	Stage 3
Organization's efforts are isolated and disjointed and are not integrated into organization's business strategy.	Organization's policies, processes, procedures, and practices are designed to be more supportive of workforce diversity.	Organization's system, culture, and values recognize employee differences as an asset.
Organization's efforts are implemented in response to a threat, crisis, or incident.	Organization's culture still highly influenced by majority group.	Organization's racial, ethnic, and gender composition reflects organization's customers and communities.
Organization expects employees to assimilate to the majority group's culture.	Employees are asked to help increase organization's reputation with customers and communities.	Organization makes intentional efforts to eliminate barriers to inclusion.
	Organization's initiatives are formalized and institutionalized.	Organization's diversity management efforts are linked to core business goals.

Diversity management is a relatively young field that is barely over twenty-five years old. It is considered a field of study or inquiry rather than a discipline such as leadership or management. Although there are numerous perspectives regarding the definition, intent, approach, and expected outcomes from diversity management, the field of diversity management has at its foundation a set of fundamental principles that serve as a foundation for a system of beliefs, behaviors, and/or reasoning for diversity professionals. Diversity practitioners translate these principles into actions on a daily basis by deciding how to respond to organizational changes, determining how success is measured, and selecting diversity-management execution strategies. Moreover, these principles inform diversity practitioners' work and guide development of their organizations' diversity-management initiatives.

Diversity-management initiatives come in a variety of forms and can include some or all of the activities that are crucial to changing the composition of the workforce, including efforts to recruit, retain, and develop employees, particularly those from underrepresented groups. Diversity-management initiatives also may include efforts to promote diversity through developing external relationships with underrepresented groups outside the organization, including nonwhite and female customers, communities, and suppliers.

Organizational performance efforts to communicate the rationale for diversity programs and to recognize and reward successes in achieving and maintaining diversity can constitute additional components. The training component is by far the most common diversity-management initiative and may consist of efforts to increase awareness of discrimination and prejudice and to improve behavioral skills of employees. Finally, a crucial component of a diversity-management strategy can be the creation of internal departments or organizations to manage organizational diversity-management strategy and initiatives.

CHAPTER 2

THE BUSINESS CASE FOR DIVERSITY MANAGEMENT

This chapter covers the business case for diversity management which includes the overall concept and approaches to diversity management, including the articulation of the proposed value of diversity management, the requirements of managing diversity management, and how diversity management is related to the culture of organizations.

Value Proposition

The field of diversity management is still evolving. While a significant number of organizations continue to focus diversity efforts on compliance and representation, an increasing number of organizations are focusing on the business case for diversity and on creating work environments where employees are valued, respected, and engaged.

The business case for diversity management as a business imperative is gaining recognition by leaders in the business world. For example, a survey of four hundred executives regarding their opinion about diversity management found that 80 percent agree that diversity-management initiatives help with managing and leveraging a diverse workforce that will contribute to organizational performance and competitiveness.

Diversity practitioners (Cox 1991b; Cox 1995; Karp, 2002; Hubbard, 2003; Iwata, 2004) argue that diversity management is beneficial to both employees and employers. Although employees are interdependent in the workplace, respecting individual differences can increase productivity. Diversity in the workforce can also reduce lawsuits and increase marketing opportunities, recruitment, creativity, and business image. In an era when flexibility and creativity are keys to competitiveness, diversity management is seen as critical for an organization's success.

Desired Outcomes

One of the primary goals of diversity management is to leverage the full potential of the entire workforce as a competitive advantage to achieve strategic goals and objectives. Other goals of diversity management are to:

- *enhance competitiveness.* Diversity practitioners (Cui & Choudhury, 2002) suggest that an organization's success and competitiveness depend upon its ability to embrace diversity and realize the benefits. When organizations actively assess their handling of workplace diversity issues and develop and implement diversity plans, multiple benefits are reported (Roberson, Kulik, & Pepper, 2004).
- *increase adaptability.* Experts in the field of diversity assert that organizations employing a diverse workforce can supply a greater variety of solutions to problems in service, sourcing, and allocating resources. Moreover, they assert that employees from diverse backgrounds bring individual talents and experiences in suggesting ideas that are flexible

in adapting to fluctuating markets and customer demands (Jayne & Diboye, 2004; Digh, 1997; Digh, 1999).

- *broaden product and service range.* Diversity managers suggest that a diverse collection of skills and experiences (e.g., languages, cultural understanding) allows a company to provide service to customers on a global basis more efficiently and effectively. A number of chief diversity officers suggest that companies that encourage workplace diversity inspire all of their employees to perform for the benefit of the organization (DiTomaso, Farris, Cordero, 1993; Hansen, 2003; Watson, Kumar, and Michaelsen, 1993).

- *increase varieties of viewpoints.* Diversity practitioners have incorporated the concept of inclusion in recent years. In many ways, this evolution reflects societal values making their way into the workplace. The values of respect, dignity, and opportunity for all represent the cornerstone of workplace diversity. Inclusiveness is thus a win-win dynamic because it generates opportunities for growth, flexibility, and adaptation in the marketplace for both employees and the organization (Jackson, Joshi, & Erhardt, 2003). Webber and Donahue (2001) argue that the collaboration of cultures, ideas, and perspectives is now considered an organizational asset, bringing forth greater creativity and innovation, with the result that many organizations are increasingly focusing their diversity-management initiatives to improve organizational performance. Indeed, more and more see it as a necessary part of sustaining their competitive position in the marketplace. Moreover, diversity practitioners suggest that a diverse workforce that feels comfortable communicating varying points of view provides a larger pool of ideas and experiences. The organization can draw from that pool to meet business strategy needs and the needs of customers more effectively (Elmes & Connelley, 1997; Hansen, 2003).

- *respond to shifting population and labor-force demographics.* Bezrukova and Jehn (2001) suggest that one of the major drivers behind the business case is the demographic changes that directly affect the labor pool and available talent. These changes are significant. In an organization, employee relationships are the backbone of success. The flow of information among employees, work teams, customers, and suppliers, for example, depends on the quality of relationships and talent in the workplace. Consequently, workplace diversity is increasingly viewed as an essential success factor to be competitive in the marketplace. Workforce-diversity issues are now considered important and are projected to become even more important in the future due to increasing differences in the US population. A number of diversity managers suggest that companies need to focus on diversity and look for ways to become totally inclusive organizations because diversity has the potential of yielding greater productivity and competitive advantages.

- *adapt to changing customer and consumer markets.* Another of the major drivers behind the business case are the changes in consumer markets that directly affect some companies' revenue and profits. In some companies, customer and consumer relationships are the backbone of success. Diversity practitioners believe that diversity management will enhance the flow of information among employees, customers, and suppliers. Gomez-Mejia and Palich (2009) suggest that diversity management is a requirement to gain competitive advantage because it improves organizational image and brand, which enhances the organization's reputation with customers, stockholders, communities, and stakeholders. Diversity management also helps penetrate nonwhite and ethnic market segments, which, in turn, helps to increase revenue and profits.

- *mitigate legal risk.* Chatman and associates (1998) argue that diversity management is an effective response to federal and state equal-opportunity legislation, which makes discrimination in workplaces illegal. These laws specify the rights and responsibilities of both employees and employers in the workplace and hold both accountable. In some organizations, diversity management not only emphasizes greater compliance with human resources' legal requirements, but also focuses on increasing the percentage of females and racial nonwhites in the organization.

- *improve organizational fairness and justice.* According to Carter, Simkins, and Simpson (2003), diversity management is rooted less in responding to moral mandates for greater equity and justice and more in responding to environmental and economic pressures for greater internal effectiveness. According to these same scholars, diversity management improves the ability to address change and improve fluidity in the organization. They also assert that diversity management increases organizational legitimacy and increases internal capabilities due to greater flexibility.

In sum, the business case for diversity management is based on assertions that it (1) increases frontline employee support for organizational programs and policies, which helps the organization achieve strategic goals and objectives; (2) increases competitiveness in recruitment and selection by enhancing the organization's reputation and ability to attract and keep the best employees; (3) promotes creative and innovative approaches to work, which improves productivity; (4) increases efficiency and reduces costs; (5) promotes fairness and justice in the workplace; and (6) helps create economic opportunity by reducing social inequality.

CHAPTER 3

DIVERSITY-MANAGEMENT THEORY

Chapter three examines the heated debate taking place between those diversity researchers who think organizations should be more diverse because it is the right thing to do and those who think organizations should be more diverse because it actually enhances shareholder value. This chapter analyzes the empirical research to determine if there is a solid business case for diversity management as a bottom line organizational strategy. Based on the research, the chapter answers the question whether there is a positive and significant relationship between diversity management and long-term organizational performance.

Angels of Mercy or Barbarians at the Gate?

The most frequently asked question by business leaders is whether diversity-management initiatives contribute to organizational success. Previous research has examined the role of diversity management as it relates to age, tenure, and product mix (Chatman, Polzer, Barsade, & Neale, 1998; Giddens, 1984; Gomez-Mejia & Palich, 1999; Richard, 2000). However, only a few studies have examined diversity-management initiatives and long-term sustainable organizational performance. The purpose of this literature review is to provide an overview of the research investigating the relationship between diversity-management initiatives and organizational-performance outcomes such as stock price, shareholder value, increased sales, and customer retention.

Many organizations have implemented a variety of initiatives aimed at managing diversity effectively. Most recently, some of these initiatives have been relabeled as aiming to increase employee inclusion (Goll & Rasheed, 2005; Gilbert & Ivancevich, 2000). Research that evaluates the performance of such initiatives remains scarce. When such research is conducted, successful initiatives are defined as those that reduce inequalities (e.g., in pay, turnover, and promotion) among demographically defined groups (Hall et. Al, 2000; Ragins, Townsend, & Mattis, 1998). Seldom has the focus been on establishing an empirical link between diversity-management initiatives and organizational performance.

It is estimated that organizations spend $8 billion annually on diversity-management initiatives (Harris & Tanner, 1996; Hansen, 2003). Organizations are seeing the need to hire a workforce that reflects their customers, communities, and labor pools. Another major factor is attracting and retaining the best available talent in the context of the current workforce demographic trends. As women and nonwhites increase in labor pools, it becomes increasingly important for organizations to be successful in hiring and retaining workers from these groups (Cox, 1993). The question business leaders often ask is how diversity management affects the bottom-line performance of organizations and whether there is any tangible evidence that there is a relationship between them. Researchers have struggled during the past two decades to improve their understanding of how diversity management influences organizations, work teams, and individual employees. Numerous empirical studies seem to confirm what business leaders already know: that the potential benefits of diversity management do not happen automatically (Jackson & Joshi, 2004).

Some studies (Jackson, Joshi, & Erhardt, 2003; Webber & Donahue, 2001) have found diversity management is associated with greater innovation, improved strategic decision making, and organizational performance; and other research shows that various types of team and organizational diversity sometimes increase conflict, reduce social cohesion, and increase turnover.

Cox (1993) argues that diversity management may also affect certain organizational processes such as communications, creativity, and problem solving, which are closely related to organizational performance. However, Watson and associates (1993) stated that the combined impact of diversity management on group processes and performance is somewhat difficult to predict from existing research.

Richard (2000) conducted a study to seek a greater understanding into the relationship between managing racial, ethnic, and gender diversity and organization performance. The results demonstrated that the positive impact of racial diversity on organizational performance has a lot to do with context.

In the absence of consideration of context, a negative relationship between racial diversity and organizational outcomes may emerge. In addition to highlighting the importance of context to a positive racial diversity effect, the results also shed light on the organizational contexts in which workforce diversity may impede organizational performance.

Workforce diversity can increase coordination costs, and the leaders of no-growth or negative-growth organizations should be particularly aware of the organizational-performance implications of a clash between diversity and downsizing. Richard (2000) cautions that the same resources that offer some organizations competitive advantage can be a performance detriment to others.

Developing a business case is more difficult for diversity management than for other business issues because evidence of diversity-management's impact on the bottom line has not been systematically measured and documented for easy retrieval and use. Given the uncertainty of whether or not diversity-management initiatives enhance performance, there is a need for a comprehensive review to link the different genres of diversity research and organizational performance.

Simply having a diverse workforce does not necessarily produce the positive outcomes that are often claimed by some of the more optimistic proponents, and Richard identified four major gaps between diversity rhetoric and research findings. Specifically, they found that increased workforce diversity does not necessarily build commitment, improve motivation, reduce conflict, or improve group performance (Huy. 2001; Jayne & Diboye, 2004).

Organizational leaders, on the other hand, assert that finding reliable answers to the question of whether or not diversity management contributes to organizational performance is difficult because diversity-management experts define diversity management in different and often conflicting ways.

Angels of Mercy—The Positive Externalities of Diversity

There is evidence in the research literature that diversity management has the potential to improve competitive advantage through improved problem solving and decision making. The rationale for this hypothesis is that increased creativity is the result of diverse groups having a broader and richer base of experience from which to approach a problem and make critical analyses when making decisions (Cox, 1993; Hess, 1995).

Different types of people see the world in different ways, and having different perspectives can be helpful when groups are trying to come up with creative ideas or solve complex problems. For example, researchers found that organizational performance increases when the senior-management team in an organization is more diverse (Itzin, 1995; Kravitz, 2003). Kravitz argues that organizations with few women, especially in senior-management ranks, are more likely to embrace stereotypical gender roles, and women in such organizations typically have less power. As a consequence, these organizations may be less attractive to women, costing organizations access to the knowledge and skills that female employees could have brought to the table.

Based on these arguments, Frink and associates (2003) found that gender diversity has a positive impact on organizational performance. Specifically, they report that performance maximized when women comprised about half of an organization's workforce. Departures from a 50-50 split in either direction would decrease diversity, and as a result, lead to lower organizational performance. Frink and his colleagues' findings are based on two studies.

In the first study, human resource managers from 291 companies reported on their organizations' gender distribution, size, and job classification. They also rated their organizations' market performance on several dimensions, such as profitability and growth in sales. On average, these companies had 624 employees, 49 percent of whom were women. They found that there was an overall positive effect of female representation on organizational performance. More importantly, organizational performance increased when female representation increased up to a maximum of 50 percent. These results were not affected by organization size or industry sector.

The second study involved a random sample of 410 publicly traded organizations in five industry sectors and covered the time period from 1990 through 2000. Frink and associates (2003) used a variety of reports and databases to obtain workforce and financial information about these organizations, which were much larger than the companies included in their first study.

On average, organizations in the second study had total assets of $534 million and nearly 28,000 employees. Female representation was lower than in the first study, with women comprising about 32 percent of the workforce on average in organizations in the second study. Moreover, in the second study, productivity (total revenue per employee) and profitability (net income before interest and taxes) were used to measure organizational performance. Frink and his colleagues found that productivity was unrelated to gender diversity, but they did find a direct relationship between the percent of female employees and organizational profitability. As the percentage of women in the company increased, so did profitability. Moreover, profitability was highest at intermediate levels of female representation. In essence, these results are consistent with the pattern found in the first study (Frink et al., 2003).

According to Homan (2007), diverse information and perspectives on work teams can potentially boost performance. Homan defines informational diversity as differences in knowledge bases and perspectives that employees bring to the team. Jehn, Northcraft, and Neal (1999) argue that organizations increasingly rely on cross-functional teams in an attempt to stimulate innovation, solve problems, and make decisions. Often, informational diversity within such teams comes hand in hand with differences, such as demographic characteristics and deeply held values and beliefs. Moreover, teams are more likely to effectively use their informational resources when group members believe in the value of diversity. He also found that diversity beliefs moderated the relationship between informational diversity and organizational performance, such that information-diverse groups performed better when they held pro-diversity beliefs.

Using the theoretical argument of cognitive-resource diversity, researchers in this area have argued that workforce diversity has a positive impact on performance because of unique cognitive resources that members bring to the team (Cox & Blake, 1991; Hambrick, Cho, & Chen, 1996; Lovato & Khoo, 1991). The underlying assumption is that teams consisting of heterogeneous employees promote creativity, innovation, and problem solving, hence generating more informed decisions (Horwitz, 2005). Nemeth (1986) found that heterogeneous teams that included nonwhite and female employees were more creative in generating ideas and nonobvious alternatives than homogenous ones. The results indicated that the heterogeneous teams were more creative in problem solving than the homogenous when controlling for ability levels.

In another study, Simons, Pelled, and Smith (1999) observed that workforce diversity in terms of education and company tenure influenced the quality of debates and thus positively impacted the decision-making process in a team of senior executives. Roberson and Jeong, (2007) found that there was a relationship between an organization's diversity reputation and book-to-market equity, which suggests that diversity reputation may send a signal to shareholders about a company's future performance. For example, capital-market investors may view *Fortune's* list of the fifty best companies for nonwhites as a quality workforce diversity reputation signal, or may view such a designation as relevant to the valuation of a company's expected stock returns (Kahan, 2006; Roberson & Jeong, 2004). The results of their study also showed a positive relationship between senior management team diversity and revenue growth, such that organizations with greater gender and racial representation in senior management tended to experience larger increases in annual revenues.

A large body of theoretical literature suggests that cultivating a diverse workforce and developing relationships with diverse stakeholders leads to improved decision making, problem solving, innovation, and creativity, which provides organizations with a strategic and competitive advantage. For example, Weigand (2007) investigated whether these advantages were discernible in organizations' financial performance. Specifically, he compared organizations recognized for exemplary diversity-management practices by *DiversityInc* magazine and *Fortune* magazine in 2004 to matched samples of peer organizations using a wide variety of accounting, financial, and market-based metrics.

Organizations listed on the *DiversityInc* and *Fortune* diversity honor rolls had a performance advantage over their peer organizations during the years immediately preceding publication of the lists, particularly in accounting-based profitability measures. These organizations were larger than the peer organizations in terms of market capitalization, assets, and sales. The study observed superior performance based on metrics directly correlated with organization size, such as net operating profit after tax and market value added.

Over most of the years of the study, Weigand found that both sets of diversity award winners also had higher profit margins, return on assets, return on equity, and economic value added compared to the peer organizations.

These advantages, however, did not directly translate into benefits to shareholders. Over the five years of the study, the risk-adjusted excess returns of the diversity and matching portfolios were identical and insignificantly different from zero. The higher profitability of the diversity award winners is consistent with the idea that diversity-management initiatives provide organizations with a strategic and competitive advantage, and is unsupportive of the view that diversity-management initiatives are merely another aspect of organizations' commitment to social responsibility (Kossek, 1996; Weigand, 2007).

Other studies examining the link between diversity management and financial performance (Kossek & Lobel, 1996; Williams & O'Reilly, 1998; Richard & Johnson, 1999; Richard, Kochan, & McMillan-Capehart, 2002) assert there is little research conducted in actual organizations that addresses the impact of diversity-management practices on financial success. While there are a large number of laboratory experiments that test specific diversity-performance hypotheses, there are few such studies in real organizations, and fewer still that assess this hypothesis using objective performance measures. An exception is a study that compared companies with exemplary diversity-management practices to those that had paid legal damages to settle discrimination lawsuits. The results of this study showed that the exemplary organizations also performed better as measured by their stock prices (Wright et al., 1995).

A review of the research reveals that diversity management can influence organizational performance in several positive ways. For example, diversity management leads to creativity, innovation, and different ideas, which results in better group performance (Knight et al., 1999). Bantel and Jackson (1989) agree that higher levels of workforce diversity in an organization can lead to more-effective executive decision making and more-positive organizational outcomes.

Supporting the above perspective, research conducted by Milliken and Martins (1996) on the impact of diversity on the decision-making patterns of work teams found that diverse groups are able to make higher-quality decisions. Increasing the number of nonwhites and females on a work team affects the team's total frequency of interaction (Hoffman, 1985; Lang, 2000).

According to Hoffman, a person's decision making is affected by his or her individual values and attitudes; therefore, individuals use discretion in the ways in which they perform on behalf of the organization. Nonwhites and females bring different perspectives about performance of tasks, thereby making the organizations more cohesive (Hoffman, 1985). Likewise, organizations with diverse management teams are positively associated with higher organizational performance. Goode and Baldwin (2005) argue that a diverse workforce stimulates the release of creative energy, which leads to more innovative solutions to problems and challenges.

The research (Cox, 1994; Joshi, Liao, & Jackson, 2006; Richard et al., 2004; Sacco & Schmitt, 2005) points out that numerous benefits of workforce diversity have been offered, including coverage of projected labor shortages, increased access to untapped consumer markets, improved corporate image, reduced legal liability, and greater creativity, problem-solving ability, employee performance, and market share.

According to Carter, Simkins, and Simpson (2003), the positive effects of workforce diversity include increased creativity, enhanced decision making, improved problem solving, and increased effectiveness. These positive impacts apply not only to team effectiveness but organizational performance as well. Other studies show that workforce diversity is valuable to the organization because it can lead to increased creativity, flexibility, and better decision making (Elsass & Graves, 1997; McLeod, Lobel, & Cox, 1996). According to Cox and Blake (1991), organizations that can successfully attract a diverse workforce will increase their revenue potential by matching the demographics of the markets they serve. Under this view, looking more like the customer base is thought to enhance marketing opportunities and increase organizational value.

Furthermore, organizations that develop reputations for increasing workforce diversity will likely attract the best talent (Carrell, Elbert, & Hatfield, 2006; McNerney, 1994). Hollowell (2007) found that a strategy of investing in a portfolio of top diversity companies would have left an investor with $1.93 versus just $1.04 for each dollar invested in the large capitalization market index from 2001 to 2004. Hollowell further asserted that in the long run, the *Fortune* top diversity organization portfolio outperformed the market, and he presented some of the first empirical evidence that links workforce diversity with multiple-year shareholder value.

According to Hollowell, workforce diversity positively affects the bottom line because it enhances ingenuity and innovation due to the variety of outlooks that emerge from a diverse work team, which causes managers to consider more perspectives and therefore leads to more informed decision making in the long run.

Barbarians at the Gate—The Negative Externalities of Diversity

Some research suggests that racial and gender diversity can have negative effects on organizational performance. For example, team coordination costs and communication time initially appear to increase with workforce diversity, but evidence exists that these effects diminish with time (Miller & Neathey, 2004; Watson, Kumar, & Michaelsen, 1993; Richard & Johnson, 2001).

Based on their *similarity-attraction theory* of workforce diversity, McKay and Avery (2005) argue that organizations need to do their homework before attempting to recruit nonwhite and female job seekers. They suggest that this homework consists of performing diversity audits to determine whether their climates are supportive of workforce diversity, developing recruitment messages that coincide with the organization's culture and placing these messages in nonwhite-rich recruitment sources, evaluating recruitment and retention performance, and eliminating workplace behaviors and norms that undermine workforce-diversity recruitment and retention initiatives. Otherwise, organizations will be apt to default on their implied recruitment promises, nonwhite and female recruits will feel misled, and some form of backlash will be probable.

The similarity-attraction theory of workforce diversity builds on previous research (Morris, 1995; O'Reilly, Caldwell, & Barnett, 1989; Milliken & Martins, 1996) when it suggests that team members' perceptions of others, as frequently inferred on the basis of similarity in demographic attributes, lead to distraction among team members. For example, attributes such as age, gender, and race/ethnicity are immediately observed and categorized by individual members, and differences tend to be negatively associated with organizational performance.

According to the similarity-attraction theory, homogenous teams are likely to be more productive than heterogeneous teams because of mutual attraction of team members with similar characteristics. Heterogeneous groups, in contrast, are hypothesized to be less productive and have lower team cohesion because of inherent tensions and relational conflicts arising from member differences. Horwitz (2005) argues that although different perspectives within a team can lead to enhanced team functioning through information elaboration, this effect may be reduced or even reversed when information diversity converges with workforce diversity dimensions such as gender, personality, attitudes, and values. Homan (2007) suggest that when different dimensions of diversity converge, the covariation of differences creates a diversity fault line that may elicit subgroup categorization or an us-them distinction. Moreover, Homan (2007) argues that such subgroup categorizations can disrupt group processes by rendering group members less trusting of and less motivated to cooperate with other group members. In addition, they are less committed to the group, increasing interpersonal tensions and conflict and lowering the performance of group communication.

Other empirical research that presents unfavorable findings on the value of diversity management was conducted by Watson, Kumar, and Michaelsen (1993), who found that homogeneous work groups are better in the short term, while heterogeneous work groups outperform other groups over an extended period of time. Moreover, Pelled, Eisenhardt, and Xin (1999) found that diversity in certain work groups resulted in emotional conflict that ultimately harmed organizational performance.

Several researchers have argued that diversity in the executive ranks of organizations can result in less communication, less effective decision making, and less-positive organizational outcomes. For example, Miller (1998) and Knight (1999) found that workforce diversity in the senior-management team of an organization has been shown to have negative effects on group cohesion and the frequency and quantity of communication, and can lead to increased conflict within the group. These negative effects arise from a lack of understanding the effects of the demographic characteristics of group members—such as race, age, sex, and education—on group interaction, but more importantly, the potential compositional effects of these variables in superior/subordinate relationships (Neill et. al., 2004; O'Reilly, Caldwell, & Barnett, 1989).

Surprisingly, although the theory of organizational racial and gender representation has been related to outcomes such as executive succession, no specific effort has been made to investigate what accounts for these findings. More research is needed to explore the processes by which organizational racial, ethnic, and gender representation influences outcomes (O'Reilly, Caldwell, & Barnett, 1989).

Lastly, William and O'Reilly (1998) found that diversity management may stimulate organizational performance through information elaboration; it also undermines organizational performance through social categorization. Pelled, Eisenhardt, and Xin (1999) found that workforce diversity variables such as race, tenure, and age can influence conflict and lack substantial ties to positive organizational performance.

Summary

The ultimate goal here is to determine whether the empirical research supports a link between diversity management and organizational performance. It is hypothesized that an examination of the literature and previous research will help provide a conceptual framework that links diversity management to organizational performance or supports an interactional model of the impact of diversity management on organizational performance.

A review of the research uncovered mixed results about the impact of diversity management. For example, of the one hundred and twenty five studies reviewed, 55 percent of the studies reported positive effects of diversity, while 45 percent of the studies described negative effects of diversity management. Moreover, the diversity of work teams has been linked to both favorable and unfavorable organizational performance. Thus, it is risky to make recommendations about the steps organizations should take to reduce potential negative consequences of diversity management or leverage diversity management to achieve positive business outcomes.

Overall, the search for evidence that directly supports the link between diversity-management initiatives and organizational performance has proved elusive. Two reasons might explain this lack of evidence. First, diversity management is extremely difficult to study in organizational settings because of the general lack of agreement of desired outcomes. In addition, some organizations are reluctant to share their experiences or data, given the legal climate and the potential for litigation. Another reason for the lack of evidence linking diversity management to organizational performance may be attributed to the fact that the relationship between diversity management and the bottom line is more complex than implied by popular rhetoric.

Decades of research on the effects of diversity within teams indicates that diversity can have negative effects as well as positive ones. The empirical literature does not support the simple notion that more-diverse teams necessarily perform better, feel more committed to their organizations, or experience higher levels of satisfaction (Williams & O'Reilly, 1998; Milliken & Martins, 1996; Jackson, May, & Whitney, 1995; Reimoeller & Van Baardwijk, 2005). Instead, the evidence suggests that workforce diversity may simultaneously produce more conflict and employee turnover, as well as more creativity and innovation (Jehn, Northcraft, & Neale, 1999; Williams & O'Reilly, 1998). This pattern of mixed results was also found in studies that examined diversity within top management teams in the banking industry. In one study, diversity in top management teams was associated with greater innovation within bank branches (Bantel & Jackson, 1989; Richard & Murthi, 2004). In another, diversity was also associated with higher rates of turnover among top management team members (Jackson et al., 1991). Thus, the research literature paints a more complex picture of the outcomes of diversity management than does the popular rhetoric.

CHAPTER 4

FRAMING THE LINK BETWEEN DIVERSITY MANAGEMENT AND ORGANIZATIONAL PERFORMANCE

This chapter presents a model of the impact of diversity initiatives on organizational performance based on the research. The model identifies barriers that may inhibit the employment, development, retention, and promotion of non-whites and females in the workplace and suggests other significant factors that may influence diversity initiatives. It identifies the primary reasons and desired outcomes for managing diversity: improve productivity, remain competitive, form better work relationships among employees, enhance social responsibility, and to address legal concerns. This chapter presents a model as well as the best strategies for managing diversity. It also discusses components of an effective diversity management strategy.

Research Model

The previous chapter exposed the mismatch between empirical research results and diversity-management rhetoric. However, the literature review also provided a conceptual framework for investigating the link between diversity-management initiatives and organizational performance. Figure 2 presents the model that guided the examination of the research studies discussed in this book. The goal of the model is to provide diversity-management practitioners with a framework that will allow them to develop and implement diversity-management initiatives based on empirical research.

The model (see figure 2) suggests that in addition to diversity management, organizational performance may depend on several aspects of an organization's diversity-management strategy, organizational culture, and human resource policies or practices. In addition, the model proposes that these effects are likely to operate through organizational behaviors such that, under facilitating conditions, diversity management is associated with positive work processes and is therefore beneficial to organizational performance, whereas under inhibiting conditions, diversity management is associated with negative work processes and is therefore detrimental to performance. Research conducted by Williams and O'Reilly (1998) supports the model and confirms that diversity management is linked to organizational behaviors such as communication, conflict, and cohesion.

Figure 2. A Framework for Understanding the Effects of Diversity-Management Initiatives on Organizational Effectiveness Outcomes

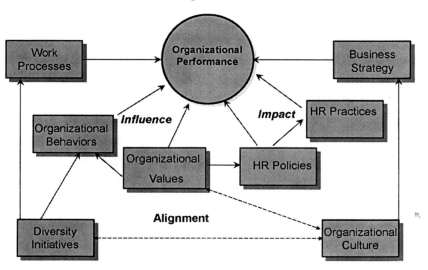

Jehn (1995) provided additional support for the model by showing that diversity management influences work-team behaviors such as cohesion and communication, which, in turn, impact organizational performance.

Some of these behaviors may be productive. For example, if they help the team avoid groupthink and bring additional points of view into the discussion, it will positively impact organizational performance. The connections shown in the model that link diversity-management initiatives to employee behaviors and then to performance seem logical, but past research has not always found strong linkages between diversity-management initiatives and organizational performance.

In fact, past research suggests that there may be no direct positive or negative relationship between diversity-management initiatives and organizational performance. In some organizations, diversity-management initiatives may improve performance, while in other organizations, diversity management may be detrimental to organizational performance (Hoffman, 1978; Jackson, 1992; Jehn, Northcraft, & Neale, 1999; O'Reilly & Flatt, 1989; Steiner, 1972). If diversity management has inconsistent effects across groups, then in studies that examine the relationship between diversity management and performance across many groups, the positive and negative effects may cancel each other out, making it difficult to assess their impact on organizational performance. Therefore, the research model suggests that the relationship between diversity management and performance outcomes may depend on the organizational context in which the work takes place.

For example, the effects of diversity management on organizational performance might be more favorable if organizations' leaders build on employees' creativity and information. Diversity management may also be more likely to improve performance when managers are trained to deal with work-process issues, particularly those involved in communicating and problem solving in diverse teams.

The model further suggests that human-resource practices such as recruiting, hiring, training, motivating, and rewarding employees partially determine whether employees and managers are skilled in communicating with and coordinating among members of diverse work teams. When human-resource practices support the creation of a workforce that has the skills needed to give the organization a competitive advantage, diversity management is more likely to lead to positive performance outcomes. In other organizations, however, human-resource practices may inadvertently result in a workforce that is diverse but unskilled in diversity management. Such organizations are more likely to experience negative outcomes, such as disruptive conflict and increased turnover.

Also shown in the model is another hypothesis linking organizational culture and organizational performance. The evidence supporting this hypothesis is derived largely from research conducted by Chatman and Barsade (1995), which examined how organizational cultures that foster cooperation and commitment can be created. Using a business simulation, Chatman and Barsade found that organizational culture moderated the effects of workforce diversity and conflict arising from team diversity. O'Reilly and his colleagues (1997) also found that an organizational culture supporting racial diversity in a company's workforce improved organizational performance.

The model suggests that the impact of an organization's human-resource policies represents another critical contextual factor that should be considered. For example, Kossek, Zonia, and Young (1996) suggest that organizational approaches to diversity management will likely be beneficial if human-resource systems are devised that alter the design of jobs and the structure of workplaces and foster employee teamwork. They argue that human-resource practices such as new employee orientation programs and diversity training socialize new employees by helping them to identify with positive, distinctive, and enduring characteristics of an organization. This identification, in turn, enables new employees to develop loyalty to an organization and support it.

Lastly, Kossek and his colleagues suggest that organizations need diversity-management initiatives like new employee orientation and diversity-training programs to create a two-way socialization process, ensuring that personal bias is reduced and nonwhite employees' perspectives are valued.

Research Questions Used to Frame the Study

The model represented by figure 2 shows the framework that guided this review and evaluation of the research on the impact of diversity-management initiatives on organizational performance. Specifically, the research study addressed the following questions:

1. *What effect do diversity-management initiatives aimed at increasing racial, ethnic, and gender representation have on the organization's talent pool?*

   Does an increase in the diversity of a group at the demographic level (i.e., age, gender, and race) have an impact on the increase in task-related knowledge, skills, abilities, experiences, and other characteristics? The research in industrial and organizational psychology has yielded a variety of standardized techniques that have been shown to be predictive of job performance (Roberson & Park, 2004; Schmidt & Hunter, 1998).

   These include behavioral interviews, biographical-data inventories, assessment centers, work samples, personality inventories, mental-ability tests, and other procedures that provide objective, quantitative assessments of knowledge, skills, and abilities. Some scholars suggest that improvements in the talent pool are best accomplished by using measures such as these rather than using racial, ethnic, or gender diversity as a surrogate of talent diversity. On the other hand, some diversity practitioners argue that while organizations should seek the most valid assessment tools, an overemphasis on selection to the neglect of training and development is likely to harm diversity-management efforts.

This research examines whether diversity-management initiatives are likely to achieve a balance between identifying and selecting people who have the right talent and experience using the best measures, and growing knowledge, skills, and abilities through training, coaching, mentoring, and other development activities.

2. *What impact do diversity-management initiatives have on employee commitment, motivation, engagement, productivity, and cohesion?*

Diversity-management advocates argue that a happier, more harmonious workplace will result from diversity-management initiatives. Unfortunately, previous research shows that diversification of the workforce often has the opposite effect.

One area of research, often called relational demography, has focused on how individual employees react to work situations in which they must work with persons who are demographically similar to themselves as opposed to situations in which they must work with persons who are dissimilar. Some researchers (Riordan, 2000; Shaw, 1993; Williams & O'Reilly, 1998) argue that working with dissimilar others is often associated with negative outcomes. These same scholars suggest that employees working with dissimilar others are likely to show lower commitment to the organization, express less satisfaction, perceive more discrimination, and display a variety of other negative behavioral and attitudinal outcomes.

3. *What effect do diversity-management initiatives have on organizational-performance outcomes such as net profit, customer satisfaction, market share, stock price, or earning per share?*

While some research has identified benefits of demographic heterogeneity on work-group outcomes such as creativity and innovation (Bantel & Jackson, 1989), other research has shown that organizations whose members are diverse in terms of their race, gender, age, or tenure have a variety of problems, including communication breakdowns, low cohesion, and turnover (Milliken & Martins, 1996; Simmons, 2001; Williams & O'Reilly, 1998).

Previous research (Bowers, Pharmer, & Salas, 2000; Webber & Donahue, 2001) has shown that workforce diversity is associated with a mix of results and that the overall relationship of homogeneity to performance based on the aggregate of these studies is very small. These findings have led many researchers to view diversity management as a double-edged sword.

The research in this book seeks to be the most comprehensive evaluation to date and examines if there is justification for the assertion that organizations that take strategic actions to manage the diversity in their workforce perform better on return on investment, profits, revenue, costs, and other financial measures.

4. *Which diversity-management initiatives, if any, improve organizational performance?*

Unlike the research on the effects of workforce diversity on individual and group-level performance, where there are a large number of case studies, there are relatively few empirical studies assessing the relationship to the performance of the organization, and the results are mixed. Some studies have shown that diversity management is related to higher performance (Smith & Barnes, 2000; Wright et al., 1995; Hartenian & Emundson, 2000), but others have shown that diversity management is actually detrimental to organizational performance (Sacco & Schmitt, 2003). Richard and associates (2003) hypothesized an inverted-U relationship, in which the highest performance results from implementation of noncontroversial diversity-management initiatives. Although this appears to be the best study so far, there are limitations, including small and possibly unrepresentative samples. Consequently, the debate on the business case for diversity management is far from over.

The present study provides a compelling intellectual contribution to the widely debated issue of diversity management by skillfully blending theory and practice in order to provide substance to the debate on whether diversity management contributes to organizational performance. As a result, diversity practitioners and business leaders can judge where their past initiatives have yielded success and what areas demand a renewed effort. The study provides practical recommended actions to guide future efforts.

Diversity-Management Initiatives

Thomas (1990, 1991, 1996, and 1999) describes diversity management as a strategically driven process whose emphasis is on building skills, making quality decisions that bring out the best in every employee, and assessing organizational mixtures and tensions as a result of changing workforce and customer demographics.

According to Thomas, organizations that exhibit a strategically driven approach with regard to diversity management respond to workforce and customer demographics by proactively initiating long-term and broad-based diversity-management initiatives. He suggests that when diversity-management initiatives are implemented effectively, organizations can expect to see performance outcomes such as an engaged workforce, satisfied customers, improved communication among employees, and improved financial performance. This critical linkage provides the foundation for suggesting that diversity-management initiatives are linked to organizational performance.

Diversity-management initiatives are described by Thomas (1992, 1996) as proactive and intentional actions taken by the organization to improve human-resource processes and enhance organizational culture. Specifically, these actions maximize the unique skills and abilities of employees in the organization, and include how the organization recruits, hires, trains, mentors, promotes, develops, and integrates underrepresented racial and ethnic groups. In theory (Thomas, 1990, 1991, 1996, 1999), diversity-management initiatives are internal strategic human-resource management processes or a pattern of planned activities intended to enable an organization to achieve its goals. In practice, few organizations strategically develop and implement diversity-management initiatives. In fact, most organizations engage in activities that are not sustainable over the long term and are unrelated to measurable organizational performance.

In a very general sense, diversity-management initiatives reflect an organizational commitment to "recruit, retain, reward, and promote a heterogeneous mix of productive, motivated, and committed employees" (Ivancevich & Gilbert, 2000, p. 77). Although that sounds like nothing more than good management, these initiatives also explicitly or implicitly are based on the assumption that without specific and intentional efforts to manage diversity, "rules, regulations, and procedures that unintentionally discriminate on the basis of race and gender" will persist (Fernandez, 1999, p. 6).

Building on Thomas's (1991) strategic diversity-management model, Cox (1994) suggests that diversity management also could be expected to relate to performance. According to Cox, diversity management is conceptualized as the degree to which an organization implements fair human-resource policies and socially integrates underrepresented employees. Cox sees diversity management as a function of several factors:

1. Individual-level factors involving the extent of prejudice and stereotyping in organizations.
2. Group/intergroup factors referring to the degree of conflict between various groups within an organization.
3. Organizational-level factors regarding such domains as organizational culture and the degree that underrepresented personnel are integrated into higher-level positions and within an organization's social networks.
4. Systemic factors pertaining to whether institutional bias prevails in an organization's human-resource systems, such as recruiting, hiring, training, developing, promoting, and compensating employees.

Cox (1994) argues that diversity management, in essence, refers to the extent that an organization's practices and social context are affected by group membership, as manifested in various forms of demographic difference (e.g., racial-ethnic, sex, age, etc.).

Although this definition of diversity management might seem similar to organizational justice, McKay (2007) argues that diversity management differs from this seemingly related concept. Organizational justice—or the general fairness of organizational policies, allocation of rewards, and interpersonal treatment of others when implementing policies—is a consideration in employees' perceptions of the efficacy of diversity-management initiatives. However, McKay argues that organizational justice concerns only the fairness component of diversity management, ignoring the structural and social-integration components. Moreover, organizational justice, which refers to general feelings of being supported by an organization, might capture some of the diversity-management components, but not fairness. The difference between the two was confirmed by McKay (2007), who used factor analyses to distinguish diversity management from organizational justice in a study on the turnover intentions of a sample of racially and ethnically diverse retail managers.

I reviewed the extensive diversity literature to identify the most common initiatives organizations implement to create better work environments and organizational cultures. Based on the research, a combination of the following diversity-management initiatives should yield valuable and measurable organizational-performance outcomes:

- *Recruitment and representation.* One of the most common diversity-management initiatives cited in the literature is enhancing the process of attracting and increasing the supply of qualified racially, ethnically, and gender-diverse applicants for employment. This often includes activities such as employee referral programs, posting and advertising jobs, targeting specific groups, sponsoring nonwhite and female conferences, attending job fairs, and targeting universities and community colleges with diverse student bodies.
- *Employee involvement.* Diversity managers assert that it is critical for organizations to implement efforts to leverage employee talents by being open to ideas, thoughts, behaviors, and attitudes that differ from conventional wisdom and the status quo. This often involves organizations attempting to open up the culture and work environment to make them more transparent and fair. Specific actions may include establishing diversity councils or employee resource groups; conducting town-hall meetings where employees are encouraged to speak their minds freely without fear of retribution; recruiting frontline employees to take concrete, positive, and public actions on the results of employee-engagement surveys; encouraging employee groups or affinity groups to talk about and celebrate their cultural and ethnic heritage; promoting qualified employee resource group members into leadership positions; holding brainstorming sessions during employee resource group meetings; and rewarding employee resource group members for business innovations that contribute

to organizational success. These are a few examples of best practices that demonstrate that the organization values and leverages frontline employees in the organization's diversity-management strategy.

- *Education and training.* Perhaps the most common diversity-management initiative implemented by practitioners is efforts to educate managers and employees about diversity management. These initiatives include conducting awareness training on the organization's diversity goals, as well as issue-based prevention training (e.g., sexual harassment or civil treatment) and team-building and group-process training. Diversity-management education and training is often designed to be highly engaging, informative, and nonthreatening, and is designed to spark dialogue within the organization about the value of diversity in decision making and teamwork. Moreover, diversity training is designed to provide managers with tools and techniques for leading diverse teams and creating inclusive work environments. The ultimate goal is to make employees more aware of how well the organization is doing in terms of achieving diversity-management goals.

- *Development and advancement.* Similar to recruitment, this diversity-management initiative is designed to broaden the ongoing, strategic process of identifying, developing, and advancing nonwhite and female talent to secure the organization's pool of potential future leaders. This initiative includes activities such as diversifying employee benefits (e.g., adoption, domestic partner, eldercare, flexible health, and dependent). It may also often include adopting work/life programs and incentives (e.g., on-site child care, flexible work schedules, and on-site lactation facilities). Lastly, it includes implementing specific development activities such as leadership-development training programs and mentoring programs aimed at advancing nonwhite or female employees.

- *Management and oversight.* Diversity-management practitioners suggest that a key diversity-management initiative is putting in place an organizational structure to develop, implement, and manage the organization's diversity-management strategy. They specifically recommend that a chief diversity officer be hired to ensure diversity-management initiatives are developed and aligned with the organization's strategic plan.
- *Leadership and support.* According to diversity-management practitioners, it is important that the CEO, executive managers, and board of directors take actions to visibly demonstrate and communicate the importance of diversity management throughout an organization. Visible actions include measures put in place to ensure that managers are responsible for diversity management by linking their performance assessment and compensation to the progress of diversity-management initiatives. Additional activities include the CEO addressing diversity at town-hall meetings, incorporating diversity into business plans, and chairing or participating in corporate and local diversity councils.
- *Supplier diversity.* The conventional wisdom among diversity practitioners is that organizations must have a robust supplier-diversity program. Supplier-diversity programs encompass due diligence efforts to include nonwhite-owned and female-owned businesses in all bid opportunities by seeking them out, assisting in their development, and encouraging joint ventures. In order to provide the maximum practicable opportunity as required by the federal government's *Small Business Liaison Office Handbook, 2005*, organizations that have contract(s) with the federal government are encouraged to advertise subcontracting opportunities, break large requirements into smaller packages, keep the playing field level, mentor/develop small businesses, and allow adequate

time for nonwhite-owned and female-owned businesses to offer proposals and submit bids.

Organizational-Performance Outcomes

Diversity practitioners for years have argued that diversity management, properly implemented, results in measurable, long-term, and sustainable benefits for the organization. For most organizations, it is believed that this shows up as decreased costs, increased productivity, lower voluntary turnover, and increased recruiting efficiency. Moreover, diversity-management experts suggest that these organizational gains are not only tangible, measurable and significant, but that the market-driven gains can quickly drive other business results, such as share price.

In theory, quantitative and qualitative performance measures help organizations translate their diversity aspirations into tangible practice. For example, an organization can track data on its workforce to evaluate the performance of the organization's diversity management efforts and the progress it is making in those efforts. Organizations also can track the return they receive on investments in such areas as diversity-management training and recruitment to evaluate the progress they are making in those efforts.

In addition to analyzing quantitative workforce data, organizations can use qualitative data derived from interviews, focus groups, and surveys for identifying employee perceptions regarding career-advancement opportunities, work environment, and organizational culture. For example, organizations can ask employees a series of general questions in such areas as retention, organizational commitment, promotions, job satisfaction, supervision, and performance evaluations. Over time, trends in responses are the types of qualitative information that can help organizations assess how their diversity-management initiatives are progressing in achieving organizational goals. Well-designed measurements share some common traits regardless of the environment in which they are used, including being based on reliable and accurate data that are consistent and compatible with existing business systems and processes.

Given the controversy around whether diversity management is an essential part of good management practice, the relationship between diversity management and organizational performance deserves empirical investigation. Therefore, in order to identify organizational performance outcomes that may be linked to diversity management, I reviewed research studies conducted on organizations of at least five hundred people in bona fide work settings. I excluded studies done in laboratory settings where participants were performing artificial tasks and focused instead on studies conducted in more naturalistic settings, such as public, private, and nonprofit organizations and publicly traded companies.

Next, various diversity-management practitioners were interviewed. The organizational outcomes that were investigated were those recommended by a majority of experts interviewed and cited by scholars in research journals. Since it is possible that other diversity-management practitioners may have identified other performance outcomes, this list should not be considered exhaustive. Based on the literature that was reviewed and discussions with experts in the field of diversity management, the following organizational-performance outcomes were identified and examined.

- *Enhanced competitiveness.* Diversity-management experts suggest that organizations' success and competitiveness depend upon their ability to manage diversity by actively assessing their handling of workplace-diversity issues and developing or implementing diversity-management strategy plans. The underlying assumption is that strategic diversity management will provide a competitive advantage in the marketplace and help achieve long-term positive business results.

- *Employee engagement.* According to most diversity-management practitioners, this organizational-performance outcome helps drive the contribution of employees to the organization. One of the underlying assumptions is that engaged employees supply a greater variety of solutions to problems in service, sourcing, and allocation of resources. Moreover, engaged employees from diverse backgrounds bring individual talents and experiences in suggesting ideas that are flexible in adapting to fluctuating markets and customer demands.

- *Increased productivity.* Diversity managers suggest that one outcome of diversity management is increased employee productivity. The underlying assumption is that organizations that implement certain diversity-management initiatives inspire all of their employees to perform to their highest ability.

- *Enhanced company reputation and increased customer retention.* Diversity-management practitioners argue that diversity-management initiatives result in a more diverse collection of skills and experiences (e.g., languages, cultural understanding), which allows a company to provide a broader service range to customers. According to these same experts, a diverse workforce that feels comfortable communicating varying points of view provides a larger pool of ideas and experiences. This, in turn, enables the organization to draw from that pool to meet business strategy needs and the needs of customers more effectively.

Data Collection and Search for Relevant Studies

In order to address the research questions, I conducted a review of empirical studies on diversity management and organizational performance during the period from 1990 to 2010 using numerous relevant key terms. This review included the leading journals in the field of diversity management, organizational behavior, and human-resource management. Some of the specific journals in this survey included the *Academy of Management Journal, Human Resource Management, Journal of Management, Journal of Management Studies, Management International Review, Management Science, Organization Science, Organizational Behavior & Human Decision Processes,* and *Strategic Management Journal.*

These journals were selected because they are widely believed to be the top journals based on several lists of journal rankings in the fields of diversity management, organizational behavior, business management, and human-resource management (Harzing, 2009; McWilliams, Siegel, & Van Fleet, 2005). In addition, they attract contributions from diversity-management scholars in general, as well as practitioners in the fields of diversity management, human-resource management, and organizational behavior. Moreover, when taken together, they employ a range of eclectic empirical methodologies in their studies to include quantitative, qualitative, descriptive, and prescriptive. Lastly, these journals represent visible, respected outlets for diversity-management scholars and practitioners interested in a cross section of diversity-management and organizational-behavior issues.

A search by word in the Business Source Complete database of journals using multiple variations to refer to diversity and organizational performance was conducted and resulted in an extensive number of positive results. Because diversity is defined differently across fields of study in the social sciences, a broad treatment of diversity was used, which resulted in an extensive keyword list. The number of keywords also reflects the large number of outcomes that could possibly be influenced by diversity management.

Some keywords were not included. For example, notable omissions were keywords that focused on personality differences. The literature on the influences of the collective personalities of group members is extensive, but it does not inform an understanding of the link between diversity-management initiatives and organizational performance. In addition to personality differences, my search did not include articles related to religion or sexual orientation.

The keyword searches for the 1990-to-2010 period generated more than ten thousand possible articles pertaining to diversity. Therefore, a major portion of the search activity involved rejecting articles that were not relevant. Three factors were necessary for a study to be included: it had to involve empirical theory testing, have a true diversity-management focus, and have results examining performance outcomes. The bottom line in selecting or rejecting a study was whether it could provide empirical evidence to answer the question *"Do diversity-management initiatives in organizations influence specific performance outcomes?"*

Although the keyword phase of the search produced numerous possible items for the study, over fifty studies published from 1990 to 2010 met all three criteria. Using the snowball method to track backward from these studies to predecessors, an additional fifty studies were identified. Using the keyword-search method, the database was updated in June 2011 to obtain studies published in 2010. An additional twenty-five studies were added to the database in the second phase. This resulted in 125 empirical studies that were examined. This approach is similar to the methodology used by Wise (1997, 2000).

Empirical studies relating diversity management to organizational performance published during the period from 1990 to 2010 that met the criteria have been included in this examination. Meta-analyses that summarized findings of earlier research on this relationship but were published during the captioned period were also included in the survey. Case studies with essentially a single organization focus that did not use any empirical method were excluded from the list as being outside the scope of this examination.

Given the time frame for this review, it serves as an update of the research, including Elsass and Graves 1997; Finkelstein and Hambrick 1996; Jackson, May, and Whitney 1995; Milliken and Martins, 1996;

Reskin, McBrier, and Kmec, 1999; Shaw and Barrett-Power, 1998; Tsui and Gutek, 1999; Webber and Donahue 2001; Williams and O'Reilly, 1998; and Wise and Tschirhart 1999, 2000.

The current analysis builds on previous efforts while attempting to avoid the bias and misinterpretation that plague qualitative reviews due to information overload. For example, Hunter and Schmidt (2004) have shown that reviews that have as few as seven studies can draw different conclusions depending on the review format (e.g., narrative versus meta-analysis). Previous research (Cooper & Rosenthal, 1980; Kulik & Roberson, 2008; Ward & Winstanley, 2004) included one-organization case studies in their review, but it is difficult in such studies to ascertain whether performance outcomes resulted from diversity-management initiatives or natural effects of organizational maturation.

The implementation of the diversity-management practices supported by empirical research may provide insights to organizations as they undertake or attempt to strengthen their own diversity-management practices. This examination considers the practical implications of the accumulated evidence and concludes with potential challenges to the continued advancement of diversity-management initiatives and the field of diversity management.

For each question, the discussion considers the strengths and weaknesses of the business case of each diversity-management initiative as stated in the diversity-management research literature. Then I examine what, if any, organizational-behavior theories support the business case. Then the study points out what, if any, empirical evidence exists in the research that could further advance our understanding of the efficacy of diversity-management initiatives in organizations.

Summary

The model shown in figure 2 illustrates the dynamics of the relationships between diversity-management initiatives and organizational outcomes. This study reviews the empirical studies that examined the link between diversity-management initiatives and organizational performance. More importantly, it illustrates the combined effect of diversity-management practices on organizational performance. The model indicates that organizational performance is an outcome of these relationships. The model further illustrates that other important variables—such as human-resource practices, organizational norms, and business strategy—also shape diversity-management strategy and organizational-performance outcomes.

Consequently, the efficacy of diversity-management initiatives warrants attention. It is hoped that the framework used in this work can be extended to broader considerations. For example, this framework may be helpful in investigating whether service organizations tend to benefit more from diversity-management initiatives than manufacturing organizations. It may also prove useful in examining whether organizations operating in turbulent environments rather than stable ones benefit more from diversity-management initiatives. Other interesting research questions will undoubtedly emerge as the framework for assessing diversity management and performance is extended.

CHAPTER 5

INCREASING RACIAL, ETHNIC, AND GENDER REPRESENTATION

In order to manage strategic demographic change in organizations, a common diversity management initiative is to increase the diversity of the workforce through hiring over time. This chapter examines organizational level consensus and valence regarding intentional and proactive efforts to increase demography toward greater diversity in race and gender composition. In addition to describing how organizations attempt to increase the female and non-white representation, this chapter gauges the efficacy of such efforts and the degree to which these efforts support selection, retention and advancement of talent.

Business Case

Organizations that take proactive and intentional steps to increase female and nonwhite representation have three major rationales that, when taken in aggregate, are believed to be positively associated with organizational performance. Diversity-management practitioners suggest that retaining nonwhite and female employees can be more difficult than recruiting them. This is especially true for organizations in less-diverse regions, where relocated nonwhite employees may feel disconnected. Organizations base their business case on one of three rationales.

Advocacy Rationale

Efforts to increase the percentage of females and nonwhites, particularly in an organization's senior-leadership ranks, increase legitimacy with frontline employees (Mathis, 1993; Milliken & Martins, 1996). Mathis argues that ethnically, racially, and gender-diverse senior leaders can serve as role models to individuals within the organization, as mentors for aspiring women and nonwhite employees, and as a signal to other women and nonwhites in the organization that their concerns and issues will be voiced through this representation.

Moreover, the presence of nonwhite and female senior managers sends an explicit signal that there are opportunities for career growth for these groups in the organization (Milliken & Martins, 1996). Ely's (1991, 1995) study of gender diversity in top management teams discovered that increasing female representation may cause women within the organization to behave differently due to a perceived access to power and opportunity. In a study on the analysis of race and gender in early career experiences, Cox and Nomo (1991) found the main reason professional and managerial women and nonwhites leave an organization is the lack of career growth and opportunities.

This increased turnover may have significant financial implications for organizations. For example, in a Fortune 500 company with 27,000 employees, costs associated with such turnover and loss of productivity were $15.3 million a year, excluding the costs of sexual harassment or racial discrimination (Robinson & Decant, 1997; Wilson & Iles, 1999). One of the key success factors of diversity management within organizations is commitment from the top of the organization (Rynes & Rosen, 1995). Therefore, when an organization has nonwhites and females on the senior-management team, this may signal a commitment to workforce diversity.

Lastly, the advocacy rationale suggests that as a result of including women and nonwhites on the senior-management team, the reputation and credibility of the organization in the internal and external labor market may improve (Daily & Schwenk, 1996; Hambrick & D'Aveni, 1992). Internally, this signals to the employees a commitment to workforce diversity. Research by Eisenberger, Fasolo, and Davis-LaMastro (1990) found that if employees perceive they are valued, supported, and cared about by their organization, attendance, dedication, and job performance will improve as a result. They also found that this perception made employees more innovative, inevitably enhancing the performance of the organization.

Thus, the benefits of having ethnic, racial, and female representation in the senior-leadership ranks are intertwined and may be mutually reinforcing. A diverse leadership team acts to increase organizational legitimacy, which provides increased access to external labor pools and internal employees. This access to critical nonwhite and female talent pools may lead to an increased ability for the organization to hire, retain, and promote valuable female and nonwhite employees and/or attract nonwhite and female managers, which in turn, acts to increase organizational legitimacy. In addition, as increased legitimacy leads to more access, this will, in turn, lead to enhanced organizational performance.

Strategy Implementation Rationale

The second argument for increasing the number of nonwhites and females, especially in the management ranks of the organization, is based on the *strategy implementation rationale* (Pearce & Zahra, 1992; Johnson et al., 1996; Wright et.al., 1995). The strategy implementation rationale suggests that one of the key roles of senior leaders involves advising the chief executive officer and top organizational managers, as well as initiating and formulating strategy (Johnson et al., 1996; Lorsch & McIvor, 1989; Mace, 1971).

In this role, the senior managers, in particular, are viewed as instrumental to the success of the organization (Baysinger & Butler, 1985; Zanoni & Janssens, 2003). Each manager brings to the organization unique skills, abilities, and talents (Kesner, 1988; Kosnik, 1990). While specific expertise is likely to be based on such characteristics as functional background, education, training, and past experiences, some of these unique attributes are the beliefs, values, attitudes, and orientation related to their race, ethnicity, or gender (Baysinger & Butler, 1985). People of different ethnic backgrounds possess different values, attitudes, and norms that reflect their cultural heritage. These values, norms, and attitudes may then affect the strategy role of the individual manager (Cox et al., 1991).

Mizrahi (1983) asserts that managers establish the framework for strategic decision making within an organization. Managers' involvement in the strategic-planning process is a role that may be positively related to performance (Judge & Zeithaml, 1992; Zahra & Pearce, 1989). Managers are increasingly involved in initiating strategies (Haunschild, 1993) and are participating in all phases of the strategic development and implementation processes (Johnson et al., 1996).

In diversity-management literature, it has been found that racially and ethnically diverse groups exhibit a greater range of perspectives and generate more alternatives to problems than homogeneous groups (Watson, Kumar, & Michaelsen, 1993). In addition, Dutton and Duncan (1987) assert that diversity of beliefs within a group leads to increased information search and increased momentum for strategic change. This may be due to the increased diversity of environmental perceptions within ethnically and racially diverse groups (Allison, 1971; Jackson et al., 1991; Larkey, 1996; Mitroff, 1982) in that members of racially and ethnically diverse teams not only notice different events in the work environment, but they also have different perspectives on these same events (Sutcliff, 1994).

Moreover, research on group performance has found that relationships between racially and gender-diverse groups result in increased quality of ideas in brainstorming sessions and increased group performance (McLeod & Lobel, 1992). There is compelling evidence that gender diversity facilitates creativity within groups (Hoffinan & Maier, 1961; Jackson, 1992; Nemeth, 1986). Thus, an organization with a high percentage of female managers may benefit not only from increased perceptions, increased information processing, identification of more alternatives to problems, and increased momentum for strategic change, but may also benefit from a higher degree of creativity.

Greater racial, ethnic, and gender representation in senior management is not always a positive, however. Greater representation may also lead to increased conflict, parochialism, and faults with the status quo (Glick, Miller, & Huber, 1993).

However, these negatives may not be entirely detrimental to all organizations. Amason (1996) asserts that there is actually a functional type of conflict within groups. Functional conflict is caused by cognitive differences arising from different positions and perspectives (Amason, 1996; Mitroff, 1982; Schweiger, Sandberg, & Rechner, 1989). That is, individuals see things differently and have different approaches to the group task. These different perspectives and approaches often lead to synthesis, a situation where the group sees more than just the sum of individual perspectives. The different perspectives and orientations that individuals have as a result of their ethnic culture or gender may lead to this functional conflict.

Therefore, the general assertion made by Glick and associates (1993) about conflict being a negative may be misleading. For senior managers, in particular, functional conflict may actually be beneficial to organizational performance due to the variety of perspectives. In addition, a critical component of the strategy role of managers is questioning the status quo. In intensely competitive markets, organizations must be ready to adapt, be flexible, and not fall prey to organizational inertia (Goodstein et al., 1994; Hannan & Freeman, 1977).

An increased ability to find fault with the status quo may again be a positive for a senior-management team that has racial, ethnic, and gender representation. Given the specific context of the work role of senior managers in an organization, negatives such as conflict and challenging of the status quo are often associated with racially and ethnically diverse groups and may actually be positive.

The problem-solving ability of racially and ethnically diverse groups has also received attention in diversity-management literature. Watson, Kumar and Michaelsen (1993) found that racial and ethnic diversity in groups often leads to less-effective problem solving early on due to the lack of a common perspective. However, the differences in performance between culturally diverse groups and homogeneous groups were found to be nonexistent after nine weeks of working together, and eventually, the performance of the culturally diverse groups exceeded that of homogeneous groups. Since managers work together over an extended period of time, this impeded initial process is not likely to affect decision making.

The nature of the task that diverse groups need to solve may also affect the relationship between workforce diversity and group performance. Janis (1982) and Watson Kuman and Michaelsen (1993) assert that increased racial, ethnic, and gender representation within groups will lead to increased performance on tasks that require a variety of viewpoints. Specifically, in nonroutine problem-solving tasks, diversity in traits, attitudes, values, and orientation lead to more-effective problem solving (Bantel & Jackson, 1989; Filley, House, & Kerr, 1976; Shaw, 1976). The tasks faced by senior managers in an organization are nonroutine by nature and typically benefit from a variety of perspectives.

Agency Rationale

The third rationale for increasing nonwhite and female representation is agency rationale (Johnson et al., 1996). Agency refers to the role managers have to act as fiduciaries of shareholders, serving to alleviate or reduce organizational costs (Fama & Jensen, 1983; Jensen & Meckling, 1976). For example, when the strategies of an organization are ineffective, managers are expected to take action.

An important factor in the agency role is the ability of managers to question the actions of the organization. As mentioned in the discussion of the strategy implementation role, racially and ethnically diverse managers are more likely than homogeneous groups to question or find fault with the status quo (Glick et al., 1993). Ethnic and gender diversity within groups leads to multiple perspectives (Jackson et al., 1991; Mitroff, 1982; Milliken & Martins, 1996) and increased information processing (Sutcliff, 1994). Multiple viewpoints within an organization ensure that the organization does not fall prey to groupthink (Janis, 1982); when a group shares the same perspective and outlook on a situation, they may be blinded to different ways of doing things that may be more effective.

So the multiple perspectives that result from increased gender, racial, and ethnic representation and the increased likelihood of questioning the status quo that results may actually increase the performance of senior-management teams in fulfilling their agency role. This increased ability to perform the agency role is closely linked to the strategy implementation role. Johnson and associates (1996) assert that many organizational-behavior experts now believe that one of the ways nonwhite and female managers are more effective in the agency function is through their cultural perspectives and experience, which contribute to better organizational decisions.

Theoretical Arguments

Social justice theory suggests that although the civil rights movement and legislation granted greater access for nonwhites to the workplace, the movement and legislation failed to fully remedy the disparate treatment many nonwhites encountered in the workplace. Initially, social justice theory was a response from the legal community to address the stagnation and rollback of civil rights legislation such as affirmative action. Some of the core tenets of social justice theory include the recognition that racism is rife in American society, that nonwhites have a voice emanating from their distinctive experiences with racism, and that concepts such as color blindness and meritocracy are misleading ideologies that have actually contributed to the backlash against race-conscious redress by camouflaging and justifying the exclusion of racial and ethnic nonwhites from positions of power (Shuford, 2001; Tate, 1997; Taylor, 1998). Given these core tenets of social justice theory, it is a powerful and relevant theoretical lens by which to examine the effects of organizations' attempts to increase gender, racial, and ethnic representation.

Substitution theory suggests that nonwhite representation is often increased at the expense of white female representation (Szymanski, 1976). Szymanski argues that African Americans and white females are underrepresented in organizations due to the same causes, namely employment discrimination and occupational segregation. However, Szymanski asserts that the nonwhite group label does not seem to apply to females equally and that nonwhite representation and white female representation vary inversely with each other. Moreover, there are a finite number of jobs in an organization; consequently, the higher the percentage of jobs held by nonwhites, the lower the percentage of jobs held by white females. Conversely, the higher the percentage of jobs held by white females, the lower number of jobs held by nonwhites.

Labor market theory suggests that organizations faced with large female and nonwhite populations and labor pools have no choice but to draw upon these pools to fill jobs. Moreover, diversity in the organization will occur when people in the labor pool are hired without making any distinction in favor of, or against, any racial or ethnic group. External labor market theory also implies that a large nonwhite or female population means a larger female and nonwhite applicant pool, a higher probability of qualified nonwhite and female applicants, and a stronger community and customer base in favor of nonwhite and female recruitment (Eisinger, 1982a, 1982b, 1983; Coleman, 1990; Lewis & Nice, 1994).

Goode and Baldwin (2005) offered a similar explanation to account for the high concentration of nonwhites and females working in municipal government. In explaining the impact of African American mayors, Goode and Baldwin suggest the increases in nonwhite and female municipal government employment were a function of increases in the nonwhite and female labor pool in large municipalities rather than the positive externalities associated with the presence of an African American mayor.

Internal labor market theory, in turn, suggests that nonwhites and females are employed more equitably in larger organizations that are increasing in terms of their number of full-time employees. Organizations that are expanding attract more capable people and have an easier time retaining them than an organization that is stagnating or shrinking. Moreover, Goode and Baldwin (2005) assert that when organizations downsize employees or outsource work, nonwhites and females suffer a disproportionate burden of job losses because they generally occupy lower-level positions, which are especially vulnerable to job layoffs and initiatives to outsource work and services.

Majority dominance theory contends that when a racial or ethnic nonwhite group reaches majority or plurality status in an organization, that group begins to obtain a disproportionate share of jobs in that organization, especially in relation to other ethnic groups (McClain, 1993). Given that a major responsibility of managers is the recruitment and selection of employees, nonwhite managers are in a special position to actively increase female, racial, or ethnic representation when they are a majority or plurality (McClain, 1993; Meier & Smith, 1994). The theory suggests that nonwhite managers are purportedly less prejudiced against members of their own group, desire to improve the status of members in their group, and are willing to take active measures to make employment policies and outcomes more favorable to their racial or ethnic group (Eisinger, 1982b, 1983).

Externality theory (Eisinger, 1982; Saltzstein, 1986; Goode & Baldwin, 2005), an economic theory used to explain gender and racial representation in organizations, suggests that the mere presence of nonwhites or females in senior leadership positions in the organization influences the degree of diversity in an organization, even when they do not take direct action to increase female, racial, or ethnic representation.

Seemingly ironic, the *passive* presence of females and nonwhite department heads has a positive unintended consequence, or external benefit, of *active* representation. Individuals forced to interact with nonwhite or female leaders may become more appreciative of nonwhite and female capabilities and more aware of potential and actual employment barriers to nonwhites and females. Perceiving that an organization headed by a nonwhite or female is more receptive to nonwhite and female job applicants, nonwhites and females are also more inclined to apply for jobs in that organization (Goode, 2000; Goode & Baldwin, 2005).

Implementation theory contends that percentage of non-whites and females decreases, in general, when organizations fail to carry out equal-employment opportunity and affirmative-action directives mandated by judicial and legislative branches of government (Farley, 1979; Howard, 1986; Thompson, 1991). Taken one step further, implementation theory specifically suggests that resistance to increasing nonwhite and female representation by white males increases as judicial and legislative pressure increases. Moreover, this quiet and passive resistance to workforce diversity efforts most likely manifests itself as tepid enforcement of judicial consent decrees and superficial support of equal-employment opportunity programs (Huckle, 1984; Pierce & Zahra, 1992; Lorsch & Mcivor, 1989; Mace, 1971).

Upper echelons theory links observable demographic characteristics of top executives to gender and racial representation (Hambrick & Mason, 1984). Key to upper-echelons theory is that visible demographic measures are systematically related to the psychological and cognitive elements of a senior manager's orientation, which works through a filtering process that leads to managerial perceptions regarding the performance of females and nonwhites. Upper echelons theory employs the use of observable demographic characteristics to predict senior managers' orientation, thereby having greater power to predict organizational outcomes such as nonwhite and female representation and retention.

In a study of senior-management team representation, Knight and associates (1999) found support for the upper-echelons theory and that senior executives make decisions that are consistent with their cognitive base or executive orientation. Additional support was provided by Bantel and Jackson (1989), who argue that innovation is associated with the racial and gender makeup of the senior top-management team. Lastly, Sowa and associates (2003) suggest that employees positively concur with management's decisions if the racial and gender composition of senior management reflects that of the group.

Research Findings

The purpose of this review is to examine whether the research provides a link between racial, ethnic, and female representation and organizational performance. Proponents of diversity maintain that different opinions provided by culturally diverse groups make for better-quality decisions (Cox, 1994; McLeod et al., 1996). Nonwhite and female views stimulate consideration of nonobvious alternatives in work settings (McLeod & Lobel, 1992; Nemeth, 1992) and appear useful for making valuable judgments in novel situations. Diversity in decision-making and problem-solving styles produces better decisions through the consideration of a wider range of perspectives and a more thorough critical analysis of issues (Jackson, 1992).

A few studies have provided support for the idea that racial, ethnic, and female diversity benefits organizational performance. For example, Watson, Kumar, and Michaelsen (1993) studied the interaction and performance of culturally homogeneous and culturally diverse groups for seventeen weeks. They reported that homogeneous groups initially scored higher on both process and performance. Over time, both types of groups showed improvement on process and performance, and the between-groups differences lessened. By week seventeen, there were no differences in process or overall performance, but the diverse groups scored higher on two task measures: range of perspectives and alternatives generated.

The business case for diversity—the view that more diversity would increase performance—is gaining momentum because of talent shortages and an increasingly diverse customer base. A study by Kochan (2003) based on a large field-based five-year research project summarizes the findings from the studies of four large organizations in the information processing, financial services, and retailing industries on the relationship between race/gender diversity and business performance. The studies measured performance, satisfaction, and turnover and related them to cultural, demographic, technical, and cognitive differences. They also measured group processes of communication, conflict, cohesion, information, and creativity within the organizational context of culture, business strategy, and HR policies. Qualitative data on business-unit cultures, HR, and managerial practices; survey data based on quality of group processes; and census data on demographic composition of teams were used to interpret the results. The studies established few direct effects of racial and gender representation on organizational performance.

The report looked beyond the existing business case by adopting an analytical approach of linking diversity-management practices to organizational performance. It supports experimentation and evaluation and not simply sticking to the old frame of the business case. The study concluded that it was important to inculcate a culture of mutual learning and cooperation; organizations should implement appropriate human-resource policies in addition to training programs for diversity management.

Horwitz and Horwitz (2007) conducted a meta-analytic review of studies published between 1985 and 2006 to provide quantitative estimates of the relationship. A total of seventy-eight correlations from thirty-five articles were included in the review for the purpose, and correlation coefficient on randomized experiments and post hoc analysis were used as tools to better understand the hypothesized relationships. Based on a dichotomization of representation variable into task versus demographic orientation, Horowitz and Horowitz tested the hypothesis of organizational performance resulting from diverse employee teams. Although demographic orientation (race and gender) were not significantly related to organizational performance, the positive impact of task orientation on organizational performance was supported.

Employing the idiom of melting pot versus tossed salad, Bachman (2006) explored what it takes to design an effective diverse team in the workplace. The study distinguished between two types of coupling in work groups: structural and cultural. Structural coupling refers to the task-related domain, and cultural coupling refers to the non-task-related social domain. The most effective diverse groups tend to have a tight coupling in the task-related structural domain and loose coupling in the non-task cultural domain.

While the former results in consensus, cohesion, effectiveness, and stability, the latter leads to accuracy, creativity, and flexibility. Structural coupling is achieved by clarifying the group's objectives, dividing group tasks into interdependent subtasks, assigning task roles, allocating responsibilities and authority, and determining the norms of task-related interactions. The cultural coupling is accomplished by creating an atmosphere of mutual respect and acceptance and signaling approachability for smoothing differences. In short, an effective work group needs to be both a *tossed salad* and a *melting pot* to produce long-term benefits for the organization.

Based on a study of 437 teams in forty-six departments of a large US company, Joshi, Hui, and Jackson (2006) concluded that in-group/out-group dynamics of diverse work groups might contribute to sales performance differences between white and nonwhites. The study employed measures such as individual demographic attributes, work-team composition, management composition of work units, and sales performance. The control variables were age and tenure of service to account for differences in employees.

Joshi, Hui, and Jackson (2006) suggest it is possible that all employees experience both in-group favoring and out-group discrimination. As the in-group size increases, the members of the in-group enjoy benefits of in-group dynamics. On the other hand, as the in-group size decreases, the group suffers from costs arising from out-group discrimination. Moreover, Joshi, Hui, and Jackson assert that status is also an important factor in the performance implications of representation. It is frequently observed that men and whites typically enjoy higher status than females and nonwhites. Because status is usually associated with skill and expertise, white males may be valued and rewarded even when they are in the minority in the organization.

Senior Leadership Representation and Organizational Performance

On the other hand, Miller (1998) asserts that empirical research on the link between representation and executive decision making is weak. There is no consistent support for either position. Miller argues that gender and race are not hypothesized to have direct effects on organizational performance, but are hypothesized to have indirect effects through differences in cognitive ability. Thus, they investigated and offered an alternative theory, cognitive diversity.

They define cognitive diversity in terms of differences in beliefs and preferences held by senior managers within the organization. They concluded that cognitive diversity is the variation in beliefs concerning cause-effect relationship and the variation in preferences concerning various goals for the organization. Cognitive diversity and racial or gender representation produce unclear effects, some positive and others negative, positive being more prevalent (Miller, 1998).

Pelled (1996) conducted field research on the impact of racial and ethnic representation on organizational performance in the banking industry. Racial and ethnic representation interacted with business strategy in determining organizational performance measured in three different ways—as productivity, return on equity, and market performance.

The results demonstrated that the positive impact of racial or ethnic representation on organizational performance has to do with context. In the absence of consideration of context, a negative relationship between racial and ethnic representation and organizational outcome may emerge. The racial representation-market performance correlation was strong and consistent with previous group-level research (Pelled, 1996; Riordan & Shore, 1997; Tsui, Egan, & O'Reilly, 1992). Absent consideration of context, no relationship between racial representation and organizational outcome was found. The results demonstrated that racial and ethnic representation does, in fact, add value, and within the proper context, contributes to organizational performance.

Board Representation and Organizational Performance

Hillman, and associates (1998) conducted a study that was the first step toward examining the relationship between racial and gender makeup of boards of directors and organizational performance. Their findings support a positive relationship between board racial and gender representation and organizational performance. Because their research was based on only 10 percent of the S&P 500 company boards that had at least one female member or ethnic nonwhite member, their empirical findings were somewhat limited. Their exploratory analysis examined the change in racial makeup of directors and performance between 1991 and 1992 and supported their cross-sectional associations. Moreover, their research examined whether board representation was positively associated with organizational performance, such as legitimacy or increased likelihood to question the status quo.

While their methodology did not pinpoint the underlying causes of the relationship, they did find the percentage of nonwhites on boards to be positively associated with organizational performance. The evidence presented in the research suggests that ethnic, racial, and gender representation is quantifiable and positive results are related to a more diverse board of directors.

Hillman and associates (1998) assert that because women and ethnic nonwhites bring unique perspectives and ties to organizations, organizations that exclude these individuals from their boards may be negatively affecting organizational performance. Moreover, regardless of the underlying reason for underrepresentation of nonwhites and females on boards of directors (e.g., discrimination, recruiting challenges, etc.), their study indicates that organizations without nonwhite or female representation may be harming their long-term performance.

Despite these important findings, Lau and Murnighan (2005) argue that racial and gender representation, measured alone, might not provide conclusive evidence of the impact on organizational performance. Therefore, they investigated the effects of demographic fault lines on the interactions within groups and subgroups. It was observed that intragroup and cross-subgroup communications affected demographic fault lines.

If members of a group fall into more than one nonoverlapping subgroup based on demographic characteristics (e.g., Asian American female or Hispanic American male), a strong fault line is said to be present in the group. Fault lines could explain better why the perceptions of team learning, psychological safety, satisfaction, and expected performance vary more than single variables, such as race or gender representation. The fault-line model used in this study suggested that when a group is split into subgroups, people associate their identities more with their subgroups than with their entire groups.

Members of strong fault-line groups evaluate members of their subgroups more favorably than do members of weak fault-line groups. The identification of subgroups could accentuate members' awareness of a subgroup's boundary and their feelings of belonging. When outcomes depend more on their subgroups' actions, people tend to focus on subgroups rather than the entire group's actions.

Group members are more likely to communicate and share information within rather than across their subgroups when demographic fault lines are strong. Groups with strong fault lines experience more intragroup conflict and poorer group outcomes (e.g., rating of their task and relationship conflict, group learning, psychological safety, satisfaction, and expected group performance) than do groups with weak fault lines. The effects of cross-subgroup communications are moderated by group fault lines.

Effective diversity management is based on recognition of commonalities and awareness of differences. Role-modeling behaviors of those who readily accept the differences could help alter the organizational culture, and thereby improve organizational performance. Globalization and diversity have increased the need for investigation into workplace attitudes toward diverse others.

Therefore, Strauss and Connerley (2003) explored the relationships between race, gender, agreeableness, openness to experience, contact and cognitions, feelings, and behaviors. The universal-diverse orientation (UDO) construct was employed as a measure of attitudes toward diversity. This metric has three components: realistic appreciation (cognition), comfort with difference (feeling), and diversity of contact (behavior).

Based on a survey of 252 undergraduate business students from two different institutions, the study found partial support for the hypothesis that women and nonwhites have more positive UDO attitudes. Gender plays a role only as a first step. Individuals who rate high on openness to experience would have more positive UDO attitudes. Surprisingly, the findings did not support the view that people living in more diverse work environments would have more positive UDO attitudes.

Contact, gender, and race would interact with openness and agreeableness to predict UDO attitudes. Women had more favorable attitudes and higher levels of openness than men. The findings suggest that the cognitive and affective components of UDO attitudes were impacted by agreeableness alone, and the behavioral component was significantly related to race, agreeableness, openness, and contact when all variables were included in the model. Agreeableness emerged as the most important predictor of attitudes.

In their study of nonwhite and female representation in the executive leadership ranks of organizations, Elliott and Smith (2001) explain why nonwhites and females occupy so few executive positions of authority in organizations. They contend that those in power tend to prefer others like themselves, especially when trust is at stake. Historically—and not much has changed in society today—the primary decision makers in organizations are white males. They, therefore, benefit most from this in-group preference.

Elliott and Smith (2001) go on to point out that nonwhites and females are underrepresented in positions of authority in most organizations because the group in charge reproduces its descriptive characteristics in those they select to join them. They refer to this process as homosocial reproduction (p. 210) or top-down ascription; and while they do not debate this theory, they believe it to be incomplete and offer an alternate position.

Group membership impacts authority attainment, and based on identity theory, elites only reproduce themselves. The closer one gets to elite status, the potential for top-down ascription increases, as well as forces bottom-up ascription at lower levels of the organization. The bottom-up ascription refers to matching the race and ethnicity of lower-level managers to the dominant race and ethnicity of their subordinates. In other words, African Americans are more likely to supervise African Americans, and Hispanic Americans are more likely to supervise Hispanic Americans.

This will maintain organizational harmony by curtailing perceptions of unfairness with respect to inequalities in opportunities for upward mobility. Elliot and Smith cite a study conducted by Lefkowitz in 1994, in which African American new employees tended to be assigned to African American managers more frequently than to white managers, even during reassignments. This segregation grew over time and was labeled ethnic drift by Lefkowitz.

Elliott and Smith (2001) contend from their findings that ethnicity and race of the work group is a significant indicator of the race and ethnicity of the supervisor, particularly among nonwhites. When increasing wages were considered, bottom-up ethnic matching significantly decreased and exclusion by white males increased with movement up the organizational chain of command. Pressures for group homogeneity increase as positions of authority become available. These positions, according to Elliott and Smith, are considered a coveted social resource that white males, as a group, are unwilling to abandon.

In a study of the US banking industry, Richard (2000) explored the relationship between representation and financial performance using a sample of sixty-three banks. The banks were drawn from three states: California for its high racial diversity, Kentucky due to its low racial diversity, and North Carolina for the banks' financial wealth and asset size. Blau's index of heterogeneity was used to assess workforce diversity of the banks. Financial information was obtained from the Shesunoff Bank Search database.

The independent variable for the study was the racial/ethnic background of bank employees (white, black, Hispanic, Asian, and Native American). The dependent variables were productivity, return on equity, and market performance. Organization size, state differences, gender, mix of loan portfolio, geographic scope, and banks' attitude toward racial diversity were controlled. Although the hypothesis that racial and gender representation is positively linked to organization performance was not supported, the organizations' business strategy was found to moderate the relationship between the two. Thus, when an organization pursued a strategy of growth, there was a positive relationship between racial representation and organizational performance, while the relationship was negative when the strategy was one of downsizing.

In a related study, Richard and associates (2004) added gender and the degree of entrepreneurial orientation of the organization to the racial diversity of manager and supervisor groups as variables, and studied the responses from 535 bank presidents and human-resource executives. Covin (1989) nine-item entrepreneurial scale was used to measure three dimensions of entrepreneurial orientation: innovativeness, risk taking, and proactiveness. Organizational performance was measured by labor productivity (net income per employee) and the average return on equity for the preceding two years. The proportions of whites and men (due to a large majority in sample), organization size, and annualized percentage of asset growth were controlled.

The hypothesized U-shaped curvilinear relationship between cultural diversity in management and organizational performance was not supported. However, it was found that the curvilinear relationship would be positive and moderately strong in organizations with an innovative orientation, and moderately negative in organizations with a risk-taking orientation when the racial, ethnic, or gender representation is very high or very low. Proactive entrepreneurial orientation had no impact on the relationship.

Broadening their study beyond the banking industry to include a range of other industries, Richard, Murthi, and Ismail (2007) investigated the impact of racial diversity on intermediate and long-term organizational performance and the moderating role of the environmental context. Using data from *Fortune* magazine's diversity survey for the years 1997 through 2002, they estimated the models, employing ordinary least squares regression (OLS). Organizational performance was measured by labor productivity and Tobin's q (ratio of market value to asset replacement value). Organization size, R&D, net income, and the cost of goods sold were controlled.

Racial representation displayed a curvilinear positive relationship to intermediate organizational performance at low or high levels of diversity. Racial representation also exhibited a positive correlation to long-term organizational performance. The type of industry was found to moderate the strength of the relationship between the two. Thus, the predicted U-shaped relationship between racial representation and organizational performance was found to be more noticeable in service industries than in manufacturing industries. The linear relationship between racial representation and long-term performance would be stronger in resource-rich environments. Environmental instability would negatively moderate this relationship. For example, the U-shaped relationship between organizational performance and racial diversity would be stronger in stable environments than in unstable environments.

Practical Implications

In sum, the research on the link between gender, racial, and ethnic representation in an organization and organizational performance clearly appears to suggest that representation in some cases can increase coordination costs or result in no growth or negative growth. Organizations should be particularly aware of the performance implications of a clash between representation and downsizing. Moreover, the same resources that offer some organizations competitive advantage can be a detriment to others. The findings from the research on representation and organizational performance make several contributions to the literature.

A review of the research on the link between representation and organizational performance uncovered several weaknesses. First, much of the research was based on studies that tended to show benefits of representation. Second, most research measured representation at the senior-management level instead of the organizational level. Examining the gender, racial, and ethnic representation in organizations (Cox, 1991a; McLeod et al., 1996; Pelled et. al, 1996) or in organizations' upper echelons (Hambrick & Mason, 1984; O'Reilly & Flatt, 1989) does not, however, capture the larger employee base that ultimately determines an organization's success (Wright & McMahan, 1992). Third, a number of research studies need to better operationally define race or ethnicity in order to establish correlations with organizational performance. For example, many studies put racial and ethnic minorities in one group and whites in the other group, a division that does not fully capture the diversity of racial groups (Kim, Park, & Suzuki, 1990).

Increasing representation is a diversity-management initiative designed to help organizations pool the best talent, reduce the gap between increasingly diverse customer bases, unleash creativity, promote innovation, and thereby enhance the competitiveness of the organization. Jayne and Dipboye (2004) proposed that crucial to changing the workforce are efforts to recruit, retain, and develop employees from underrepresented groups, as well as efforts to create internal structures to sustain an effective diversity-management program.

Using behavioral interviews, biographical data inventories, assessment centers, and work samples to assess knowledge, skills, abilities, experiences, and other characteristics, Jayne and Dipboye (2004) suggest that effective diversity-management programs should strike a balance between identifying right knowledge or skill and enhancing them through training. Employing a "relational demography" method, the study found that working with dissimilar others often results in negative outcomes.

Increased group-level diversity does not necessarily lead to higher performance, and a diverse group is not always a better-performing group. The research clearly shows the benefits of increasing gender, racial, and ethnic representation are contingent on situational factors such as organizational culture, human-resource practices, and the environmental context.

Diversity-management initiatives like recruiting and retaining females and nonwhites should be based on specific goals and not quotas for nonwhite groups. The research makes the important point that the success of diversity-management initiatives such as increasing nonwhite and female representation depends on how they are framed. Rather than as threats to overcome, they should be framed as challenges and opportunities. Comparing the relative efficacies of alternative approaches to framing, the integration and learning perspective (rethinking primary processes) is recommended as the most effective in sustained motivation of management and employees for long-term success. Having racial, ethnic, and female representation on the senior-management team is the most powerful way to signal the support for diversity management.

Summary

Based on the rationales reviewed above, organizations strive to increase gender, racial, and ethnic representation as a diversity-management initiative with the underlying assumption that there is a positive and significant relationship between representation and organizational performance. For example, the advocacy rationale for increasing racial, ethnic, and female representation is associated with increased information; access to critical external constituents (such as customers and individuals in the external labor market); increased organizational benefits, such as reduced turnover, increased organizational commitment, engagement, and productivity among female and nonwhite employees; legitimacy; credibility; and reputation.

The strategy implementation rationale suggests that increased racial, ethnic, and gender representation is positively and significantly associated with a greater range of perspectives and alternatives generated to solve problems, increased information search, increased momentum for strategic change, higher-quality brainstorming ideas, increased group performance in solving nonroutine problems, and increased creativity.

Finally, the agency rationale asserts that organizations pursue increased gender and racial representation as a diversity-management initiative because nonwhite and female managers are more likely to question the status quo, and their diverse perspectives may lead to increased ability to monitor organizational performance on behalf of shareholders.

Drawing upon social-identity theory, the research suggests encouraging managers to know each other as individuals so as to overcome stereotyping, prejudice, and intergroup conflicts. In general, these few studies indicate the value obtained from increasing gender, racial, and ethnic representation. Based on a review of the literature and previous studies, the present examination suggests that greater racial, ethnic, and gender representation in an organization leads to more effective problem solving and increased organizational performance.

CHAPTER 6

INCREASING ENGAGEMENT THROUGH BUSINESS RESOURCE GROUPS

This chapter covers affinity groups, employee resource groups and business resource groups. It describes the efforts of organizations to engage and invest in their employees. It explores the way employee networks are organized and evaluates whether the organization benefits from the efforts of these networks. Lastly, it gauges the programs and benefits provided to resource groups to meet the specific needs and concerns of their members.

Business Case

Diversity-management practitioners assert that involving employees in diversity management improves employee engagement and inclusion. Employees may become involved in their organizations' diversity-management efforts by forming employee diversity task forces, diversity councils, employee resource groups, or affinity networks to identify issues, recommend actions, and help drive initiatives. Organizations that establish employee resource groups that include employees from many specific groups typically do so because they believe that employee resource groups play a vital role in organizations' diversity-management efforts by promoting a safe place for employees to communicate (Koonce, 2001). Social gatherings and business meetings, where members listen to each other's concerns and provide feedback, are good ways to create dialogue. Employee resource groups are also recommended to provide employees access to business information and career opportunities. Employee resource groups also provide an avenue for employees to receive constructive, critical feedback about career mistakes and successes (Flagg, 2002).

Cox's (1994) interactional model of cultural diversity provides a framework that explains the effects of employee resource groups on organizational performance. The model provides support for the proposition that employee resource groups affect organization-level outcomes, such as attendance, turnover, productivity, work quality, and recruiting. Cox further asserts that employee resource groups may also impact individual-level outcomes, such as job success, career advancement, organizational identification, and commitment.

Some organizations deploy employee resource groups as a diversity-management initiative based on the proposition that these groups enhance employee engagement, which ultimately fosters greater organizational performance. The underlying assumption is that employee resource groups foster a stronger identification with the company among employees, which makes them feel that the organization serves their best interests. This, in turn, increases the probability that employees will view the organization's fate as their own, and they perform actions for the benefit of the organization (Hogg & Terry, 2000). Several studies (Hicks-Clarke & Iles, 2000; Hopkins, Hopkins, & Mallette, 2001; McKay, 2007) have shown employees who participate in employee resource groups report higher employee engagement. Applying this logic to their overall diversity-management business case, organizations expect that employees who are members of employee resource groups will expend greater effort to meet organizational goals and that participation in such groups is significantly and positively related to organizational performance.

Lastly, organizations deploy employee resource groups as a diversity-management initiative to socially integrate female and nonwhite employees in hopes that they will perceive the organization and its human-resource policies more favorably. Cox (1994) suggests there may be a strong relationship between employee resource groups and their perception of an organization's diversity climate. Specifically, Cox found a positive correlation between organization-level factors, such as the degree that female and nonwhite employees are integrated into management positions and within an organization's social networks, and whether institutional bias prevails in an organization's human-resource systems (e.g., promotions, talent acquisition, leadership development, etc.). Organizations embrace employee resource groups because employees' combined perceptions of the organizational culture and human-resource practices are affected by employee resource group membership.

Theoretical Arguments

The origin of employee resource groups can be traced back to seminal work by Mark Granovetter (1974), whose *social-network theory* provided insights about how social networks helped people find jobs. This was followed by the work of Blair-Loy 2001; Burt 1998; Ibarra 1992, 1995; McGuire 2000; and Petersen, Saporta, and Seidelm 1998, who suggested that differential network contacts and differential resources accruing from these contacts may explain part of the continuing differences in promotion rates between whites and blacks and between men and women. According to these social-networking theories, white men are more likely than others to find good jobs through network ties because their networks are composed of other white men who dominate the upper tiers of organizations. Social networks also encourage trust, support, and informal coaching (Baron & Pfeffer, 1994; Burt, 1998; Kanter, 1977).

Although networking programs were pioneered in the 1970s, they were revived in the 1990s as part of diversity-management efforts (Castilla, 2005; Fernandez & Fernandez-Mateo, 2006; McBrier, 2000; Mouw, 2003; Wernick, 1994; Winterle, 1992). Today, employee resource groups are thought to provide useful contacts and information. Employee resource groups vary in structure. Some take the form of regular brown-bag lunch meetings, whereas others include large national conferences (Crow, 2003). Employee resource groups may be initiated by employees or by diversity departments. They provide a place for members to meet and share information and career advice. Some networks also advocate policy changes, such as those involving work-life balance policies and domestic-partner benefits (Briscoe & Safford, 2005). Although networking may occur without any organizational impetus, it has become a prevalent diversity-management initiative, as evidenced by the fact that numerous organizations support it through release time off for employees, meeting space, funding, communication, and communication resources such as newsletters and e-mail lists.

The implementation of employee resource groups as a diversity-management initiative is also supported by social-categorization theory research (Brewer, 1995; Jackson, 1995; Williams & O'Reilly, 1998). Social-categorization theory has been used to predict and understand how diversity-management initiatives influence individual attitudes and behavior as well as team dynamics. To explain the effects of employee resource groups on employee performance, the basic argument is that a person's similarity on visible and relatively immutable traits influences feelings of identification (Tsui, Egan, & O'Reilly, 1992).

Within employee resource groups, identification based on demographic similarity is associated with in-group biases and team conflict. By extending the logic of theories that explain individual attitudes and behavior, diversity-management researchers have found a strong theoretical rationale for making predictions about how employee resource groups are likely to influence social processes within teams and organizations (Jehn et al., 1999; Pelled, Eisenhardt, & Xin, 1999). Although social-categorization theory and social-identity theory were developed originally to explain the effects of gender, race, and ethnic diversity, some researchers have used these theories to explain the effects of employee resource groups on organizational performance (Thomas, 1999).

Drawing from social-identity theory, several researchers (Stryker, 1968; Tajfel & Turner, 1986) recognized the potential link between employee resource groups and organizational performance. Social-identity theory proposes that people categorize themselves and others into social groups based upon salient characteristics such as race-ethnicity, sex, age, national origin, and religion. Two principal tenets of social-identity theory are that people are psychologically linked to in-group outcomes due to their implications for self-esteem and that people seek out environments and situations that affirm their identity group (Ashforth & Mael, 1989; Hogg & Terry, 2000).

Given the subordinate social status of nonwhites in most organizations and the workplace discrimination they experience routinely (Bell, Harrison, & McLaughlin, 1997; Deitch et al., 2003; Ridgeway, 1991), it stands to reason that nonwhites, more so than whites, will appreciate organizational efforts to offer employee resource groups (Kossek & Zonia, 1993; Linnehan et al., 2003; Mor Barak, Cherin, & Berkman, 1998). Given this greater relative importance, nonwhite and female employees should find employee resource groups as more affirming of their identity groups, which likely promotes greater motivation to advance organizational goals (Blau, 1964).

Corroborating this reasoning, Ely and Thomas (2001) reported nonwhite and female employees in organizations that effectively managed diversity felt more valued by their organizations when employee resource groups were present and supported. Moreover, other researchers (Avery et al., 2007; Gilbert & Ivancevich, 2001) found white-nonwhite differences in productivity were greater in organizations that embraced employee resource groups.

In their review of the literature on racial-ethnic differences in job performance, Roberson and Block (2001) identified four theoretical perspectives to explain the relationship between employee resource groups and organizational performance.

The *internal-trait model* suggests that racial-ethnic differences in job performance are due to differences in ability and motivation. However, the *bias and discrimination model* proposes racial-ethnic differences are a function of biases held by decision makers, which lead to inequitable performance ratings and discriminatory treatment that detracts from actual performance. As nonwhites become aware of bias and discrimination against their social-identity groups, they develop strategies (e.g., self-limiting behavior, psychological disengagement) designed to protect their self-images from identity threats such as discrimination. These mechanisms form the basis of the *coping model.* Finally, the *organizational-context model* suggests both employee race-ethnicity and aspects of the organizational context (e.g., structural integration, cultural distance, diversity climate) influence individual responses, with implications for organizational performance.

Research Findings

Intensive efforts to measure the impact of employee resource groups and their impact resulted in mostly positive findings about their effect on organizational performance. For example, Kmec (2007) examined the relationship between employee resource groups and job turnover, and found that social similarity eases communications, fosters trust, strengthens personal bonds, and predicts that information-sharing between socially similar individuals differs in quality and content from information between dissimilar pairs.

Additional research confirmed Kmec's *homophlilly theory* (i.e., Bell, Harrison, & McLaughlin, 1997; Deitch et al., 2003; Kossek & Zonia, 1993; Linnehan et al., 2003; Mor Barak, Cherin, & Berkman, 1998). These researchers all conclude that given the subordinate social status of nonwhites in most organizations, it should be expected that nonwhites appreciate organizational efforts to employ employee resource groups. Given this greater relative importance, nonwhite employees find organizations with employee resource groups as more affirming of their identity groups, which likely promoted greater employee engagement and inclusion.

Ely and Thomas (2001) reported nonwhite employees in organizations that had employee resource groups felt more valued by their organizations. Moreover, other researchers (Avery et al., 2007; Gilbert & Ivancevich, 2001) found white and nonwhite differences in absenteeism (a performance outcome) were smaller in organizations perceived to place greater value on employee resource groups, business support groups, or affinity groups.

McKay (2008) conducted perhaps the first study to examine the moderating effects of employee resource groups measured as mean racial-ethnic differences in employee sales performance. Their study suggests a link between employee resource groups and certain organizational outcomes and demonstrates that implementing employee resource groups is an effective diversity-management initiative because it has bottom-line implications.

McKay's study is a departure from previous research, which focused primarily on demographic diversity (Joshi et al., 2006; Sacco & Schmitt, 2005) to the relative exclusion of the role of employee resource groups as an effective diversity-management initiative. The study conducted by McKay (2008) consisted of a sample of 6,130 sales employees working in seventeen departments in a retail company that maintained individual sales figures. Sales associates were expected to manage the customer interaction on the sales floor and to show additional choices to customers or suggest add-on purchases. These sales associates had sales goals in their performance plan, and store sales goals were reviewed daily during storewide meetings. Sales associates handled transactions and customer complaints as well, but their primary function was to create a positive customer experience and deliver sales results. Sales associates received a significant amount of their compensation based on their ability to sell larger amounts and higher-quality items from their area and therefore had an incentive to close the sale.

The study found significant Hispanic-white but not black-white mean differences in sales performance, and employee resource group membership moderated racial and ethnic mean differences in sales performance. McKay (2008) concluded that the stronger results may be possible in organizations with similar approaches to diversity management. However, employee resource group presence in the organization failed to impact gender mean differences in sales performance. McKay speculated that gender differences in sales possibly reflected differential responding by female salespersons and their nonwhite counterparts to the survey items. Moreover, females might hold gender as a focus of employee resource group participation more so than nonwhites, for whom race-ethnicity could be of greater importance.

McKay's study has several limitations. First, there was some indication of survey nonresponse in the data set. Some employees' propensity toward nonresponse might have been heightened due to the nonanonymous nature of data collection. Survey nonrespondents tended to be younger, be lower in job level and with less organizational tenure, be part-timers, and generate fewer sales per hour. It should be noted, however, that nonrespondents were less representative of the bulk of store employees in terms of age, work schedule, and tenure.

Second, the nonanonymous survey administration may explain why McKay derived a different pattern of racial-ethnic and sex mean differences in individual performance climate than those observed in earlier research (e.g., Kossek & Zonia, 1993; McKay 2008; Mor Barak et al., 1998). Perhaps respondents were reluctant to report lower perceptions due to fears of retaliation. Although these issues may lessen somewhat the internal validity of results, reduced variance in scores on relevant study variables lessens the likelihood of obtaining statistically significant interaction terms (McClelland & Judd, 1993). Thus, the results of McKay's research may signify a conservative examination of the presence of employee resource groups' moderating effects on mean racial-ethnic differences in sales performance.

Practical Implications

Employee resource groups are company-sanctioned organizations formed by employees with common interests, backgrounds, or lifestyles. The research shows that most organizations have such groups formed by female employees; gay, lesbian, and bisexual employees; ethnic nonwhite employees; parents; disabled employees; and faith groups. However, several studies clearly indicate that there is no mechanism for investing the employee resource groups with formal power or authority to influence the organization's diversity-management strategy. They are, rather, perceived as helpers or supporters of the company's diversity-management initiatives.

Within this framework, diversity-management research indicates that the activities of employee resource groups involve helping their organizations in recruiting and retaining diverse employees, participating in community projects, and supporting diversity initiatives in the organization. Most important, employee resource groups are seen by their respective organizations as important resources providing insights to diverse markets and supporting the marketing of the company's brands among diverse segments of the population.

Accordingly, the diversity-management research is full of narrations of success stories about employee resource groups helping their respective organizations to achieve a greater market share among ethnic nonwhite, female, gay, lesbian, bisexual, and transgender customers. Moreover, research suggests that employee resource groups are not identity or pressure groups in the traditional sense, but they are company-sanctioned organizations with clear aims in terms of their business impact in making the company an employer of choice or brand of choice for diverse communities.

This statement should not obscure the potentially political principle that brings these employees together in the employee resource groups—that is, their identities in terms of being members of disadvantaged demographic groups. What is striking in the business-case rhetoric for employee resource groups is the focus on the employers' interest. For example, employee resource groups' interests are issues of consideration as long as they contribute to business goals. This focus on organizational benefit is very well illustrated in the case of most organizations' perception of the employee resource groups as mediums with which to leverage the diversity of their employees in order to sell more products to a diverse customer base.

There are a number of practical implications for the field of diversity management. McKay and associates' (2008) findings illustrate that beyond racial-ethnic demographic diversity, the presence and effective management of employee resource groups had positive ramifications for female and nonwhite employees' job performance and, cumulatively, organizational performance. Furthermore, employee resource groups were not associated with declines in individual performance among white employees, as diversity-management backlash arguments might suggest (e.g., Linnehan & Konrad, 1999).

The empirical research also suggests there is a dollar value associated with effectively deploying employee resource groups as a diversity-management initiative. Also, the benefits of leveraging employee resource groups as an effective diversity-management initiative extends beyond increasing the percentage of nonwhites and females in the workforce to improving organizational performance.

Numerical workforce diversity targets do not alone equate to successful diversity management. McKay and Avery (2005) found only a slight correlation between the percentage of nonwhite employees and the presence of employee resource groups. Such superficial approaches to diversity management do not ensure that employees in an organization feel included, perceive human-resource policies to be fair, or experience the social integration of diverse employees into the work environment. Consequently, organizations must be intentional and strategic about deploying employee resource groups so that they are advantageous to the organization's long-term business success.

CHAPTER 7

CONDUCTING DIVERSITY TRAINING AND EDUCATION

This chapter explores how organizations conduct diversity management awareness education and skill-building training, and the integration of such training into the overall training and development of employees in their organizations. The chapter takes a close look at the extent to which diversity management training are provided equitably to enable all to enhance both employees individual performance and organizational performance.

Business Case

By the late 1970s and into the 1980s, there was growing recognition within the private sector that while legal mandates were necessary, they were not sufficient for ensuring the effective management of diversity within organizations. Although the workforces of many organizations became more diverse, entrenched organizational cultures, which remained inhospitable to traditionally underrepresented groups, were slow to change.

To promote the development of more positive organizational cultures that would support the effective development of more diverse workforces, organizations began to offer training programs aimed at *valuing diversity*. These efforts focused on changing employees' attitudes and eliminating behaviors that reflected more subtle forms of discrimination and exclusion, which often inhibited effective interactions among employees. The widespread adoption of such training programs expanded the concept of diversity as people began to realize that visible, legally recognized demographic differences such as race and gender were not the only types of differences that affected work relationships among employees.

Gradually, training initiatives proliferated, encouraging employees to value the wide range of physical, cultural, and interpersonal differences that would, presumably, enhance decision making, problem solving, and creativity at work. Unfortunately, however, most studies show that such training rarely leads to the desired long-term changes in attitudes and behavior (Bezrukova & Jehn, 2001).

For the purposes of this book, diversity training is defined very broadly in order to capture a wider sample of studies that incorporate diversity training. Using a broad definition of diversity has been associated with greater perceived success of diversity training (Rynes & Rosen, 1995). Diversity training can incorporate subject matter specific to certain subgroups, for example, race (Randolph, Landis, & Tzeng, 1977; Stewart et al., 2003) or be broad and generic (Davis, 2008; Sanchez & Medkik, 2004). The goal of diversity training can be either to raise awareness of diversity-related issues, teach skills relevant for diversity management, or both (Kulik & Roberson, 2008). Diversity-management training may also involve teaching about the effects of stereotypes and bias on decision making, learning how to resolve conflicts that may arise between individuals from different subgroups, or learning what is appropriate behavior in the workplace.

According to some diversity-management practitioners, training can help an organization's managers increase their awareness and understanding of workforce diversity, as well as help them develop concrete skills to assist them in communicating and increasing productivity. Such training can provide employees with an awareness of their differences—including cultural, work style, and personal presentation—and an understanding of how diverse perspectives can improve organizational performance.

Diversity-management training also teaches employees about the importance of the organization's diversity goals and gives them the skills required to work effectively in a diverse workforce. In addition to increasing employee performance in a diverse environment, diversity-management experts recommend that diversity training include team building, communication styles, decision making, and conflict resolution. This view is consistent with President Barack Obama's executive order 13583 to federal agencies, which requires that agencies train supervisors and managers to increase their communication and interpersonal skills so that they can more effectively manage diverse work teams.

Initially, organizations instituted diversity training in response to legal concerns (Anand & Winters, 2008). Gradually, organizations abandoned this conception of diversity training and adopted the business case model. This perspective recognized that a diverse workforce is beneficial to productivity. In fact, a number of companies reported that they conducted diversity training for the purposes of improving productivity and relations between employees. Thus, organizations have shifted their focus to include skill development in addition to raising awareness and changing attitudes and behaviors through diversity training (Bendick, 2001; Page, 2007).

Employer surveys of diversity-management initiatives reveal that training has mushroomed in the past decade. Twenty years ago, it was virtually absent from lists of the most common diversity practices. Ten years ago, diversity training was being offered in an estimated 50 percent of large organizations. Between 2002 and 2006, the percentage of members of the American Management Association who reported having training as a formal component of the diversity-management strategy rose from 46 percent to 50 percent (Lynch, 2007). A 2005 survey of the fifty largest industrial organizations in the United States reported that 70 percent had formal diversity-management programs with training as a major component of strategy and an additional 8 percent were developing such a program (Lynch). Sweeney (2002) found that 67 percent of employers surveyed conducted gender- or race-related diversity training. Lee (2003) reported that several companies were increasing their budgets for diversity training, although exact figures were not reported.

Diversity-management training has tended to focus on content related to race and gender, but since the 1980s, training has included cross-cultural and intercultural content.

Cross-cultural training focuses specifically on training individuals for expatriate assignments (Bean, 2006). In contrast, intercultural training focuses more broadly on improving the ability of individuals to interact with people from cultures other than their own (Fowler, 2006).

Theoretical Arguments

Numerous scholars have criticized organizations for failing to conduct evaluations of their diversity-training programs (Hite & McDonald, 2006; Perry et al., 2009; Rynes & Rosen, 1995). Often, social and political pressures dictate the extent to which training is evaluated (Gutiérrez et al., 2000; Lynch, 1997). When organizations do evaluate, they tend to use reaction measures rather than more rigorous tools, such as knowledge assessments or behavioral measurements (Bennett, 2006; Rynes & Rosen, 1995). Reaction measures are easy, quick to administer, and cost-effective. Therefore, they are used more frequently than any other training evaluation tool.

Some organizations analyze diversity training from a more theoretical perspective, using the Kraiger, Ford, and Salas (1993) model of training evaluation. This emphasized three types of learning outcomes: affective, cognitive, and skill-based. These outcomes draw on various theoretical domains (e.g., social, cognitive, instructional psychology, etc.). Further, the Kraiger, Ford, and Salas model distinguished between different types of specific outcomes within each of the three broad categories. For instance, verbal knowledge is only one component of the cognitive domain (knowledge organization and cognitive strategies are two other categories).

Affective-Based Diversity Training

The most common outcome evaluated within diversity training is affective learning. Affective learning refers to attitudes, self-efficacy, and motivation. Kraiger (1993) defined affective-learning outcomes as measures of internal states that drive perception and behavior. In examining this learning outcome, Kraiger excludes reaction measures because they are designed to assess affective reactions to the training rather than changes in diversity-related effects resulting from training (Curtis & Dreachslin, 2008; Kraiger, 1993).

Attitude change reflects the extent to which people have changed the way they perceive others. Some research has suggested that training is not a viable option for changing attitudes toward others (Bendick et al., 2001; Kalev et al., 2006). However, other research has found positive effects for diversity training on attitudes (Bailey, Barr, & Bunting, 2001; Pruegger & Rogers, 1994; Robb & Doverspike, 1998). Kulik and Roberson (2008a) suggested that the observed effects depend on the focus of the training. For example, they found negative or inconclusive effects for studies focusing on attitudes toward specific groups, but they observed positive effects for diversity training when one measured diversity attitudes and when training was predicated on the business case or displayed organizational importance.

Similarly, Hollister, Day, and Jesaitis (1993) suggested that attitude change is likely to occur within a supportive transfer environment and that diversity training has different effects on change in explicit versus implicit aspects of attitudes. However, very few studies have investigated implicit attitude change in regard to diversity training (Castillo et al., 2007; Rudman, Ashmore, & Gary, 2001).

Self-efficacy reflects another affective outcome. Self-efficacy is an important construct within the training and job performance domains (Bandura, 1997; Stajkovic & Luthans, 1998). Combs and Luthans (2007) suggested that instead of measuring reactions to training, one should measure self-efficacy as a training outcome. Measuring one's internal belief structure for dealing with organizational diversity is likely to be important for inferring how individuals will behave in diversity-related contexts.

Cognitive-Based Diversity Training

A second organizational-performance outcome evaluated within diversity training is cognitive learning. Cognitive outcomes can encompass assessments of knowledge about diversity and related processes. Cognitive outcomes also can include strategies employed by the participants to overcome thoughts and practices that may be detrimental to team performance. Even further, one can measure the cognitive organization of diversity knowledge. Previous research focused on the verbal knowledge attained by participants (Gulick et al., 2009; Holladay & Quiñones, 2008; Roberson et al., 2001; Sanchez & Medkik, 2004; Williams, 2005).

For example, research investigating the reduction of sexual harassment in workplaces has examined the effects of these interventions on sexual-harassment knowledge (Perry, Kulik, & Schmidtke, 1998; Robb & Doverspike, 2001). Very few, if any, studies have investigated other cognitive outcomes, such as cognitive structures. Kulik and Roberson (2008) reported overall positive effects of diversity training on cognitive-based outcomes in their review.

Skill-Based Diversity Training

A third outcome evaluated within diversity training is skill-based learning. There has been a greater focus in skill-based learning on assessments of procedural knowledge and skill compilation than on automaticity (Barker, 2004; Hanover & Cellar, 1998; Moyer & Nath, 2004; Perry et al., 1998; Sanchez & Medkik, 2004). This is largely due to the fact that diversity-related behavior tends to be more complex and require more working memory capacity than traditional psychomotor skills. Procedural knowledge, behavioral observation, and role-plays are common skill-based evaluation tools used by diversity trainers. Skill development has moved toward generalizable skills such as conflict resolution and interpersonal skills training and away from diversity-specific skills (Kulik & Roberson, 2008). Whereas the overall effect of diversity training on skill-based learning has been positive, most of the studies have evaluated skills using self-assessments, and few have investigated objective, behavioral skills (Kulik & Roberson, 2008).

Research Findings

What, if any, relationship exists between diversity-management training programs and organizational performance? Bezrukova and Jehn (2001) concluded that diversity training can result in meaningful intercultural understanding, attitude change, and even behavioral change. However, they concede that more research must be conducted to understand how the design and context of diversity training influences organizational performance if diversity training will eventually be as useful as it is popular.

There are three streams of diversity-training research. One stream of research has focused on managers', employees', and participants' perceptions of diversity training. Some of this research has used company surveys and interviews as a means of assessing managers' and employees' perceptions of diversity-training practices within their organizations (Bendick, Egan, & Lofhjelmm, 2001; Gutiérrez et al., 2000; Rynes & Rosen, 1995). The results of this research stream have suggested that diversity training, at best, is perceived as having only modest effects on organizational performance.

At worst, managers' and employees' perceptions of diversity-training interventions were mixed, reflecting both positive and negative perceptions (Rynes & Rosen, 1995). In a similar vein, some research has examined employees' perceptions of experimentally varied characteristics of diversity-training programs. Participants responded to descriptions of programs in which characteristics of the program (e.g., group composition, training focus, training title, trainer's race or gender) have been experimentally varied. Typically assessed are reactions and backlash, as well as perceptions of trainer effectiveness, credibility, and expertise (Hanover & Cellar, 1998; Holladay et al., 2008; Holladay et al., 2003; Holladay & Quiñones, 2005, 2008; Kath, 2004; Liberman, Block, & Uyekubo, 2010).

A second stream of research has examined learning outcomes of individuals participating in diversity-training programs that vary in terms of characteristics of the training design, trainer, trainee, and training environment (Hanover & Cellar, 1998; Holladay et al., 2003; Holladay & Quiñones, 2005, 2008; Kulik et al., 2007; Roberson, Kulik, & Pepper, 2001). The focus of this stream of research has been on investigating the factors that explain when and for whom diversity training will be effective. However, much of this research has not adequately compared diversity training with a control group. Thus, the research could not definitively state whether improvements in organizational performance are due to diversity training itself.

Kulik and Roberson (2008) focused on organizational performance in their qualitative review. They reviewed diversity training within educational, laboratory, and organizational contexts, examining effects on affective, knowledge, and skill-based outcomes, as suggested in Kraiger, Ford, and Salas's (1993) model of training evaluation.

The third stream of research focuses on the effectiveness of diversity training. For example, several scholars (Combs & Luthans, 2007; Rudman, Ashmore, & Gary, 2001; Sanchez & Medkik, 2004; Stewart et al., 2003) have examined simultaneously some of the above contextual factors discussed previously, as well as compared diversity training against a control group on learning outcomes.

Hanover and Cellar (1998) examined the effects of the work and social environments on learning outcomes while testing the effects of diversity training against a control group. For sexual-harassment training interventions, some studies have investigated the likelihood to sexually harass (i.e., an individual difference variable) as an important control variable during experimental manipulation of training interventions (Perry, Kulik, & Schmidtke, 1998; Robb & Doverspike, 2001).

Practical Implications

This chapter focused on the factors within the research model that could help explain or clarify the relationship between diversity training and organizational performance. Specifically, I examined how the training was designed, who received the training, and the circumstances that impacted the effectiveness of diversity training. Another goal of this chapter was to examine evidence that diversity training influences organizational performance in regard to design of, participation in, and context of diversity training. A third goal was to examine effects on organizational performance. To accomplish this goal, I assessed the extent to which diversity training improved organizational performance. I also examined research regarding the extent to which diversity training affected organizational goals such as recruitment procedures, hiring practices, or promotion policies.

Based on my review of the research, it appears that regardless of the specific training content, organizations generally seem to favor training that targets individual attitudes and behavior. This approach may give too little weight to the powerful social dynamics that arise within natural work teams, which increasingly emphasize teamwork. Future training programs should shift the focus of diversity-management training from the individual to the team level. Training teams to manage and leverage their own diversity may prove more beneficial to the entire organization.

Unfortunately, there is no guarantee of success. It mainly depends on the manager's ability to understand what is best for the organization based on teamwork and the dynamics of the workplace. According to Roosevelt Thomas (2001), managing diversity is a comprehensive process for creating a work environment that includes everyone. When creating a successful diverse workforce, an effective manager should focus on personal awareness. Both managers and employees need to be aware of their personal biases.

Therefore, organizations need to develop, implement, and maintain ongoing training, because a one-day session of training will not change people's behaviors (Koonce, 2001). Managers must also understand that fairness is not necessarily equality. There are always exceptions to the rule. Diversity management is about more than equal-employment opportunity and affirmative action (Losyk, 1996). Managers should expect change to be slow, while at the same time encouraging change (Koonce, 2001).

A second key finding from the research that has significant implications for diversity-management practitioners is that organizations seem fixated on raising awareness of workplace inequities instead of building skill sets for diversity management. Awareness training encompasses knowledge of stereotyping as the first step toward behavioral change (Kulik & Roberson, 2008). Most studies that have examined awareness and knowledge issues rather than skill-based training concluded that few organizations assess beyond the awareness level (Curtis & Dreaschlin, 2008; Hite & McDonald, 2006).

However, research casts doubt on the ability of diversity training to enact the proposed benefits of awareness training (Kulik &

Roberson, 2008b; Sanchez & Medkik, 2004). Moreover, awareness training may not even align with the organizations' desired skill sets for managers. Organizations are more interested in skill-building and leadership skills as opposed to knowledge or awareness of specific cultures (Day & Glick, 2000). Skill-based training also may decrease the negative ramifications of backlash by broadening the approach of diversity training (Gutiérrez et al., 2000; Holladay et al., 2003).

Further, focusing on skill-based training may improve organizational performance more so than if training focused solely on raising awareness. For example, skill-based training may provide practice in appropriately applying awareness knowledge. Therefore, organizations should design and develop both types of diversity training as opposed to awareness training alone.

One criticism of diversity training is that one cannot expect much attitudinal or behavioral change within short, one-time sessions (Kalev et al., 2006). Mobley and Payne (1992) suggested that diversity training that is too brief, too late, or too reactive will result in employee backlash. Change is likely to occur when diversity training is spread out over multiple sessions and does not appear to punish particular individuals. Stereotypes develop over extended periods of time, and one might surmise that it should take at least an equal amount of time to relearn or adjust one's attitude toward or knowledge of other cultures.

Kulik and Roberson (2008) suggest that attitudes have produced inconsistent results, although knowledge gains seem to be fairly consistent across contexts and length of sessions. Thus, the evidence so far has been mixed. Regardless, research on overlearning would suggest that increased practice would improve retention levels and retrieval on subsequent testing (Driskell, Willis, & Copper, 1992). Driskell, Willis, and Copper defined overlearning as the percentage of practice beyond one errorless trial. In other words, if one needs five trials to produce one errorless trial, then ten additional trials of practice would reflect 100 percent overlearning. Overlearning produces stronger effects for cognitive tasks than psychomotor tasks.

Diversity training is more cognitive than physical. Whereas it is difficult to ascertain the level of overlearning within diversity-training studies, one can assume that longer diversity-training sessions would utilize greater amounts of practice of learned skills, which should increase organizational performance.

Summary

Diversity training alone is not sufficient for an organization's diversity-management strategy. A strategy must be created and implemented to create a culture of diversity that permeates every department and function of the organization. Effective managers must be made aware that certain skills are necessary for managing diverse teams and creating inclusive work environments. First, managers must understand discrimination and its consequences. Second, managers must recognize their own cultural biases and prejudices. Diversity is not about differences among groups, but rather about differences among individuals. Each individual is unique and does not represent or speak for a particular group. Finally, managers must be willing to change the organization, if necessary. Organizations need to learn how to manage diversity in the workplace to be successful in the future.

CHAPTER 8

RECRUITING, DEVELOPING AND ADVANCING MINORITIES AND FEMALES

This chapter describes how organizations attempt to ensure diversity in their hiring and selection processes, and whether these efforts help create an organizational culture that increases diversity, advances non-whites and females into leadership positions while enhancing organizational performance.

Business Case

Diversity-management practitioners contend that recruitment, a key process by which organizations attract a supply of qualified nonwhites and females for employment, is the first step toward establishing a diverse workforce. To ensure that they are reaching out to diverse pools of talent, they suggest that organizations widen the selection of schools from which they recruit to include, for example, historically black colleges and universities, Hispanic-serving institutions, women's colleges, and schools with international programs.

In addition, diversity-management experts argue that it is important for organizations to build formal relationships with such schools to ensure the cultivation of talent for future leadership pools. Moreover, diversity-management professionals suggest that organizations should also consider partnering with multicultural professional organizations and speaking at their conferences to communicate their commitment to diversity to external audiences and strengthen and maintain relationships. Although the focus of recruitment efforts in the diversity-management literature is with colleges and universities, given the number of employees who are eligible for retirement in the next few years, there will be a need to also recruit midcareer employees, which are defined as employees who are generally forty and over and have ten or more years of work experience.

The underlying assumption behind diversity-management initiatives aimed at recruiting nonwhites and females is that organizations should increase their numbers of women and racial and ethnic minorities to better match the demographic characteristics of their significant customers in order to achieve a competitive edge in the market (Cox, 1994). As racial and ethnic populations increase as a proportion of the total population, it behooves companies to adjust their human-resource mix to reflect the target market they are attempting to reach. Moreover, as organizations reach out to a broader customer base, they need employees who understand particular customer preferences and requirements (Morrison, 1992). The insights and cultural sensitivity that women and nonwhite employees bring to a marketing effort may improve an organization's ability to reach different market segments (Cox & Blake, 1991).

Recruitment as a diversity-management initiative is also designed to help an organization gain competitive advantage through one of a company's most important assets: its people. Employees may give an organization enduring competitive advantages to the extent that they remain scarce or hard to duplicate, have no direct substitutes, and enable companies to pursue opportunities (Barney, 1991; Lado,

Boyd, & Wright, 1992). As other sources of competitive advantage, such as technological and physical resources, have become easier to emulate, the crucial differentiating factor between organizations can be how employees work within an organization (Pfeffer, 1994).

The concept of *human-capital theory* is that people have skills, experience, and knowledge that provide economic value to organizations. Barney and Wright (1998) noted that in order for employees to contribute to sustainable competitive advantage, they must create value, remain hard to imitate, and appear rare. Workforce diversity in an organization serves as a source of sustained competitive advantage because it creates value that is both rare and difficult to imitate.

Organizations may also select women and nonwhites to gain alternative perspectives necessary in changing or turbulent environments (Cox, 1991; Cox & Blake, 1991). Nemeth (1992) maintained that encouraging nonwhite viewpoints improves the quality of thought, performance, and decision making. If an organization overcomes resistance to change in the area of accepting diversity, it may be positioned well to handle other types of change (Iles & Hayers, 1997).

Diversity within decision-making teams may also lead to changes in corporate strategy or organizational flexibility that may be advantageous in a particular market context (Amason, 1996). Many valuable resources are protected from imitation not by property rights, but by knowledge barriers. Proponents of the resource-based view recognize the nature of human resources by focusing on their subjectivity, ambiguity, and creativity (Kamoche, 1994; Pfeffer, 1994). Employees, particularly those from diverse backgrounds, are protected by knowledge barriers and appear socially complex because they involve a mix of talents that is elusive and hard to understand (Lippman & Rumelt, 1982).

Knowledge-based resources depend upon large numbers of people or teams engaged in coordinated, creative action, providing an organization a competitive advantage (Barney, 1991; Hart, 1995).

Therefore, an organization with a diversity of perspectives should have more resources to draw on and should be more creative and innovative. For example, knowledge-based resources such as racial, ethnic, and gender diversity enable organizations to succeed because they gives the organization the skills needed to adapt products or services to market needs and meet competitive challenges.

Advanced capabilities accumulate from skills, in part because rivals do not know that workforce diversity contributes to success. It is difficult to discern what in a rival's employee mix makes it effective; therefore, an effective mix is difficult to imitate. Miller and Shamsie (1996) noted that knowledge-based resources may eventually be imitated but that this normally takes time, and by then, the imitated organization may have developed its skills further.

The value obtainable from a large number of diverse individuals who work together is quite high, and in most cases, a given organization's mix is impossible for competitors to imitate. In addition, the socially complex dynamics in diverse organizations are not transferable across organizations, benefiting only the organization in which the relationships develop. Hence, the value obtained from cultural diversity seems hard to imitate.

A strategic asset must be rare in order to offer sustained competitive advantage (Barney & Wright, 1998; Russo & Fouts, 1997). If it is assumed across organizations that workforce diversity as a human-capital strategy does not create value, when in fact it does, there is tremendous potential for an organization to exploit the rare characteristics of a diverse employee base for competitive advantage. In fact, in some cases, organizations still fail to address workforce diversity beyond attempting to increase the number of females and nonwhites in the organization.

Furthermore, many organizations have interpreted workforce diversity as a human-resource cost to be managed instead of a human-resource asset to be fostered. Additionally, since workforce diversity has not been shown to impact the bottom line, many companies' top managers do not see the value in it (Robinson & Decant, 1997; Wright, Perris, Hiller, & Kroll, 1995).

Lastly, advocates of recruiting nonwhites and females as a diversity-management initiative point out that recruitment is the front door to succession planning, which is a comprehensive, ongoing strategic process that provides for forecasting an organization's senior-leadership needs, identifying and developing candidates who have the potential to be future leaders, and selecting individuals from among a diverse pool of qualified candidates to meet the organization's executive-leadership needs.

Succession planning can help an organization become what it needs to be rather than simply recreate the existing organization. Innovative organizations go beyond a replacement approach that focuses on identifying particular individuals as possible successors for specific top-ranking positions and engage in broad, integrated succession planning and management efforts that focus on strengthening both current and future capacity. They anticipate the need for leaders and other key employees with the necessary competencies to successfully deal with complex business challenges. Succession planning also is tied to the organizations' opportunity to change the diversity of the senior-management team through the promotion of nonwhites and females.

Theoretical Arguments and Research Findings

Human-capital theory suggests that an organization's workforce diversity is impacted because the human wealth that nonwhites and females possess is not marketable (Becker, 1962; Mincer, 1994). In other words, nonwhites do not possess sufficient knowledge, skills, abilities, experience, aptitude, training, or education in sufficient quantity demanded by employers.

This view is not without its opponents. For example, it is well established in the literature that major human-capital theories are inadequate in accounting for the experiences of nonwhites and females. Phelps and Constantine (2001) observed that race and ethnicity have not been included as variables in many of the major human-capital theories and models. The recruitment, and advancement behavior and patterns of nonwhites have been evaluated, in large part, based on white male norms and behavior patterns. The sociopolitical and sociohistorical (e.g., racism, sexism, bias, and discrimination) realities and experiences of nonwhites have not been considered along with their personal and individual realities.

The considerations of position, culture, context, and historical experiences are all important when framing theories of talent acquisition to be used with women and nonwhites. The lack of consideration for nonwhites in human-capital theorizing has limited the relevance and applicability of major theories to recruitment as a diversity-management initiative. Certainly, employment data confirm that the experiences of nonwhite men are distinct from their white counterparts. Thus, it is an error to equate the career behaviors and advancement of white men to those of nonwhites and females.

Several scholars (Barrett, 2000; Cheatam, 1990; Humphrey, 2007; Thomas & Alderfer, 1989) agree that more research is needed before major human-capital theories can be broadly applied to diversity-management initiatives. Recognizing the increasing diversity in the workplace and the lack of attention to race in talent acquisition and development, some scholars have moved to address the gap. For example, Cheatam and Thomas and Alderfer developed talent-acquisition and development models specifically relevant to African Americans.

Cheatam's (1990) *heuristic model of African American acquisition and development* emphasized the need to consider the sociopolitical and sociohistorical context of African American recruitment, development, and advancement. While Cheatam's model provides insight about the talent-acquisition and development processes that lead to their initial recruitment and selection, Thomas and Alderfer

(1989) focused on what happens in African Americans' career development after they join the organization.

Both of these theories are important constructions in the diversity-management literature and are relevant to this present study because they center on the issue of race and racism and advance a more holistic lens through which to view nonwhite and female recruitment, development, and advancement as a diversity-management initiative in organizations. Other theories have also emerged since the earlier traditional theories were developed, but the prevailing thought remains that no single, comprehensive model of nonwhite and female recruitment exists that addresses the issues of the recruitment of racial and ethnic minorities (Barrett, 2000; Hackett & Byars, 1996; Humphrey, 2007; Osipow & Littlejohn, 1995).

Practical Implications

Bailyn (2000) suggests that backlash and resistance may be occurring among white males at the top level of organizations in response to recruitment efforts aimed at increasing the number of females and nonwhites. Initially, women and nonwhites enter organizations with relatively equal resources to white men, as supported by the HR policies, processes, and practices. However, by the time women and nonwhites reach midlevel manager, subtle discrimination processes occur in how human-resource policies are applied, such as lower access to resources, promotions, and poor climate.

Despite the increase in upward mobility, the representation of women and nonwhites at the top is still relatively low. Ely (1994) found that if women are underrepresented at higher organizational levels, relations between women at lower levels might be of lower quality due to increased competition and negative gender dynamics in the larger social system. If diversity-management strategies that alter the distribution of existing resources across organizational and demographic groups are to be successful, they must take into account not only tipping points in terms of overall organizational representation, but more importantly, how tipping points are distributed in demographics across the hierarchies of work groups or departments.

Nonwhite and female recruitment strategies that bring in many new hires of different backgrounds may have negative ramifications for social functioning in groups, particularly if new members are not supported by organizational policies and processes that allow them to enter work groups on an equal footing or if their work groups do not have leadership that mirrors their demographic identities. As Kanter (1983) found, identity groups must be equal in their access to power resources if contact is to produce improvement in attitudes. There must also be time for the new members to be socialized and integrated into the culture.

Harrison (1998) found that the longer the length of time that members worked together, the greater the effects of deep-level attitude similarity. Organizations are increasing surface (demographic) and deep-level (attitudinal) diversity simultaneously, which is likely to have negative short-term ramifications for the consensus and direction of climate. Organizational recruitment efforts must not only focus on the surface level—reflecting structural and demographic attributes—but also simultaneously on deep-level characteristics, reflecting values within the context of specific groups at all organizational levels.

In sum, recruitment as a diversity-management initiative should focus on initiatives that relate to the joint alignment of group members' multiple characteristics (e.g., demographic, hierarchical status, task) in work groups—that is, to examine group contextual influences (Wharton, 1992).

CHAPTER 9

HIRING A CHIEF DIVERSITY OFFICER TO MANAGE STRATEGY

This chapter covers the way organizations structure or organize the diversity management function so that that it effectively carry out the organizations diversity management strategy. The role of the Chief Diversity Officer is specifically examined to look at the way they measure diversity management initiatives and whether they use research to support diversity management strategies.

Business Case

Diversity-management practitioners have consistently emphasized the importance of assigning accountability for guiding the organization's strategic diversity-management efforts. According to these same practitioners, appointing a chief diversity officer is a key element to ensuring success of an organization's diversity-management strategy, because this person can ensure that managers in the organization are trained to create inclusive work environments and lead diverse work teams. Moreover, chief diversity officers can advocate that the organization make managers' performance ratings and compensation dependent, in part, on their success in achieving diversity-related goals.

A survey of diversity practitioners found that almost 70 percent of the Fortune 500 companies make it a common practice for the chief diversity officer to ensure diversity-management goal accountability by integrating diversity goals into the performance appraisal criteria of senior executives in the organization (SHRM, 2007). The chief diversity officer is also responsible for informing managers that success and a positive evaluation will include an assessment of how they contribute to the organization's diversity-management strategy, and emphasizing that diversity management is essential to attracting, developing, and retaining a qualified workforce.

Diversity experts argue that because it can take five to seven years to successfully implement diversity-management initiatives in most organizations, it is important that the chief diversity officer institutionalize initiatives by integrating them into organizations' strategic-planning efforts. Moreover, diversity-management practitioners assert that effective oversight of the organization's diversity management requires eight specific competencies:

1. *Leading.* Gains agreement among senior leadership about the desire to move forward.
2. *Visioning.* Develops and champions a diversity vision. Develops programs and strategies to include a well-thought-out plan for specific managerial accountabilities.
3. *Diagnosing.* Analyzes organization's readiness to move forward.
4. *Learning.* Facilitates efforts to increase awareness of the benefits of diversity. Performs diversity audits and conducts exit interviews. Encourages managers to research best practices.
5. *Changing.* Investigates ways to change organizational culture and structure. Conducts focus groups to identify barriers and develops plans to attract diverse employees. Helps leaders move away from simple compliance with equal-employment

opportunity guidelines and conducts cultural scans and assessments.

6. *Sustaining.* Drives leaders to find ways to better support diversity strategy. Promotes employee networks, support groups, or affinity groups and conducts compensation-equity analysis. Creates mentoring programs and designs career-development programs. Advocates for alternative dispute resolution to review diversity-related issues.

7. *Maximizing.* Strengthens managers' ability to lead diverse work teams more effectively. Integrates diversity in key human-resource management systems such as performance management, selection, recruitment, succession planning, leadership development, and promotions. Introduces, adapts, or changes policies such as domestic-partner benefits. Takes intentional steps to ensure the organization's workforce mirrors the demographic composition of the labor pool or population.

8. *Reinforcing.* Monitors the work culture and work environment's early-warning signs that indicate whether employees feel they are treated as unique individuals whose identities and abilities are respected and appreciated. Develops accountability measures to ensure the organizational change is in place in the form of policies, systems, and processes. Designs early-warning detectors that signal if the organization is retreating from efforts to attract, retain, and develop employees with diverse backgrounds and qualifications.

The chief diversity officer is also responsible for integrating diversity management into an organization's strategic plan in order to foster a culture change that supports and values differences. Diversity-management practitioners point out that an organization must link diversity management to its overall strategic plan to ensure that diversity management initiatives are not viewed as an extraneous program, which could make them vulnerable to budget cuts.

The role of the chief diversity officer is considered important to the organization because this individual can help the organization focus on diversity management in order to make the organization more inclusive, which contributes to business success. Diversity scholars argue that the chief diversity officer must advocate the business case that diversity management makes good business sense, emphasizing that it enhances productivity, stimulates innovation, and helps expand services to meet the needs of a more diverse customer base.

Lastly, the business case in favor of hiring a chief diversity officer asserts that this individual could help foster a diverse and inclusive workplace that helps the organization reduce costs by reducing turnover, increasing employee retention across demographic groups, and improving employee morale. According to SHRM (2007), the average diversity department has five employees. Aside from staff, the chief diversity officer may also have budget for data collection and analysis, internal and external communications, and legal and compliance issues. Further, depending on the company, the chief diversity officer budget may include staff for diversity recruiting, talent development, supplier diversity, and supporting employee resource groups.

Chief diversity officers typically focus on the workforce and the work environment, and specific responsibilities often include increasing engagement and productivity, decreasing regrettable loss, increasing the quality of the labor pool, reducing exposure to potential liabilities (lawsuits), and recruiting top talent. Organizations that had a chief diversity officer for five years or more primarily focused diversity efforts on market penetration or growth and had budgets for areas like marketing, sales development, emerging market development, global business development, and public relations. The most advanced organizations also use their diversity departments to understand how to foster and grow innovation (SHRM, 2007).

Research Findings

Ten current and former chief diversity officers were interviewed for their thoughts on the current state of and future challenges for the field of diversity management and the role of the chief diversity officer in addressing those challenges. It is interesting to note that over half of the chief diversity officers were diversity-management professionals and practitioners, in the sense that they had worked with diversity management in more than two organizations and had over ten years of experience in diversity management or human-resource management. The others had been temporarily reassigned by their organization from operational roles to the position of chief diversity officer for the purpose of enhancing the breadth of their career experience. Eight out of the ten chief diversity officers interviewed were African American, Hispanic, female, or a combination of these characteristics. The remaining two were white males.

They were asked directly, "Does a person have to be a nonwhite or female to be an effective chief diversity officer?" The consensus was that it may be an advantage because a female or nonwhite could probably relate from personal experience to the subtle difficulties that females and nonwhites in their organization were facing.

When asked about future challenges, surprisingly, several of them responded that legal challenges stemming from racial discrimination, sexual harassment, and retaliation kept them awake at night. They indicated that although their organization had initiated numerous diversity-management initiatives, there was still a fear of litigation over issues of equity and fairness. They all expressed regret over the fact that their department was largely viewed as a mitigating factor against employees' lawsuits. They observed, however, that this reality is both reassuring for the continued existence of their diversity department and troublesome because the legal perspective is only a very small portion of their organization's diversity-management strategy.

Another future challenge that they all agreed must be addressed is the perception that diversity management is designed to benefit only females and nonwhites at the expense of white men. They lamented that in most organizations there is an entire segment of employees that they are not reaching. To quote one interviewee, "One of the goals of our overall strategy is engagement and inclusion, but how can we achieve this goal if over half of our organization [white men] believe there is no benefit to them?"

During the interview, talent management was mentioned by several of the chief diversity officers as a continuing challenge. They acknowledged that a long-term sustainable diversity-management strategy includes taking into account that the pool of qualified employees is becoming increasingly diverse and that this demographic pattern will continue to increase. They agreed that diversity management is an inescapable business issue.

The chief diversity officers who were interviewed in this study often mentioned organizational culture as one of the challenges they see organizations facing today. They believe that employees who do not mesh quickly with the organizational culture, such as midcareer hires, experience a longer runway to success. It runs counter to diversity management that the reality for most of these people is that they must adapt and assimilate to the organization's dominant culture. For example, they must quickly learn that "the way we do business around here" is a necessary component for individual success. One chief diversity officer summed up this paradox this way: "Unfortunately, the diverse background, along with a diverse perspective, that led the organization to hire the person in the first place may actually be a disadvantage to that new employee, who has to work in an organization with a strongly ingrained and dominant culture."

One of the most surprising issues mentioned by chief diversity officers as a future challenge was performance management. They all agreed that overt expressions of bias are rare and are the easiest situations to handle because most organizations currently have policies and procedures to handle such issues. Most issues that happen in the workplace are not considered as issues related to diversity management. They are considered to be performance-management issues. In the pressured environment following the 2009 recession, everyone must produce results and multiple outcomes that benefit the overall organization. Unfortunately, the consensus among the chief diversity officers is that rarely is performance management ever discussed in terms of individual differences and how those differences should be leveraged to benefit the organization. Instead of the focus being on candid, timely, and honest feedback to facilitate the person's development, growth, and performance, the main focus is on the final rating.

Several of the female chief diversity officers interviewed thought it shameful that after three decades of focused and dedicated diversity-management initiatives, women still substantially experience a glass ceiling. The chief diversity officer of one large company stated that, "When we did a study of the most successful people in our organization, we noted that the most successful women were over the age of forty and did not have children. On the other hand, it is interesting to note that the most successful men were under forty and did have children."

The research (Kalev & Dobbin, 2006; Williams & O'Reilly, 1998) shows that female executives have to adapt to the organization's leadership style in order to be successful. A study of over one thousand female executives in over two hundred Fortune 500 companies done by Wise and Tschirhart (1999) found that over 70 percent of the female executives had received private coaching sessions on how to modify their interaction patterns to fit those of the male senior executives in the organization.

The chief diversity officers again agreed that it runs counter to the goals of diversity management that female executives have to alter their communication pattern and leadership style just to play the game according to the men's rules, while also being vigilant not to be seen as soft or overly emotional.

The chief diversity officers were asked directly, "Are chief diversity officers as proactive as they need to be in addressing contemporary and future challenges?" The chief diversity officers responded with a resounding "No way!" They were asked, "How should the chief diversity officer approach these issues?" They acknowledged that although progress in some areas has been slow, chief diversity officers still need to exercise patience. Chief diversity officers need to remember that they are working for long-term organization and culture change, which in most cases occurs over a significant period of time. As one of the interviewees put it, "Small improvements will lead to eventual cultural change within the organization."

Chief diversity officers interviewed for this study realize that because they are expected to be cultural-change agents, they should be accountable for objectives that are long-term and sometimes difficult to measure. For example, they acknowledge the impact of employee-engagement survey results, quality of work/life perceptions, job-satisfaction ratings, and retention rates on performance outcomes such as productivity.

But they also acknowledge that this relationship is very difficult to measure. The chief diversity officers expressed frustration about the fact that most organizations tend to measure results quarter over quarter, but the work of diversity management involves making systemic changes that may take years. As a result, those chief diversity officers who had come from an operational role indicated that they think of the diversity job as a short-term position. All expressed the desire to return to an operational role, where they could more easily demonstrate their ability to get results ahead of schedule and under budget.

The ultimate role of the chief diversity officer is to weave diversity-management strategy and initiatives into the core operations of the organization in an effort to help it achieve long-term sustainable success. Understanding this prime directive constitutes the most important work of a chief diversity officer. Essentially, diversity management requires intentional and strategic actions aimed at a mix of employees working together in an organization, with the objectives of bringing about cultural change that ameliorates racism, sexism, and other forms of discrimination, and increasing all employees' equal opportunity and access. Moreover, the core work of a chief diversity officer is to manage and lead an organization whose objective is to increase inclusion, improve engagement, and eliminate all forms of discrimination by effectively implementing organizational and cultural change. The result of this work, when done effectively by a chief diversity officer, is an innovative, high-performing, inclusive organization that delivers sustainable stakeholder value.

Practical Implications

The research clearly shows that there has been significant growth in the position of chief diversity officer; however, it also indicates there are a number of areas for improvement. For example, the research (Williams, 2009; Metzler, 2009) points out that many chief diversity officers are not strategic in their approach to diversity management. Consequently, their efforts have not changed the culture of their organizations.

Moreover, the research (SHRM, 2007) confirms that most chief diversity officers reside in the human-resource function and are too far removed from the core operations of the organization to effect meaningful change. Frankly put, diversity management is more than a human-resource process, and putting the chief diversity officer in the human-resource department without unfiltered access to the CEO and other senior organizational decision makers limits the ability of the chief diversity officer to influence change that benefits the entire organization.

Finally, it appears from the research that chief diversity officers still have some work to do to improve their business acumen. Metzler (2009) argues that chief diversity officers must become better students of the business. He states that it is unreasonable and unrealistic for chief diversity officers to expect organizational leaders to value diversity management when chief diversity officers refuse to master the business.

CHAPTER 10

SECURING CEO COMMITMENT

Chapter 10 discusses leadership and accountability. It covers the responsibilities of the organizations' leadership in shaping, guiding and leveraging diversity management. It also covers the accountability methods for the CEO and other senior leaders in organizations.

Business Case

Diversity-management practitioners suggest that one of the most important actions an organization can take to advance its diversity-management strategy is to secure the support of the CEO and other senior leaders. CEO support is considered a fundamental element in the implementation of diversity-management initiatives. It is not enough that the CEO speaks articulately about diversity management; he or she must also have the knowledge, tenacity, and courage to effect large-scale and long-term organizational change.

The CEO, in particular, must be willing to take risks and deal with the ramifications of these risks. Authentic diversity leadership requires that the CEO lead by example and make decisions reflective of that leadership. A CEO who is authentic in his or her leadership of the organization's diversity-management strategy not only articulates why diversity management is vital to the organization's success, but he or she believes it and acts on it with determination (Metzler, 2003).

According to diversity-management practitioners, senior leaders within organizations are also responsible for the success of diversity management because they must provide the visibility and commit the time and necessary resources. A leader committed to diversity management communicates the organization's support for diversity management in newsletters, policy statements, speeches, meetings, and websites. Communication from senior leaders sends a clear message to others in the organization about the seriousness and business relevance of diversity management.

In a study on the role of the chief executive officer in the top fifty companies for diversity, Frankel (2008) discovered that 84 percent of chief executive officers signed off on goals and achievements for diversity-management initiatives, 70 percent had mandated diversity training, and 88 percent directly approved the budget for diversity-management initiatives that exceeded $2 million.

Diversity-management messages from the CEO and other senior leaders are most effective when they share their values on a regular basis, as routinely as budget reviews and reports on other programs. Handfield (2005) asserts that the CEO and members of the senior-management team should demonstrate personal commitment to diversity-management initiatives through participation in diversity events, meetings with affinity groups, chairing diversity-council meetings, meeting with nonwhite and female suppliers, spreading diversity-management success stories, and communicating results and achievements through formal communications within the organization. Lastly, it is suggested that the direct engagement of senior leadership can result in measurable improvements in diversity-management initiatives and, subsequently, organizational performance (Rodriguez, 2008).

Research Findings

With a few exceptions, the interplay between CEO leadership and diversity management remains largely unexplored. This is somewhat surprising in light of the rhetoric espoused by diversity practitioners. The absence of relevant theoretical frameworks may be one explanation for the lack of research on chief executive officers' visible demonstration of commitment and diversity-management performance. However, Turner and Haslam's (2001) discussion of the ways in which social-identity processes may influence leaders and followers promises to move such theoretical discussion forward.

In addition, Kochan (2003) argues that unless the CEO shows strong public support for diversity management as being critical to the strategic business goals of the company—and without the CEO holding senior executives accountable for employing diversity management in every line of business—the organization's diversity-management strategy will not be successful. Specifically, Kochan found that in a financial services organization that has forty-five diversity councils and one thousand active employees, the CEO in each organization chartered and chaired the diversity council. In each case, the CEO also required each business unit have its own diversity council chaired by its respective business executive.

Support from Senior Leaders

Earlier research studies typically explored the direct link between senior-management team diversity and organizational performance, presumably due to ready availability of demographic data. The support for the relationship was, at best, modest, or the findings were mixed. In contrast, Certo and associates (2006) employed confirmatory factor analysis to investigate the moderating influences in this relationship.

They assessed senior-management team diversity using four measures: size, organizational tenure, functional diversity, executive tenure and educational level. Organizational performance was defined in terms of return on assets, three-year average return on assets, return on assets growth, three-year average return on equity, and sales growth. The study concluded that senior-management team size and financial performance are partially correlated with a positive and significant relationship between senior-management team size and sales growth, but there is no evidence of the effect of senior-management team size on return on assets or return on equity. There is also a partial positive relationship between senior-management team heterogeneity and organizations' financial performance, with functional diversity and executive tenure and educational level being positively related with return on assets. The study also found that several senior-management team variables were significantly related to performance variables, such as diversification, research and development, and internationalization.

Support from Board of Directors

Applying the theoretical lenses derived *Signaling Theory* and *Externality Theory* of Organizational Behavior, Miller and del Cannen (2009) investigated how organization reputation and innovation mediated the board diversity-organization performance relationship. The independent variables in the study were board diversity, innovation, and organization reputation. Board diversity was assessed on the basis of race and gender. Innovation was measured by research and development expenditures. Organization reputation was based on the 2004 *Fortune Corporate Reputation Survey.* Organization performance was measured using the accounting-based measures of return on investment. Organization age, liquidity, size, product diversification, customer diversification, and industry were controlled.

The study, based on a sample of Fortune 500 organizations, found a positive relationship between board racial diversity and both organization reputation and innovation. Reputation and innovation both partially mediated the relationship between board racial diversity and organization performance. Moreover, there was a positive relationship between board gender diversity and innovation.

Kilduff, Angelmar, and Mehra (2000) investigated the role of cognitions in the board-diversity-organization performance relationship. The diversity-management variables included in the study were nationality, age heterogeneity, and thinking styles. Organization performance was measured by net contribution margin and market share. The study, conducted on a sample of 159 managers split into thirty-five teams, revealed that the higher the interpretive ambiguity of top-management teams, the greater the organization performance.

Earlier research studies paid little attention to the relationship between senior-management team diversity and organizational performance outcomes. Boone and Walter (2009) sought to address this gap by investigating how team mechanisms such as collaborative behavior, accurate information exchange, and decision-making decentralization moderate the impact of senior-management team diversity on the financial performance of thirty-three information technology organizations. All the organizations operated in software services and products industries, and senior-management team diversity was defined in terms of functional background and organizational size.

While the former could potentially enhance decision quality and organizational performance, the latter could lead to relational conflict and thereby adversely impact organization performance. The study found that functional background diversity is positively related to organization performance. A senior-management team's collaborative behavior and information exchange are prerequisites to reap the performance benefits of functional background diversity. Further, decentralized decision making, while enhancing the performance of functionally diverse teams, also reinforces the negative consequences of organizational size on organization performance. Researchers generally tend to overlook the impact of nationality diversity within subsidiary senior-management teams on subsidiary performance.

Drawing on theoretical insights from knowledge and legitimacy perspectives, Gong (2006) investigated this important dimension of diversity using a large sample of 370 subsidiaries' senior-management teams, with a total of over two thousand managers in twenty-eight organizations. Organization performance was measured using subsidiary labor productivity, industry, senior-management team size, number of years a subsidiary was in operation, and capital investment.

The study concluded that there was a significant positive correlation between team diversity and subsidiary performance. Furthermore, as the number of years the subsidiary was in operation increased, the effect of subsidiary senior-management team diversity became more positive. Thus, racial and ethnic diversity becomes more important when it is more pertinent to a team's work.

Practical Implications

Examining the impact of chief executive officers, boards of directors, and senior leaders on efficacy of diversity-management initiatives is an area ripe with opportunity. Investigating new organizational outcomes goes hand in hand with conducting research aimed at understanding the dynamics of diversity-management initiatives (e.g., securing CEO support and commitment) in large organizations. Whereas many studies of diversity-management initiatives have been reported, little is known about the link between CEO support of diversity and organizational performance.

For example, at the organizational level, chief executive officer and senior-management team dynamics may provide useful insights about how to more effectively manage joint ventures, mergers, acquisitions, and various forms of strategic alliances (ambrick et al., 2001; Jackson & Schuler, 2003; Li et al., 2002; Schuler, Jackson, & Lao,

2003). Understanding the relationship between the chief executive officer and diversity-management performance may also be useful for understanding patterns of knowledge flows in organizations. Contributions to the literature on understanding organizational leadership might be made by diversity-management research that takes into account chief executive officer leadership characteristics and the relational similarity of the chief executive officer to other top-management team members (see Barsade et al., 2000; Pitcher & Smith, 2000).

CHAPTER 11

INCREASING ECONOMIC INCLUSION BY DIVERSIFYING SUPPLIERS

This chapter surveys the process organizations use to select, contract, and interact with the organization's small vendors and disadvantaged suppliers in a manner that supports and enhances economic inclusion along the supply chain. It gauges organizations' recognition of the diversity of its potential supplier base and its sensitivity to the nuances of languages and strategies used to attract and recruit prospective vendors.

Business Case

Diversity-management practitioners suggest that a key component of an organization's diversity-management strategy should be proactive and intentional efforts to develop a supplier base that reflects the gender and race of the community in which corporations reside and includes the consumers who buy their goods and services, namely, women and nonwhites. They also suggest that supplier-diversity initiatives become infused in the culture of the organization when economically driven as a business imperative (Nesbitt, 2008).

The federal government's *Small Business Liaison Office Handbook, 2005 defines* diverse supplier classifications as small business, small disadvantaged business, woman-owned business, veteran-owned business, service-disabled veteran-owned business, black-owned business, Latino-owned business, Asian/Pacific Islander-owned business, and American Indian-owned business. In addition, military veterans are recognized as an equity group in recognition of their service to country (Glover, 2000). These groups qualify as diverse suppliers because they have been historically excluded, underserved, or economically disadvantaged. Supplier diversity, as a diversity-management initiative, is designed to counterbalance economic inequities by providing an avenue for disadvantaged groups to establish coalitions and economic summits to present their business case to organizations' purchasing agents. Moreover, supplier-diversity programs encompass intentional actions on the part of the organization to help increase the skills of small or disadvantaged business owners so that they acquire an understanding of the organization's operations and its purchasing processes (Creswell, 2003).

The business case for supplier diversity is more compelling because it has been supported by a favorable public policy and legislative actions. Several laws require organizations that qualify as federal contractors to help small and disadvantaged businesses gain access to large public contracts that might otherwise not be available to them if a supplier-diversity program did not exist. Being awarded huge federal contracts is the reward some organizations seek or the pay for having a socially responsible purchasing group (Worthington, 2009).

Diversity-management practitioners argue that companies that have state or federal contracts should assess their risks and ask themselves if they can afford not to have a supplier-diversity program. As a result, organizations not only comply by giving opportunities to diverse suppliers (e.g., nonwhite, female, veteran, small disadvantaged), but they also take steps to educate senior managers about the increased market share, profits, and shareholder value that economic inclusion brings via the organization's supplier-diversity program.

King (2009) suggests that organizations with robust supplier-diversity programs are often involved at the local and national levels of the National Minority Supplier Development Council. In addition, these organizations require senior-leader involvement in minority supplier efforts, conduct periodic training for internal buyers and key managers, and track second-tier spending. The most advanced organizations, according to King, have a strategic communication plan, innovative supplier-development initiatives, and a program that is fully integrated with marketing and sales, and a minority purchasing process that involves all business units.

Theoretical Arguments and Research Findings

Social-justice theory suggests that supplier diversity as a diversity-management initiative increases economic inclusion by creating access to structures of organizations and helping nonwhite and female suppliers gain access to economic opportunities (Whitfield, 2003; Creswell, 2003). Federal legislation was enacted to ensure the fair, just, and equitable implementation of public policy and the commitment to promote fairness, justice, and equity in the formation of public policy (Bebea, 2005). Appearing periodically in diversity-management literature has been the impact of public policy and demographic change in driving the development of supplier-diversity programs (Worthington, 2009). Strategies implemented include procedural fairness in the awarding of contracts and equal access.

Social-justice theory suggests that because it is increasingly difficult to steer significant revenues toward strategies to ameliorate social and economic inequities, efforts should be made by the government to level the playing field (Creswell, 2003). Consequently, the federal government has mandated that prime contractors implement a supplier-diversity program that includes the annual documenting of the total amount of money spent with diverse suppliers, methods used to identify potential sources for solicitation purposes, administration of subcontracting plan and program, specific job duties, and efforts taken to assure diverse suppliers have an equitable opportunity to compete for subcontracts.

Empirical research on supplier-diversity programs is quite limited. The research investigating supplier-diversity programs and organizational performance is even more scarce (for exceptions, see Cummings, 2004; Handfield & Edwards, 2005; King, 2009; Whitfield, 2003; Worthington, 2009). Despite researchers' efforts, the literature offers mixed results regarding the relationship between supplier diversity as a diversity-management initiative and long-term sustainable organizational performance.

King (2009) found statistically significant relationships between supplier diversity as a diversity-management initiative and organizational performance. For example, King found that when some organizations measured the effectiveness of the supplier-diversity program objectives and reviewed the annual performance of the supplier-diversity program, the probability of the program improving organizational performance was enhanced. Moreover, King suggests that women in senior management and set-aside programs increased the probability of the supplier-diversity program improving. There was also a significant positive correlation between the diversity of the senior-management team, set-aside programs, and supplier-diversity program effectiveness.

Some organizations do just enough to get by and have failed to see the strategic value of nonwhite supplier development. For example, Moore (1996) found that 64 percent of senior managers did not champion their organization's supplier-diversity management initiatives. Moore argued that organizations should demonstrate more significant involvement in supplier-diversity activities by advocating supplier diversity internally and reviewing annual performance of the supplier-diversity program. In a survey of 6,500 managers, Moore found that a low percentage of senior managers (38 percent) were being trained in supplier-diversity compliance policies annually and only 47 percent were aware that supplier-diversity goals were incorporated into the organization's mission or vision statement. Moore concluded that some companies did not see supplier diversity as being important to their long-term success. Despite the increased visibility, the major challenge to the success of supplier diversity as a diversity-management initiative is whether senior management regards supplier diversity as simply a tactical program or embraces it as a strategic issue.

Based on the premise that organizations with an effective supplier-diversity program tend to exchange and share knowledge with external constituencies such as customers, organizational experts, and others outside the group, Cummings (2004) conducted a field study of 182 Fortune 500 companies and found that supplier-diversity spend increases when such groups are structurally more diverse.

Structural diversity is operationalized in terms of employee differences in geographic locations, functional assignments, reporting managers, and business units. External knowledge-sharing was measured using supplier surveys, and performance was estimated using customer-satisfaction ratings. Cummings concluded that the interaction of external knowledge-sharing and geographic locations was significantly associated with organizational performance. The greater the external knowledge-sharing, the better the performance when there were more geographic locations. It was also found that external knowledge-sharing was related to better organizational performance when there were more functional assignments. The interaction of external knowledge-sharing and supplier diversity was also significantly associated with organizational performance. However, there was only partial support for the effect of structural diversity based on the number of business units (Moore, 1996).

A number of researchers (Handfield & Edwards, 2005; King, 2009; Worthington,, 2009) investigating the long-term impact of supplier-diversity programs found that when goals and objectives are tied to the organization's supply-chain management strategy, minority supplier participation is increased, which resulted in positive outcomes for the organization. Long-term sustainable outcomes cited by these same researchers include organizations increasing their access to ignored and untapped markets, improving their ability to leverage flexibility and insight from minority suppliers, and realizing significant cost savings. They suggest that federal government agencies are an exception to these findings because performance outcomes are still a challenge for government agencies, as they have yet to implement evaluation mechanisms that show that specific outcomes are the result of the supplier-diversity policy and program implementation.

Practical Implications

The research shows that for supplier-diversity efforts to contribute to long-term sustainable business outcomes, the program must be fully integrated with other key organizational processes. Moreover, the program must have senior-management support linked to the organization's annual performance objectives. This requires that the supplier-diversity efforts be tracked and measured and that the program focus on mission-critical primary-supplier development, a productive second-tier program, and a superior communication plan that includes a strategy for communicating to those within the organization that make buying decisions. In addition to a person dedicated fully to managing the supplier-diversity program, organizations should employ cross-functional process-improvement teams to enhance their supplier-diversity process.

CHAPTER 12

PRAYING FOR ANGELS WHILE FIGHTING BARBARIANS

Organizations have experimented with numerous approaches to diversity management. Some organizations have focused on establishing organizational responsibility for diversity management, others have directed the lion's share of the organization's efforts on moderating managerial bias through diversity training and education, and still other organization have experimented with reducing social isolation of non-white and female employees. These approaches find support in diversity management theories of how organizations achieve goals (Cox 1991a, Kochan et.al, 2003, how stereotyping shapes recruitment, selection and promotion (Kravitz & Klinberg, 2002; Chatman, Polzer & Barsade, 1998) and how employee networks influence organizational commitment (Ely & Thomas, 2001). This is the first systematic analysis of their efficacy. The analysis relies on 125 empirical studies describing the impact of diversity management on organizational performance from 1990 to 2010, coupled with interview data on current diversity management practices.

The research shows that efforts to moderate managerial bias through diversity training and education are least effective at increasing the percentage of non-whites or females in senior management or enhancing other organizational outcomes. Efforts to attack social isolation through structured or organized networking efforts such as affinity groups, business groups and employees resource groups show modest effects. Efforts to establish responsibility for diversity management strategy lead to the broadest increases in organizational performance. Moreover, organizations that establish responsibility in the form of a chief diversity officer, see better effects from diversity education, recruitment, selection, and promotion. Organizations that are federal contractors and subject to federal affirmative action compliance regulations, typically see stronger results from some diversity management initiatives. This work lays the foundation for an organization theory for the enhancement organizational culture and performance.

Increasing Female and Nonwhite Representation

A review of the research on the relationship between increasing females and nonwhites in various levels and jobs in the organization and certain organizational-performance outcomes were closely examined, and the results were mixed. For example, a study of the impact of increasing female representation on organizational performance found that increasing gender diversity influenced the performance of women, but not the performance (ratings) of men (Cox, 1994; Morrison, 1992; Norton & Fox, 1997; Pazy & Oron, 2001; Thomas, 1996; Wilson, 1997).

Other studies examining the role of gender representation found that increasing the percentage of women in an organization was related to some measures of performance but not others. Overall, the research on the impact of gender found its effects on performance are sometimes positive (Jackson & Joshi, 2003; Rentsch & Klimoski, 2001), sometimes negative (Jehn & Bezrukova, 2003), and sometimes not significant (Fenwick Neal, 2001; Richard, 2000; Watson, Johnson, & Merritt, 1998).

Research regarding racial and ethnic representation on senior-management teams' performances was also mixed. For example, even if one considers only the CEO and direct reports on top-management teams, some studies reported positive effects of racial representation on organizational performance (Kilduff, Angelmar, & Mehra, 2000), while others reported no significant effects (Bunderson & Sutcliffe, 2002; Simons, Pelled and Smith, 1999). In a study on racial representation, Timmerman (2000) found that race was unrelated to organizational performance when the work teams required little interdependence and negatively related to organizational performance when work teams required more interdependence. The pattern of mixed results also holds for studies of ethnic diversity. Some studies found its effects on performance were positive (Earley & Mosakowski, 2000; Elron, 1997), but others found that ethnic diversity was detrimental to performance in the long run (Watson et al., 1998).

There are two exceptions to the general pattern of mixed findings. First, results seem to support the conclusion that gender, racial, and ethnic representation improves organizational performance at some levels (Barsade et al., 2000; Carpenter, 2002; Jehn & Bezrukova, 2003; Krishnan, Miller, & Judge, 1997; Pitcher & Smith, 2000). Organizations that engage in creative change management may gain the most from increased female and nonwhite representation (Simons et al., 1999; Tjosvold et al., 2003). However, the positive effect of racial and ethnic representation may depend on the particular measurement approach used in the study (Bunderson & Sutcliffe, 2002).

Second, the evidence that supports the often-made claim that racial and ethnic representation improves performance is limited. One study found no significant relationship (Jehn & Bezrukova, 2003). Some studies reported negative effects of racial and ethnic representation on organizational performance (Jackson & Joshi, 2003; Kirkman, Tesluk, & Rosen, 2001; Leonard, Levine, & Joshi, 2003; Townsend & Scott, 2001). One study (Timmerman, 2000) found that racial and ethnic representation was detrimental to performance for a task that required high interdependence and it was unrelated to performance for a task that required little interdependence. Moreover, Richard (2000) found that racial and ethnic representation in an organization was beneficial to performance when a growth strategy was being pursued, but it was detrimental to organizations that were downsizing.

Increasing Engagement Through Employee Resource Groups

Strong evidence was found in the research supporting the link between employee resource groups and organizational performance. Numerous researchers encourage the development of formally constituted groups representing specific categories of nontraditional employees such as women, African Americans, or gays and lesbians (Cox, 1994, 1998; Digh, 1997; Dobbs, 1996; Morrison, 1992; Thomas & Gabarro, 1999; see Norton & Fox, 1997 for disagreement with this approach). The assumption is that employee resource groups can help mitigate the potential isolation of employees in these groups and may provide leadership in resolving conflicts. A variant of this approach is to establish advisory groups that include representatives from many distinct groups in the workforce (Fine, 1995; Wilson, 1997).

The research investigating employee resource groups and organizational performance is promising. There is evidence showing that the percentage of females participating in employee resource groups impacts female performance (Cohen, Broschuk, & Haveman, 1998; Hultin & Szulkin, 1999). Research conducted by Powell and Butterfield (2002) illuminated the effects of employee resource groups on employee performance ratings and employment decisions and related both to increasing employee engagement and job satisfaction. Such findings appear to answer the question of whether workforce diversity can impact organizational-level performance outcomes.

Conducting Diversity-Management Training

Whereas many studies of diversity training have been reported, there is little known about whether this diversity-management initiative is linked to long-term sustainable organizational outcomes. For example, based on a review of over 125 empirical studies, it appears that diversity training can be useful for improving patterns of communication flows in organizations and can result in moderate increases in employee productivity (Chambers & Riccucci, 1997; Cox, 1994; Fernandez, 1999; Gardenswartz & Rowe, 1993; Hudson & Hines-Hudson, 1999; Mathews, 1998; Riccucci, 2002; Thomas, 1996; Wilson, 1997). However, more research is needed to understand how the design and context of diversity training influences overall organizational performance (Roberson, Kulik, & Pepper, 2001).

Numerous researchers (Chambers & Riccucci, 1997; Cox, 1994; Fernandez, 1999; Gardenswartz & Rowe, 1993; Hudson & Hines-Hudson, 1999; Mathews, 1998; Riccucci, 2002; Thomas, 1996; Wilson, 1997) generally agree that it is in any organization's long-term best interest to ensure that employees are taught about the importance of diversity goals and the skills required to effectively manage a diverse workforce. However, they also agree that investigating new organizational outcomes goes hand in hand with conducting research aimed at understanding the dynamics of diversity training in organizations.

Regardless of the specific training content, organizations generally seem to favor training that targets individual attitudes and behavior. This approach undershoots the true potential of diversity training. Organizations should shift the focus of training efforts from the individual to the team level. Training teams to leverage their diversity may unlock previously untapped innovation and creativity inherent in diverse teams.

For example, at the team level, diversity training and education may provide useful insights about how to more effectively leverage diverse teams engaged in workforce planning, joint ventures, strategic planning, mergers, and acquisitions (Hambrick et al., 2001; Jackson & Schuler, 2003; Li et al., 2002; Schuler, Jackson, & Lao, 2003). If this can be accomplished, then perhaps diversity training will eventually be as useful as it is popular.

Recruiting, Developing, and Advancing Females and Nonwhite Employees

Research findings regarding the link between nonwhite recruitment and organizational performance are mixed. However, there is strong evidence to support the link between the mentoring of diverse employees and organizational performance. For example, several researchers (Cox, 1994; Dugan et al., 1993; Fernandez, 1999; Fine, 1995; Morrison, 1992; Thomas & Gabarro, 1999; Wilson, 1997) point out that when mentors are formally assigned to nonwhites and females, they serve an important role in communicating organizational expectations to employees who are interested in advancement.

The body of evidence concerning the effects of diversity-management initiatives such as recruiting and mentoring nonwhite and female talent has grown substantially in recent years. Studies have been conducted in a wide variety of field settings, and the majority of these studies used comparable research designs. Because multiple variables of nonwhite and female recruitment were often included in these studies, diversity-management practitioners should be somewhat confident that effects are accurately attributed to the correct diversity-management initiative. In addition, this work is grounded in a set of clearly articulated theoretical perspectives, including social-identity theory, social-categorization theory, upper-echelons theory, and human-capital theory. Therefore, it is easier to identify empirical trends across studies.

Despite these strengths, there were some notable weaknesses in the research on the relationship between recruiting and mentoring diverse talent and organizational performance. One weakness is that researchers have mostly ignored individual experience and specific skills. Experience and skill are often suggested as the facilitators of nonwhite recruitment and development; however, none of the studies reviewed for this book attempted to measure the status of individual team members or the degree of status differentiation within teams.

Similarly, while few diversity-management researchers would deny the importance of relevant skills and abilities in determining who is recruited and promoted (Krishnan et al., 1997), research on organizational performance has usually ignored the content and structure of task-specific skill diversity as an independent variable and its relationship to organizational performance. Arguably, this criticism is less applicable to research on female recruitment and advancement to top management, which often includes measures of education and occupation. But even in these studies, usually no attempt is made to assess the degree of match between the personal backgrounds of females to the demands of their jobs and rate of advancement.

Hiring a Chief Diversity Officer to Manage Diversity-Management Strategy

The research shows that federal executive orders and consent decrees, which lead to assigning a person to be responsible for diversity management, appear to catalyze certain diversity-management initiatives and subsequent organizational performance. Moreover, numerous researchers (Elsass & Graves, 1997; Finkelstein & Hambrick, 1996; Jackson, May, & Whitney, 1995; Kalev & Dobbin, 2006; Milliken & Martins, 1996; Reskin, McBrier, & Kmec, 1999; Shaw & Barrett-Power, 1998; Tsui & Gutek, 1999) argue that organizations must appoint chief diversity officers and give them authority to achieve diversity-management goals. They also assert that diversity-management initiatives targeting employee bias or isolation may be less effective than establishing a department responsible for managing the organization's long-term diversity-management strategy.

Diversity-management initiatives that are not linked to the everyday core operations of an organization have no value. Therefore, Kalev and Dobbin (2006) suggest that appointing a chief diversity officer with responsibility for culture change linked to sustainable business outcomes is likely to be more effective than conducting training or developing scorecards that monitor racial or gender representation, advancement, recruitment, and development efforts.

As diversity-management theorists claim (Baron, 1984; Kalev & Dobbin, 2006), there is more to diversity management than training rogue managers and supervisors who have overt biases. Thus, hiring a chief diversity officer who has sufficient staff and budget for recruitment and promotion processes may be more effective than training managers on topics such as micro-inequities, civil treatment, or valuing differences. The argument that organizations should have a chief diversity officer or someone responsible for managing diversity-management strategy seems obvious; however, the most prevalent and popular diversity-management initiatives often focus on changing the hearts and minds of employees. Organizations continue to develop and implement training solutions aimed at managers' biases, with the idea that most problems of management are problems of values rather than leadership skills.

Securing CEO Commitment

With a few exceptions, the interplay between CEO support of diversity management and organizational performance remains largely unexplored. This is somewhat surprising in light of the growing interest in authentic leadership. Contributions to a greater understanding of authentic leadership might be made by diversity-management research that takes into account CEO personality characteristics and the race or gender similarity of the CEO to other top-management team members (Barsade et al., 2000; Pitcher & Smith, 2000). The absence of relevant theoretical framework for authentic leadership may be one explanation for the lack of research on CEO and diversity management. Turner and Haslam's (2001) recent discussion of the ways in which authentic leadership processes may influence culture and organizational behavior promises to move such theoretical discussion forward, however.

Diversity-management researchers have all too often ignored status differentials among employees. They do so even when studying senior-management teams, where authority hierarchies are usually quite apparent: CEOs, board members, and executives who do not serve on the board are not all created equal when it comes to status and authority. The large pool of studies that have already been conducted on senior-management teams presents a unique opportunity for testing new conceptual models that incorporate the effects of the CEO on diversity-management progress. In many instances, existing data could simply be reanalyzed by acknowledging personality type and considering it more explicitly. Future research may also begin to clarify how various aspects of the CEO's background influence diversity-management initiatives. Expanding the range of organizational-performance outcomes considered in studies of diversity management is another opportunity.

Increasing Economic Inclusion by Diversifying Suppliers

The research supporting the link between organizations' supplier-diversity efforts and organizational performance is virtually nonexistent. The little research that does exist tends to focus on identifying those factors most important in explaining the performance of supplier diversity as a diversity-management initiative. For example, King (2009) revealed that there are statistically significant relationships between senior-management team representation and supplier-diversity program performance.

According to King, the percentage of women on the senior-management team of an organization is directly related to the organization achieving its supplier-diversity program objectives. Moreover, King found that when the chief executive officer is directly involved in reviewing the annual performance of the supplier-diversity program, the probability of the organization achieving its spending targets with nonwhite-, female-, and veteran-owned businesses is increased.

Research Limitations

Research quality is multidimensional in form and involves a balance of different concerns. For example, for any particular study, the issue of appropriateness of methods involves trade-offs and choices among reliability, generalizability, and applicability. The diversity-management literature reviewed for this analysis had several weaknesses.

Reliability

One measure of reliability is consistency in findings across different studies. If all studies concluded that racial diversity were associated with organizational performance, for example, it could be reasonably concluded that increasing the number of females and nonwhite employees as a diversity-management initiative is a good approach to achieving high organizational performance.

Studies of diversity management's impact on organizational performance have flourished in recent years. Nearly 35 percent of the studies reviewed were conducted between 2005 and 2010. Organizational performance was typically measured using financial indicators. My examination of these studies yielded few discernible patterns in the results. For most diversity-management initiatives, the findings across studies were mixed. For example, in one study, employee resource groups were positively related to diversity management in terms of sales performance and share performance (Neuman et al., 1999). However, in other studies (O'Reilly, Caldwell, & Barnett, 1989; Smith et al., 1994; Wiersema & Bantel, 1992), the impact of nonwhite and female representation on organizational performance was less than favorable.

Unfortunately, researchers investigating the effects of nonwhite and female representation have not been inclined toward repetition or replication. My search for empirical research on certain diversity-management initiatives and their link to organizational performance uncovered only a few studies in some cases. Thus, it was difficult to conduct an analysis of empirical findings across diversity-management initiatives in the diversity literature.

Generalizability

Subjects are likely to behave differently in simulated situations than they do in the field. This generalizability problem was demonstrated by Krieger and Ford (1985), who conducted a meta-analysis of seventy-four laboratory and field studies from the period 1966 to 1981 of the effects of race on performance ratings. The researchers found that both black and white raters gave significantly higher ratings to members of their own race in real-world settings than they did in laboratory simulations. Many studies examined in this analysis focused more on representation and less on organizational performance.

A number of studies on diversity management were not included in my analysis because they involved artificial situations that involved subjects performing simple tasks, class assignments, or tasks that have a gamelike element. These tasks may not be adequate proxies for group problem solving in the real world (Watson, Kumar, & Michaelsen, 1993). The task complexity and the context in which the task occurs may function as intervening variables in the diversity management-organizational performance relationship. In other words, the task and the context may influence the impact of the diversity-management initiative. Artificial scenarios also cannot duplicate other critical factors, such as organizational size, structure, technology, and organizational communication mechanisms. In addition, artificial scenarios lack the historical, political, instrumental, and emotional contexts that real diversity-management initiatives must address. Lastly, the simulations have no real consequences for personal well-being and do not put at risk personal need fulfillment.

Another limitation with generalizing from studies of diversity-management effects is the cultural setting of much of the work. Perhaps it goes without saying that results for one diversity-management initiative or outcome cannot be assumed to apply to other initiatives or outcomes, but some scholars and practitioners make the mistake of thinking they can. The lack of carryover was a pattern in the analysis of the diversity-management literature.

Not all diversity-management initiatives appear to have the same effects. An outcome can be affected by one type of diversity-management initiative but not another. This finding is consistent with the research of Sackett, DuBois, and Noe (1991), who concluded that findings regarding the effects of gender diversity on performance ratings were not generalizable to racial diversity. Other researchers also have made the point that findings regarding group diversity based on sex and personality are not transferable to culturally diverse groups (Watson, Kumar, & Michaelsen, 1993; Sackett, DuBois, & Noe, 1991).

Applicability

Factors related to time are important in assessing research applicability—earlier findings may not be relevant to today's workplace. Certain types of differences may once have been influential in determining workplace relationships, but these differences may no longer be salient or may not provoke the same level of emotional or behavioral response. For example, employment barriers that were significant for certain racial and ethnic groups in the 1960s may not be as prevalent in the 2000s. Similarly, male subordinates of a female manager may have felt more uncomfortable in such relationships in the 1980s than they did in the 1990s. Research regarding attitudes toward different nonwhite groups and how they change over time is sparse, suggesting that the observations reported in some of the empirical work that was uncovered may be outdated. Perhaps only research conducted in the last five years is relevant to current diversity-management efforts.

Lack of a common model made it more difficult to accumulate comparable findings over time and impeded efforts to learn from the accumulating evidence. One useful element of a common model would be for researchers to agree to some expectations for research designs. One expectation might be that it is preferable to assess multiple dimensions of a diversity-management initiative.

Consider, for example, how quickly our understanding of sex, race, ethnic, and age diversity would advance if the majority of studies that assessed any one of these variables also included the others. Including multiple diversity measures could be accepted as appropriate even if a researcher's primary interest lay elsewhere. Consider how much easier it would be to interpret findings about age or tenure diversity if researchers included measures of both in their studies rather than one or the other. It would also be worthwhile to provide more sensitive and precise measures of racial representation measures, as suggested by Carroll and Harrison (1998).

Another useful element of a common paradigm would involve ensuring that analyses are conducted to control for central tendency composition when assessing the effects of demographics variance. Under certain conditions, measures of variance are influenced by mean values as well as dispersion (Bedeian & Mossholder, 2000). Furthermore, there is some evidence that central tendency- and dispersion-based measures of diversity management can have unique effects on organizational performance (Barrick et al., 1998; Thomas, 1999). Yet I found that central tendency indicators were examined in conjunction with variance measures only 35 percent of the time.

Finally—especially in studies of ethnic, racial, and gender representation—it may be helpful for diversity-management researchers to consider the specific contours of diversity within an organization and pay more attention to the differential experiences of each identity group. It is apparent that individuals respond differently to their nonwhite status (De Vries & Pettigrew, 1998). It is also likely that the experience and meaning of being a nonwhite member varies considerably depending on a person's own specific attributes (Tsui et al., 1992). By extension, organizational performance also may be influenced by the specific structure and content of workforce diversity present, not simply the degree of heterogeneity or homogeneity (Randel, 2002).

Summary

Many organizations claim to have implemented a variety of diversity-management initiatives effectively. Most recently, some of these initiatives have been relabeled as aiming to increase inclusion (Gilbert & Ivancevich, 2000). However, research that evaluates the impact on organizational performance of such initiatives remains scarce. When such research is conducted, successful diversity-management initiatives are defined as those that reduce turnover, increase representation, or enhance job satisfaction (Ragins, Townsend, & Mattis, 1998). Seldom is the focus on improving organizational performance. Thus, it is risky to make recommendations about the steps organizations should take to leverage diversity management to achieve specific business goals.

The research shows clear evidence that structural diversity-management initiatives (e.g., chief diversity officer, chief executive officer, and diversity management department) are followed by increases in organizational performance; however, cultural and behavioral diversity-management initiatives that target employee biases and stereotypes through education and training are not followed by measurable increases in organizational performance. On the other hand, cultural and behavioral diversity-management initiatives designed to address social isolation among women and nonwhites (e.g., employee resource groups, affinity groups, and employee councils) are followed by modest changes. Procedural diversity-management initiatives (e.g., representation, recruitment, retention) are not linked to increases in organizational performance.

Moreover, the research shows that the effects of these initiatives vary across groups, with white women benefiting most, followed by African American women. African American men benefit least from the initiatives designed to increase and retain nonwhites and females. The research shows that other procedural diversity-management initiatives, such as mentoring and developing nonwhites and females, are more effective. These empirical research findings support diversity-management theory that builds on key precepts of organizational behavior.

In general, there was a paucity of research that examines how diversity-management initiatives affect organizational performance. It appears from the research that organizations continue to focus most of their attention on shaping the thoughts, feelings, behaviors, and long-term career outcomes of nonwhite and female employees. Given the lack of sufficient or compelling research evidence to substantiate the rhetoric that these particular diversity-management initiatives contribute to organizational performance, it would appear that diversity managers are using largely untested assumptions as a basis for diversity strategies, practices, and actions.

Moreover, studies of organizational outcomes show that organizations have largely ignored focusing diversity-management initiatives to achieve long-term sustainable outcomes that would benefit the organization. Some examples of measurable outcomes that would be most valued by organizations include:

- Demonstrating that cost savings from reduced turnover are linked to diversity-management initiatives aimed at retaining nonwhites and females.
- Demonstrating that departments with increased racial, ethnic, and female representation come up with more innovative cost-cutting ideas.
- Showing that diversity-management initiatives aimed at brand enhancement and customer retention were a key factor in retaining a valued client who accounts for a sizable portion of the company's revenue.
- Documenting increased sales when women and African American employee resource groups do blitzes with sales teams focusing on women and African American accounts.
- Demonstrating a correlation between CEO and senior-leader commitment to diversity and inclusion, and increased productivity.
- Tracking increases in the number of products sold following targeted campaigns to underserved consumer markets.

Organizations are investing significant financial resources, time, and energy into diversity-management strategies and initiatives. Yet empirical evidence about the outcomes of diversity management in organizations is limited, and many of the existing studies present conflicting and inconclusive findings. Consequently, diversity managers who want to integrate cost-effective, battle-tested initiatives into their overall diversity strategy are likely to have a difficult time identifying best practices from the research literature that can be reliably applied to actual business situations. As a result, diversity-management scholars need to conduct more research focusing on how specific diversity-management initiatives can best be designed and implemented to produce long-term positive and sustainable results for organizations.

Lastly, diversity managers must apply research-based discipline to their efforts to redesign institutional systems to be more inclusive. Talent-management programs, recruiting practices, promotion systems, performance management, and career-development practices can unintentionally block efforts to build a more inviting and inclusive culture. Left unchanged, these policies, practices, and processes can have a reverse or chilling effect on the progress diversity management has made in the last three decades.

CHAPTER 13

ADDRESSING THE CHALLENGES AHEAD FOR DIVERSITY MANAGEMENT

This chapter discusses the current state of diversity management in organizations, describes realistic short-term and long-term goals, and challenges diversity practioners to set and stretch standards in order to achieve the desired state

Defining Organizational Outcomes

A number of conclusions can be gleaned from this study; diversity practitioners should take note of the following general conclusions because they pose significant challenges for the field of diversity management. Based on a review of the empirical literature, it appears that contemporary diversity-management efforts suffer from several shortcomings, which include but are not limited to:

- focusing too much on compliance;
- emphasizing primarily racial, ethnic, and/or gender representation;
- accepting outcomes that are too narrow in scope;

- abandoning long-term focus;
- perpetuating stagnation, inertia, and the status quo; and
- placing too much attention on awareness rather than skill training

Over twenty diversity-management professionals were interviewed for this book, and some of them defined diversity in terms of what it is—its dimensions, traits, and the characteristics that make individuals different and similar. Others focused on what you do with diversity—such as recognizing, appreciating, and embracing diversity—or on how you do it, with a focus on training-awareness programs, communications, development, recruitment, and retention. Still other diversity-management practitioners focused on the desired state when asked to define diversity, referring to a respectful, trusting work environment that promotes team building and collaboration while fostering creative solutions or resolutions to business problems and effective strategies.

This was consistent with the various definitions and schools of thought offered by diversity-management practitioners in the research literature (Watson, Kumar, & Michaelsen, 1993; Sackett, DuBois, & Noe, 1991, pp. 263–267), which can be characterized by the following:

- ***Compliance and representation.*** Focuses on achieving the desired workforce numerical profile with respect to various demographic categories such as race, gender, and ethnicity.
- ***Harmony in the workplace.*** Focuses on achieving respectful and harmonious relationships across racial, gender, ethnic, and cultural groupings.
- ***Inclusive work environment.*** Focuses on creating an organizational culture that embraces a broader mixture of diversity; leverages and values the skills, abilities, experience, and contributions of all of the organization's talent; and ensures opportunities for all to reach their full potential.

- **Strategic business integration.** Focuses on integrating diversity-management practices throughout the organization and externally, including with vendors and suppliers, customers, communities, new business ventures, new products/services, mergers, and acquisitions.

Understanding Organizational Context

The benefits of diversity-management initiatives are contingent on the situation. The accumulated research and theory in diversity management provide little comfort for those who seek simple programs, processes, policies, procedures, and practices that apply across all situations. Based on the research, a variety of contingency models have been proposed for diversity-management initiatives. Moreover, there is unlikely to be one best way with regard to diversity-management programs (Roberson, Kulik, & Pepper, 2003). The probability of success is likely to depend on situational factors, such as the organizational culture, strategies, and environment, as well as the people in the organization and their jobs.

In one study, Cox (1991) described organizations as ranging from monolithic, where there are relatively few nonwhite employees and diversity-management efforts are subject to resistance, to the multicultural organization, in which there are females and nonwhites at all levels of the organization. One cannot, on the basis of the twenty years of diversity-management research, conclude with confidence that a diverse work group is a better team. As previously stated, success likely depends on organizational culture, implementation strategies, and work environment.

Moreover, organizational performance may depend on whether organizational behavior and diversity management are incorporated as basic values in corporate culture. Diversity-management initiatives are more likely to be accepted in organizations with strong diversity cultures (Elsass & Graves, 1997) and in organizations that are growth-oriented rather than engaged in downsizing (Richard, 2000). None of this is particularly surprising, but what *is* surprising is the frequency with which diversity-management programs are implemented with little or no attention to the specific situation to which they are applied.

Developing Specific Goals

Successful diversity-management initiatives are based on specific goals, with feedback provided on how well the initiatives achieve desired outcomes. In its simplest form, goal-setting theory states that explicit goals that are difficult but also acceptable lead to higher performance on a wide variety of tasks than goals that are ambiguous, easy, or nonexistent (Locke & Latham, 1990). Goals are used here to refer to whatever the diversity-management initiatives are designed to achieve. Goals should not be confused with quotas. Although increasing an organization's workforce diversity is one potential goal, the use of quotas in hiring, promotion, or placement can result in charges of discrimination.

Consequently, diversity-management initiatives should be designed with broad goals in mind rather than quotas with specific timetables. For example, an organization could have goals for improved relations with nonwhite communities, mentoring of nonwhites, cross-cultural knowledge, and a variety of other outcomes, in addition to goals for numbers of nonwhites and women hired and promoted. Furthermore, any goal regarding workforce representation should be developed in conjunction with legal counsel to ensure it is consistent with applicable employment law. Whatever the specific nature of the goals, they should be realistic and based on a careful assessment of the current organization and translated into specific targets against which diversity-management initiatives can be evaluated.

To achieve the full benefits of goal setting, progress must be evaluated and feedback provided on progress in achieving goals.

Goals focus attention on what needs to be achieved, encourage the development of effective strategies, and energize efforts to achieve them. There is little reason to believe that specific goals set for diversity-management initiatives do not have the same benefits. On the other hand, stating vague and ambiguous objectives (i.e., leverage diversity) without specific goals to accomplish measurable results is likely to do little to focus attention, generate strategies, or energize employees.

Engaging the Organization

The success of diversity-management initiatives depends on how they are framed. Research in diversity management shows the powerful influence of organizational culture and value-framing on how messages are perceived and how employees respond to them (Howard-Grenville, Hoffman, & Wirtenberg, 2003). An implication of previous research on the framing of goals in organizations is that diversity-management initiatives should be framed as challenges and opportunities rather than as threats to overcome (Drach, Zahavy, & Erez, 2002).

Ely and Thomas (2004) contrasted three frames. The *integration and learning perspective* approaches diversity-management initiatives as a vehicle for rethinking the primary tasks and processes of the organization. In the *access and legitimacy perspective*, diversity-management initiatives are seen as a strategy of gaining entry into markets through hiring employees who are similar to customers. The *discrimination and fairness frame* approaches diversity-management initiatives as a way of eliminating discrimination and providing equal opportunity.

Based on qualitative data, Ely and Thomas concluded that all three perspectives can succeed to some extent, but only the *integration and learning perspective* contains a rationale that will motivate management and employees in a sustained manner to ensure the long-term success of diversity-management initiatives. Needless to say, their research also suggests that the messages and actions of management must convey strong support for the programs.

For example, based on a survey of 785 human-resource professionals, Rynes and Rosen (1995) concluded that the factor that was most strongly related to successful diversity-management initiatives such as employee resource groups and mentoring of female and nonwhite employees was the perception that top management supported these initiatives. Having a senior-management team that is diverse is perhaps the most powerful way of conveying this support. Given that diversity-management initiatives usually include efforts to increase the hiring and promotion of women and nonwhites, the research on how increasing nonwhite and female representation is framed as a diversity-management initiative is particularly important to consider.

It appears that efforts to increase nonwhite and female representation are less likely to be accepted to the extent that they emphasize the group identity of the recipients and deemphasize merit (Kravitz & Klineberg, 2002). Moreover, descriptions of diversity-management initiatives that focus the attention of employees on the race, gender, or ethnicity of an employee who is the beneficiary of these efforts can stigmatize the beneficiary as incompetent (Heilman, Block, & Stathatos, 1997).

Shifting from Group Identity to Organizational Membership

Diversity-management initiatives are more likely to succeed when employees identify with their teams and the organization. Social-identity theory suggests that people are motivated to view themselves as positively as they can and that a primary means of achieving this goal is to identify with a group of people who are similar to themselves. Consequently, there is a tendency to sort people into in-groups and out-groups and to attribute to members of the out-group the negative attributes of the group (Ashforth & Mael, 1989). The implication is that factors in the workplace that trigger such categorizations are likely to interfere with diversity-management initiatives by encouraging stereotyping, prejudice, and intergroup conflict, whereas those that encourage the adoption of a common identity facilitate diversity-management initiatives.

There are powerful forces at work in the typical organization that encourage employees to associate with those like themselves and to reject out-group members (Lefwitz, 1994; Waldman & Avolio, 1991). Organizations should attempt to counteract these divisive pressures and encourage people from different demographic groups to place priority on their team identity over their demographic-group identity. The research suggests that organizations take a crucial first step by implementing programs that encourage managers to get to know their employees as individuals.

Harrison, Price, and Bell (1998) distinguished between visible aspects of diversity in terms of race, gender, appearance, age, and physical disability and nonvisible aspects of diversity with regard to attitudes, beliefs, and values. Diversity in terms of surface-level features had negative consequences in the short term, but as persons interacted over time, deep-level diversity emerged as a more potent force that benefited the group. Time and contact are critically important to the success of diversity-management initiatives such as employee resource groups and diversity councils (Gaertner et al., 1994).

Rewarding Inclusive Leaders

The empirical research and theory reviewed for this book suggests that the task and reward structures in the organization must foster cooperation and motivate managers to form trusting and meaningful relationships with their employees (Brickson, 2000). When the task and the rewards require managers to create inclusive work environments and lead diverse work teams effectively, relationships become more important than the demographic differences among individuals.

On the other hand, competitive or individualistic task designs, reward structures, performance-appraisal practices, and compensation systems create barriers to cooperative interaction and prevent realization of the benefits of workforce diversity (Chatman, Polzer, & Barsade, 1998). Actions to foster an inclusive and trusting culture include leadership emphasis on the common good, basing part of managers' compensation on organizational outcomes, giving and receiving performance feedback on group members' performance from a variety of perspectives (e.g., peers, customers, subordinates), and celebrating successes on a regular basis (Chatman, 1998; McCloskey, 2005).

The failure of diversity-management initiatives may be attributed to an organization's lack of attention to the needs-assessment process (Roberson, Kulik, & Pepper, 2003). For example, the culture audit proposed by Cox (1993) is one of the most widely recommended methods for needs-assessment before conducting diversity training. This audit involves a comprehensive assessment of organizational culture and human-resource systems, including recruitment and selection, training and development, performance appraisal, and compensation.

The objectives of the audit are to uncover subtle sources of bias and identify ways in which organizational culture is inconsistent with diversity-management goals. Some researchers argue that the crucial needs-assessment process should involve organizational analysis because diversity-management initiatives are often viewed as a vehicle for changing organizational culture. Information from organizational analyses can uncover sources of bias and identify ways in which the organizational structures and climate are not meeting the needs of a diverse workforce (Cox, 1993). Audits also ensure that diversity-management efforts fit into overall organizational goals and provide a valuable means for evaluating the progress of the organization's overall diversity-management strategy (Roberson, Kulik, & Pepper, 2003).

Engaging White Men as Diversity Champions

In some organizations, the terms *diversity* and *white men* are treated as mutually exclusive. White men often report feeling left out of their organizations' diversity-management initiatives, which can result in anger, confusion, or indifference toward these diversity-management initiatives. Experts (Proudman, Morris, & Welp, 2005) encourage dialogue to overcome the white guy equals bad guy stereotype. In fact, Proudman, Morris, and Welp suggest that the important thing is for organizations to engage white males in a conversation about their experiences with diversity. They contend that it is important to provide white males and others with the chance to learn more about the norms that have dominated white male behavior and influenced many corporate cultures.

Because only a handful of companies have had the insight and courage to appoint white men to head up the organization's diversity department, empirical research on the link between this practice and organizational performance is missing from the literature. According to some diversity-management experts (Bachman, 2006; Boone & Hendricks, 2009; Howard-Greenville & Hopkins, 2002; McCloskey, 2005; Proudman, 2005; Riccucci, 1997), this issue is important in order to get diversity-management initiatives off the sidelines and into the mainstream of the business. Encouraging white men to champion diversity efforts—particularly those who work in the core business lines and operations—can help bring other white males on board as full partners in the organization's diversity-management efforts.

Since underrepresented groups do not have the power and influence to effect change in most large organizations, the senior leaders in the organization must recognize the critical role that white men play in organizational change. Several experts (Bachman, 2006; Boone & Hendricks, 2009; Howard-Greenville & Hopkins, 2002; McCloskey, 2005; Proudman, 2005; Riccucci, 1997) suggest that any diversity-management initiative that does not engage white men by showing them that they will benefit from the initiative is doomed to fail. Moreover, these same experts argue that if white men are not present at the table when the diversity strategy is conceived, they will not be fully committed to or genuinely supportive of the strategy or the desired outcomes.

The research (Bachman, 2006; Boone & Hendricks, 2009; Howard-Greenville & Hopkins, 2002; Riccucci, 1997) clearly points out that several diversity-management initiatives make white men feel defensive. The remedy to this dilemma is for organizations to take intentional actions to engage white men in the organization's diversity effort. Organizations will find it very difficult to sustain their diversity efforts if white men think that there is nothing in it for them. Therefore, organizations should start by helping white male managers gain a deeper understanding of diversity management and its relationship to the organization's business goals. This is best accomplished by emphasizing that diversity-management initiatives (e.g., diversity training) can help them create a more inclusive work environment and effectively manage high-performing diverse work teams.

Some experts (Bachman, 2006; Boone & Hendricks, 2009; Howard-Greenville & Hopkins, 2002; Riccucci, 1997) suggest that it would be beneficial if more chief diversity officers were white men who came out of the core-operations side of the business. However, the research suggests that for the first time in their lives, white males are worrying about their future opportunities because of widespread layoffs and corporate restructuring. As a result, white men are feeling threatened by organizational efforts to increase racial, ethnic, and gender representation. This fear is, in part, a new manifestation of the old backlash against affirmative action. At the heart of the issue for many white males is the question of merit. In other words, as organizations pursue the goal for a more diverse workplace, white males believe they will lose out to nonwhites and females. Although this is an old argument that has little empirical foundation or support in the research, experts believe that it has been a powerful deterrent for some white men who believe that an assignment as chief diversity officer will derail their careers.

This is an important issue that has been overlooked by most organizations in the development of their diversity-management strategy. This oversight can be mostly attributed to the fact that organizations believe that the business case for diversity-management initiatives is not legal, as it is with affirmative action, but rather economic (e.g., in terms of competitiveness and viability). Consequently, this results in the belief that diversity-management initiatives will be accepted unconditionally by white males, unions, and even white-male managers.

But as organizations are seeing the nationwide assault against race- and gender-based employment programs, this has not been the case. The tepid support of diversity-management initiatives on the part of white males stems from organizations' failure to address the concerns of white men about the effects of policies and programs aimed at promoting nonwhites and females (Bachman, 2006; Boone & Hendricks, 2009; Howard-Greenville & Hopkins, 2002; Riccucci, 1997). As a result, organizations will need to work with white males so that they understand that the organization's diversity-management goals are based on inclusion, not exclusion. Moreover, diversity managers must emphasize that the organization's diversity-management initiatives do not seek to displace white males, but rather to prepare employees and managers to work in a trusting and inclusive work environment—one where everyone is valued, respected, and engaged—to help the organization achieve long-term, sustainable success.

For example, diversity-management initiatives should go beyond race, gender, ability, and age to cover, for example, career-development planning for everyone. Boone and Hendricks (2009) assert that organizations will be challenged by a critical dilemma as they address the needs and concerns of white males. They assert that organizations must not ignore the concerns of white women and people of color, who may resent efforts to win over or pamper white males.

Critical race theory suggests that having white male voices dedicated to the goals of diversity management is critical to long-term, sustainable success of organizations. Some diversity-management experts suggest that appointing white men as chief diversity officers is counterintuitive and that employees in affected organizations will question their qualifications. While divided on several aspects of this issue, most experts agree that the onus is on white men to show that they are truly committed to creating a diverse workforce and that their efforts to make sure diversity-management initiatives include white males do not come at the expense of sacrificing the larger agenda. Whether or not this will work is an empirical question that is worthy of future research.

Thinking Globally But Acting Locally

Increasing attention is being given to global diversity management. As the global marketplace continues to increase in complexity, diversity management is the obvious choice to provide organizations with the necessary tools to better understand, engage, and leverage the similarities and differences within these new surroundings. It remains to be seen, however, whether global diversity will be just an additional focus of diversity management or if it will generate new methodologies as well. It is not clear when organizations announce that they are now engaged in global diversity-management work whether they have grown methodologically and graduated to a grander scale or whether they are using the same methodology to address a different geographical area.

Facing Certain Realities—Doctor, Heal Thyself

There is still a lot of disagreement on the definition, intent, approach, and expected outcomes from diversity management. Some diversity-management practitioners admit openly to being confused and frustrated by the lack of clarity in the field. The field of diversity management is at a critical crossroads, as evidenced by the fact that the term *diversity* is not clearly defined or understood and its relationship to business results is not completely substantiated. For example, my review of over 125 research studies found that almost 27 percent of organizations did not have an official definition of diversity. Moreover, when referring to diversity in the workplace, there were many variations in the terminology that organizations used. The most common terms were *diversity, workplace culture,* and *diversity and inclusion.* My interviews with over twenty diversity practitioners found that over half of them expressed concerns regarding the state of the field of diversity and less than one-third of them expressed optimism about the future of the field in the next ten years. The most frequent concerns cited by these diversity practitioners were: (1) the field is not well-defined or understood, (2) the field still has a long way to go, and (3) the field focuses too much on compliance.

The results of my research have a number of significant implications for the field of diversity management. From a practical standpoint, the link between diversity management and long-term organizational success is still in question. Moreover, my research suggests that we are not likely to see a direct, positive relationship between diversity management and organizational performance. Instead, the effects are likely to be determined by the strategies an organization pursues and by how organizational leaders and employees respond to diversity-management initiatives. The results also highlight the importance of leveraging diversity management as a business strategy that is consistent with an organization's values and that helps achieve competitive advantage.

While the field of diversity management is continually evolving, it still faces many challenges and obstacles. Diversity-management practitioners were asked, given their assessment of the field of diversity management, what changes they would like to see made. Greater emphasis on business results, expanding focus away from racial and gender representation, and identification of standard professional credentials were all recurring themes provided by diversity managers. The strongest theme to emerge was consensus among diversity-management practitioners that they would like to see stronger ties between diversity-management initiatives and business outcomes.

One former chief diversity officer suggests that changes are necessary but believes progress is most likely to transpire through a change-management approach to diversity. As he put it, *"After working in this field for several years, I am convinced that without a change-management approach that combines the what, how, and when of diversity management and the things that drive change— such as leadership, communication, involvement, education, training, and accountability—organizations will not make progress. Most organizations unfreeze their employees and mobilize them, but never realize the change in behavior that is needed to establish a real culture of inclusion."*

Another chief diversity officer was even more candid in her observations and believes that diversity management should never be driven solely by diversity-management practitioners. *"Diversity-management professionals tend to be nonstrategic in their thinking, and they tend not to be at the table when strategy is discussed. They tend to like the soft side of the work—advocating for one group or another. It's not enough to just quote phrases like 'this is a business issue.' Understanding and managing change and strategy are crucial to remaining an active part of the long-term health of any business."* She continued, *"Diversity-management professionals have to confront the fears and unintentional discounting and lack of trust that the culture they are a part of is causing. We [diversity-management professionals] have got to reinvent ourselves inside out and operate in a consultative capacity to transfer that knowledge to other leaders in the company."*

One former chief diversity officer believes that the most significant change needed is increasing the relationship to business results. *"When a diversity-management strategy directly aligns with and helps achieve key business objectives, many of the other factors mentioned will follow naturally. Although some progress has been made in the field [diversity management], the link between business and diversity has to be analyzed, quantified, and measured. A diversity-management scorecard remains an essential tool that organizations should implement. We need more effective methods for training and educating diversity-management practitioners and organizational leaders. The diversity-management field needs standards, and it should be considered a normal business process."*

Trevor Wilson, CEO and global human-equity strategist at TWI Inc., would like to see business schools teach diversity management as part of their core curriculum. According to Wilson, people in training to be our future business leaders cannot be left to stumble onto the value of diversity management. Wilson, who specializes in the area of equity and diversity as a business issue, is also author of the highly acclaimed book *Diversity at Work: The Business Case for Equity*. Wilson argues that additional focus needs to be placed on linking measurement systems with diversity-management results.

"There has been much written about the business case for diversity. Unfortunately, not enough organizations are willing to invest sufficient resources in studying their culture to gain a clear understanding of their management practices and employee workplace behaviors," Wilson says. *"When organizations begin to invest more time, energy, and resources in understanding their strengths and weaknesses regarding diversity management, we will see an increase in the value that this business strategy delivers to organizations' long-term, sustainable success."* (Wilson, 1998, p. 62)

The results of my research further suggest that diversity-management practitioners also need a better knowledge of business strategy and other areas traditionally beyond the human-resource domain in order to make diversity-management initiatives align with business strategy. If diversity-management practitioners meet this challenge, they can take advantage of what workforce diversity may offer their respective organizations.

Moreover, in many organizations, diversity-management professionals, along with their senior-management peers, have important roles leading and managing diversity-management initiatives. In order for diversity-management initiatives to gain commitment from all stakeholders, the individuals leading and managing these efforts need to demonstrate passion and energy around these initiatives.

Given present-day reductions in formal external pressures, like equal opportunity and race and gender efforts, it is up to the chief diversity officers and other senior managers in organizations to take a proactive stance toward promoting workforce diversity, not only for the sake of corporate social responsibility, but also in the interests of long-term and sustainable organizational success. Unfortunately, a Society for Human Resource Management (2007) study found that diversity-management initiatives in most companies are often misunderstood, are too narrowly defined, or lack a clear, common language to contribute to an organization's long-term success. Moreover, the study found that in many organizations, diversity-management programs tend to focus too much on race and gender while excluding other dimensions of human and organizational diversity. Lastly, the study asserted that diversity-management practitioners lacked the discipline and understanding of what diversity means beyond race and gender or how success should be defined. The findings are astonishing, especially when considering that they come after more than three decades of promoting and defending the diversity-management business case.

Professionalizing the Field of Diversity Management

An inescapable conclusion is that further growth of the diversity-management field will require professionalization. The characteristics of professionalization include common language, foundational body of knowledge, metrics, requirements for mastery, entry requirements, fostering of thought, and self-governing mechanisms.

A single body authorized to certify practitioners would help improve overall competence in managing workforce diversity, enhancing employees' diversity-management skills, and creating healthy work environments. A singular certifying authority, with the authority to establish common standards, would be extremely influential to the advancement and development of the field of diversity management.

A singular certifying authority could spur changes in the field, such as placing more focus on business outcomes, facilitating the sharing of information, best practices, and practical tools. In addition, a certifying agency could oversee the training and educational materials for diversity-management professionals. A singular certifying authority could also help alleviate current weaknesses in the field, such as the preoccupation with race, ethnicity, gender, and equal-employment-opportunity and social-equity issues. Moreover, a certification agent could further enhance buy-in and support from executives by showing that there is a clear business case linking diversity management to long-term, sustainable organizational success.

Professionalization directly or indirectly would address most of these issues and some additional core flaws in the field, such as the possibility that the field will become obsolete and irrelevant; a chasm between state-of-the-art theories and practice; a lack of agreement on terms, models, and requirements; and a lack of a code of ethics. Clearly, one could conclude that the field of diversity management is at a crossroads, with its identity in question.

Lastly, an implication of these conclusions is that as diversity-management practitioners design and develop diversity-management strategies and initiatives, they will have to understand the various schools of thought, differentiate among them, and determine the relevancy of each with respect to the needs and issues in question. A singular certifying authority could help diversity-management practitioners leverage each school appropriately, which would ultimately further development of the field of diversity management. Research suggests that organizations seeking straight-line correlations between diversity-management efforts and bottom-line results may be well served by switching from having human resource-based people to having revenue-driving partners be responsible for their diversity-management strategy and initiatives.

Some Final Thoughts

Diversity management continues to evolve as a field and as a concept. Twenty years ago, only a handful of organizations recognized diversity management as a priority, and even among those pioneers in the field, it had little impact beyond increasing representation among women and nonwhites. Today, diversity management is no longer limited to an affirmative-action program, a training intervention, or something nice to do. Diversity management is considered a necessity by forward-thinking organizations that want to empower employees, expand market share, and sustain long-term success.

That being said, diversity management is often portrayed as a double-edged sword in the research literature. At one end of the spectrum, proponents of diversity management stress positive effects on organizational outcomes, whereas others counter that many diversity-management initiatives lead to dysfunctional team interaction and suboptimal organizational performance. In the realm of the research literature, these competing assessments of diversity-management initiatives have also been manifested, with mixed empirical findings, hence perpetuating a lack of consensus on how diversity-management initiatives influence organizational performance (Hurwitz & Hurwitz, 2007). Considering the conflicting findings in the research literature, it is not surprising that some contend that there are no consistent long-term and sustainable effects of diversity-management initiatives on organizational performance.

It is my conclusion that the effects of diversity-management initiatives on organizational performance are highly complex and very powerful; thus, the understanding of these effects should be a high priority for diversity-management practitioners and business leaders alike. Some diversity-management initiatives can be very useful in developing a workforce that is creative and skilled at problem solving and focused on achieving long-term, sustainable success for an organization; however, there must be some form of organizational assessment to assess and determine the types of diversity-management initiatives that are most needed for an organization. One size does not fit all when it comes to diversity-management strategy or initiatives, and it is essential to base them on empirical research and tailor them to the organization.

Diversity management is the key to organizations realizing the potential benefits locked up within their workforces. Research-based strategies for leveraging these benefits and minimizing potential losses have been offered in this book. This book clearly shows that some organizations are undoubtedly employing diversity-management practices that are consistent with these strategies. Unfortunately, researchers have not yet focused much attention on understanding how these practices contribute to organizational performance. By the end of this decade, perhaps another review of diversity-management research will yield usable suggestions for how to generate the organizational outcomes originally promised by diversity-management pioneers more than three decades ago.

APPENDIX A

SUGGESTED ADDITIONAL READINGS

Understanding the Link between Representation and Organizational Performance

Bell, E.L.J. & Nkomo, S.M. (2001). *Our separate ways: Black and white women and the struggle for professional identity.* Boston: Harvard Business School Press.

Drawing on surveys of both black and white female managers, the authors show the profound impact of early life lessons on women's professional identities and reveal how geography and social location, when combined with race, play a powerful role in their professional development.

Broadnax, W.D. (2000). *Diversity and affirmative action in public service.* Boulder, CO: Westview Press.

When it comes to creating a representative bureaucracy, *Diversity and Affirmative Action in Public Service* draws upon the most influential research and thought in the public administration literature to create a diverse public administrative work environment. Equal-employment opportunity, gender and age discrimination, and disability issues are also examined in detail.

Fernandez, J.P., & Davis, J. (1998). *Race, gender and rhetoric: The true state of race and gender relations in corporate America*. New York: McGraw-Hill.

Even though the authors admit that neither racism nor sexism can be fully eliminated, they insist each issue can be minimized by systematic and holistic strategies adopted to address broader human-resource issues. The book argues that after thirty years of effort, corporate America has failed to effectively deal with such challenges posed by diversity. The authors outline six major steps that employees should embrace in order to enhance their career opportunities. This interesting book of theory and practice deserves widespread discussion.

Hopkins, W.E. (1997). Ethical dimensions of diversity. Thousand Oaks, CA: Sage.

This book takes an in-depth look at the relationship between the multiple dimensions of diversity and the ways diversity affects decision making within organizations. The book uses a theoretical overview to identify points of potential conflict and subsequent effects on ethical paradigms. It also suggests ways of reconciling conflicts. *Ethical Dimensions of Diversity* gives diversity professionals the analytical skills and sensitivity necessary for dealing with difficult ethnicity and diversity issues.

Thomas, D. A., & Gabarro, J.J. (1999*). Breaking through: the making of non-white executives in corporate America*. Boston: Harvard Business School Press.

Few nonwhite executives break through to the highest executive levels in corporate America, many times against odds. The aim of this book is to explain the processes of growth and advancement that produce nonwhite executives. *Breaking Through* examines both the individual and organizational factors influencing nonwhite promotion.

Thomas, R. R., Jr. (1992). *Beyond race and gender: unleashing the power of your total workforce by managing diversity.* New York: AMACOM.

In the modern workforce, it is believed that only one in seven employees is a white male. The ability to manage such diversity successfully has now become a basic strategy for corporate survival. *Beyond Race and Gender* supplies an action plan, case studies, and a series of tough questions and answers to provide readers with the ability to think deeply about elements that are blocking the full use of their employees.

Thomas, R. R., Jr., Thomas, D.A., Ely, R.J., & Meyerson, D. (2002). *Harvard Business Review on managing diversity.* Boston, MA: Harvard Business School Publishing Corporation.

This book is a collection of classic and cutting-edge articles, case studies, and first-person accounts of affirmative action. Additional topics on career development for nonwhites and women, as well as other human resource-related policies are also included in this helpful book for managers.

Implementing a Strategic Approach to Diversity Management

Gardenswartz, L., & Rowe, A. (1998). *Managing diversity: a complete desk reference and planning guide* (Rev. ed.). New York: McGraw-Hill.

Although many organizations understand the need for diversity awareness, many of them lack an effective organizational strategy. This book is packed with information, work sheets, charts, and other valuable features for program implementation, as well as program evaluation and measurement. It also provides processes for conducting diversity audits and maximizing the talents of employees.

Gardenswartz, L.& Rowe, A. (1998). *Managing diversity in health care: proven tools and activities for leaders and trainers.* San Francisco: Jossey-Bass.

Sensitivity to and the understanding of cultural diversity have become mandatory issues for professionals in health care. This is reflected in new cultural competency requirements for health-care organizations. Most health-care professionals have little or no training, however, when it comes to dealing with the challenges of cultural diversity. *Managing Diversity in Health Care* will teach effective strategies fundamental to creating a culturally diverse health-care system.

Thomas, R. R., Jr. (1999). *Building a house for diversity: a fable about a giraffe and elephant offers new strategies for today's workforce.* New York: AMACOM.

Beginning with a short fable about how friendship between a giraffe and an elephant is threatened when the giraffe's house—built for tall, skinny giraffes—cannot accommodate his elephant friend, this story is a vivid metaphor for difficult issues inherent in diversity. *Building a House for Diversity* goes on to demonstrate how managing diversity can be seen as a set of useful skills that anyone can learn and use.

Thomas, R. R., Jr. (2006). *Building on the promise of diversity: how we can move to the next level in our workplaces, our communities, and our society.* New York: AMACOM.

Dr. Thomas believes most organizational leaders, as well as society, have come to accept a politicized definition of diversity, a definition that is now a code word for affirmative action. Such a definition positions diversity as a win/lose power struggle. It seems society views diversity through the lens of struggle because that is how society understands differences. This book will clarify the reader's understanding and thinking about diversity and show how to improve one's ability to manage diversity.

Advancing Diversity-Management Initiatives

Hayles, R., & Russell, A.M. (1996). *The diversity directive: why some initiatives fail and what to do about it.* New York: McGraw-Hill.

Organizations across the nation have implemented diversity programs designed to produce multicultural corporate environments. *The Diversity Directive* will help readers guide their organizations through the process of planning and implementing a diversity program that sustains real and lasting cultural change, as well as realizes the rewards of their efforts.

Kiselica, M.S. (1998). *Confronting prejudice and racism during multicultural training.* Alexandria, VA: American Counseling Association.

Confronting Prejudice and Racism during Multicultural Training examines multicultural-training program components in order to assess how trainees adopt, digest, or resist multicultural principles and practices. There are two parts to this book. The first part, "Theoretical and Practical Considerations," speaks of theory as well as issues of putting theory into practice. The second section, "Recommendations for Multicultural Educators," discusses recommendations for multicultural training.

Lasch-Quinn, E. (2001). *Race experts: how racial etiquette, sensitivity training, and new age therapy hijacked the civil rights revolution.* New York: W. W. Norton & Company.

Probing the intersection of the Civil Rights struggle and modern social psychology, Lasch-Quinn highlights the overthrow of the social code of segregation and the adoption of etiquette of black assertiveness and white submissiveness. Such an adoption of etiquette has produced a *harangue-flagellation* ritual that does not advance the goal of racial equality, according to the author. It seems such etiquette will make interaction between the races a social minefield, discouraging contact. Lasch-Quinn also discusses how cottage industries have perpetuated differentiation among the races.

Loden, M. (1995). *Implementing diversity: best practices for making diversity work in your organization.* New York: McGraw-Hill.

A practical and provocative guide that provides strategies and tactics used by organizations committed to implementing diversity management within their organization. This book focuses on the necessity for strategic-change initiatives when it comes to diversity management. *Implementing Diversity* discusses how to position diversity-management initiatives for maximum support, proven strategies for managing resistance, and the classic mistakes made when implementing diversity-management initiatives and how to avoid them.

Martin, J. (2001). *Profiting from multiple intelligences in the workplace.* Burlington, VI: Gower Publishing Company.

Economic competitiveness depends on having the most intelligent workforce possible. Organizations that want to survive and prosper need to be open to new ways of uncovering and developing their employees' abilities. *Profiting from Multiple Intelligences in the*

Workplace, Martin's revolutionary theory of multiple intelligences, introduces user-friendly tools for understanding and assessing employees' skills and abilities. As a result, organizations will have the necessary tools to uncover the mosaic of abilities needed for multi-skills, multitasking, and efficient teamwork.

Orey, M.C. (1996). *Successful staffing in a diverse workplace: a practical guide to building an effective and diverse staff.* Irvine, CA: Richard Chang Associates.

From recruiting to orientation, the way an organization staffs its workforce determines how such a workforce performs as a team. This guidebook shows how managers can successfully deal with each element involved in staffing a diverse workforce.

Examining Gridlock in the Field of Diversity Management

Lester, J.S. (1994). *The future of white men and other diversity dilemmas.* Berkeley, CA: Conari Press.

The author suggests ways to handle oneself in culturally sensitive situations. As a spokesperson and news-column writer on diversity issues, Lester expresses thoughts that are straightforward and easily understood, such as being sensitive to others' backgrounds, including ethnicity, gender, and age. Destruction of stereotypes and ethnic humor are also discussed.

Marsden, D. (1999). A *theory of employment systems: micro-foundations of societal diversity.* New York: Oxford University Press.

This book discusses why there are great international differences in the way employment relations are organized within organizations.

Taking account of the growing evidence that international diversity is not being eradicated by globalization, it begins with the theory of the organization and explains why organizations and workers need to use the employment relationship as a basis for economic cooperation.

Examining the Link between Diversity Management and Organizational Culture

Albrecht, M.H. (2000). *International HRM: Managing diversity in the workplace.* Malden, MA: Blackwell Business.

This collection of articles and case studies helps readers develop the knowledge, skills, and attitudes managers need for success when working in culturally diverse environments. Three key questions are addressed within the book: (1) What are the trends and current issues in global diversity that affect management and human resources? (2) What are the solutions? (3) What is needed to implement these solutions? This step-by-step book provides diversity managers with the skills necessary to become culturally competent practitioners. The book's process draws on the author's twenty years of cultural-diversity work, as well as the fundamental premise that cultural competence is an ongoing, multilayered process that involves personal, interpersonal, and organizational levels. Divided into four skills, including cultural awareness, understanding, interpersonal techniques, and organizational change, each chapter combines cognitive and experiential learning.

Cox, T., Jr. (2001). *Creating the multicultural organization: a strategy for capturing the power of diversity,* (1st ed.). San Francisco: Jossey-Bass.

Organizations are seeking proven methods for leveraging workforce diversity as a resource, especially as the war for talent rages on. *Creating the Multicultural Organization* challenges organizations to stop counting their diverse workforce for the government and begin creating effective strategies that will create a positive approach for managing diversity. This book utilizes a model outlined in Taylor Cox's previous work and shows readers the many practical and innovative ways that successful organizations address diversity issues to secure and develop talent within their workforce in order to succeed.

Thiederman, S. (1995). *Getting culture smart: ten strategies for making diversity work*. Broomfield, CO: Cross-Cultural Communications.

This book is applicable to all types of diversity. It is perfect for anyone who works or lives around diverse people. Designed as a desk reference tool, *Getting Culture Smart* is ideal for those who need to know about diversity, but lack the time to do in-depth reading. *Getting Culture Smart* discusses ten strategies for dealing with diversity, such as finding commonalities between people, diffusing stereotypical thinking, and developing skills for communicating respect.

Thiederman, S. (2003). *Making diversity work: seven steps for defeating bias in the workplace*. Chicago, IL: Dearborn Trade Publishing.

Bias lies in every heart and mind, according to Sondra Thiederman. The heart and mind are also where the answer lies to defeating bias. By focusing on individual rather than organizational processes, powerful focus for bias-busting can be obtained within the workplace. Utilizing case studies, politically incorrect questions, and insightful strategies, Thiederman guides readers through the discomfort of self-discovery.

Evaluating the Link between Diversity Management and Organizational Performance

Arredondo, P.M. (1996). *Successful diversity management initiatives: a blueprint for planning and implementation.* Thousand Oaks, CA: Sage.

Outlining specific steps for a diversity-management process, Patricia Arredondo brings a fresh, insightful, and helpful blueprint for beginning, as well as advancing, diversity-management initiatives. The book discusses the rationale for procedures, identifies potential roadblocks, and explores how barriers can be managed. Specific examples based on the author's research and experiences with organizations are given to help readers obtain an integrative and systematic perspective about issues involved in diversity management.

Chang, R.Y. (1999). *Capitalizing on workplace diversity.* San Francisco: Jossey-Bass-Pfeiffer.

Few issues present such a unique combination of challenges and potential benefits in the workplace as that of diversity. *Capitalizing on Workplace Diversity* is a guidebook that goes beyond handling the challenges of diversity and focuses on how diversity can be tapped as core strength to an organization. This book will provide managers with a practical guide on creating a diversity vision, building commitment, ensuring worker capability, and reinforcing success.

Cox, T., Jr., & Beale, R.L. (1997). *Developing competency to manage diversity: reading, cases, and activities,* 1st ed. San Francisco: Berrett-Koehler Publishers.

The ability to successfully manage diversity is a major initiative for many organizations. *Developing Competency to Manage Diversity* organizes learning and skill building for diversity management around activities that can change behavior, address a wide variety of diversity issues, integrate ideas from academia with real-life experiences, and provide managers with tools they need to manage a diverse workforce successfully.

Cross, E.Y., & White, M.B. (Eds.). (1996). *The diversity factor: capturing the competitive advantage of a changing workforce.* Chicago: Irwin Professional Pub.

With the changing face of America, the workforce of the twenty-first century will include a growing number of women and people of color. Organizations must develop new management skills if they want to remain competitive in this new environment. This book compiles the most requested articles from *The Diversity Factor*, a quarterly journal, and provides both theoretical and practical information that will help organizations learn to manage diversity successfully.

DeLong, D.W. (2004). *Lost knowledge: confronting the threat of an aging workforce.* Oxford University Press.

This book shows how losing human knowledge in a technology-intensive era can seriously affect organizational performance. It also explains what executives can do to retain critical knowledge as veteran workers leave. The author has loaded the book with anecdotes and case examples and reveals how this hidden problem, which threatens virtually all industrialized nations, is becoming extremely serious for many organizations.

DiversityInc. (2006). *The business case for diversity,* 5th edition. Newark, NJ: DiversityInc.

Workplace and marketplace diversity are marks of a well-managed company. This book illustrates how creating an inclusive culture benefits the bottom line. This is a must-read for diversity leaders, as this book includes advice and examples from top-performing companies, evidence of how diversity increases retention, information about the cornerstones of successful diversity-management initiatives, and much more important and relevant information.

Esty, K., & Griffin, R. (1995). *Workplace diversity: a manager's guide to solving problems and turning diversity into a competitive advantage.* Avon, MA: Adams Media.

This book will assist managers of diverse workforces in solving problems and turning a diverse work environment into a competitive advantage rather than a liability.

Flood, R. L., & Romm, N. R. A. (1996*). Diversity management: triple loop learning.* New York: J. Wiley.

Diversity Management provides a strong intellectual contribution to the widely debated issue of diversity management. It carefully blends theory and practice in order to provide substance to the debate on managing diversity in the social and systems sciences. It is thoughtfully illustrated with case studies and brings an overall awareness to the process of diversity management so it is more reflexive and those involved can operate more intelligently and responsibly.

Gentile, Mary C. (1996). *Managerial excellence through diversity cases.* Chicago: Irwin.

Gentile explains that diversity is not a problem to be managed away. It is, however, an opportunity to develop greater personal and organizational performance. This book includes all dimensions of diversity in the workforce and customer base, including race, gender, ethnicity, and nationality, just to name a few, and teaches professionals how to respond effectively to the increasingly diverse business environment.

Hanamura, S. (2005). *I can see clearly*. New York: Renaissance Publishers.

Intended to show leaders and decision makers new possibilities for leading a diverse workforce, *I Can See Clearly* uses the power of personal stories as the catalyst to introduce creative thinking on how to address workplace challenges and ensure that all members of society have become contributing members of the workforce.

Pearn, M. (Ed.). (2002). *Individual differences and development in organizations*. West Sussex, England: John Wiley & Sons, Ltd.

This handbook provides a unique and authoritative review of relevant research, theoretical developments, and current best practices in the management of individual development. This book is designed to be a practical guide and support for those whose role it is to bring out the development of people in the workforce.

Measuring the Impact of Diversity Management on Organizational Performance

Hubbard, Edward E. (1997). *Measuring diversity results*. Petaluma, CA: Global Insights Pub.

Measuring Diversity Results provides formulas for measuring results. It is beneficial to organizations that promote only those individuals who fall into a certain mold. By determining results, changes can be made that are beneficial to the entire workforce, not just a chosen few.

Hubbard, E.E. (1999). *How to calculate diversity return on investment*. Petaluma, CA: Global Insights Pub.

The approach found in this book will help diversity managers calculate their organizations' return on investment, reduce the cycle time to create diversity measures, link diversity efforts to organizational goals, provide a way to combine diversity and organizational measures, and provide options for valuing the process given the type of organizational work or process being measured.

Hubbard, E.E. (2003). The *manager's pocket guide to diversity management*. Amherst, MA: HRD Press.

This pocket guide will provide managers with the skills required to effectively manage a diverse workforce. It will help diversity professionals gain awareness, tools, knowledge, and techniques necessary to raise morale, improve processes, and enhance productivity while improving the bottom line. *The Manager's Pocket Guide to Diversity Management* contains workplace applications for weaving diversity into recruitment and selection, employee retention and development, and team building. This pocket guide is an invaluable tool for managers and leaders.

Hubbard, E.E. (2005). The *diversity scorecard: evaluating the impact of diversity on organizational effectiveness*. Burlington, MA: Elsevier Butterworth-Heinemann.

The Diversity Scorecard does not focus on just one particular sector of diversity management. It provides strategies, tactics, and communication approaches for all types of organizations. It takes readers from theory to practice and shows how professionals can develop their own diversity management scorecard from beginning to end.

Exploring the Link between Leadership and Diversity Management

Cobbs, P. M., & Turnock, J. L. (2003). *Cracking the corporate code: the revealing success stories of 32 African American executives.* New York: AMACOM.

The authors of this book surveyed more than thirty influential African American executives to discuss their strategies for dealing with racial, cultural, and organizational challenges. The content combines strong narrative and stirring quotes and tackles a number of issues, including race and gender bias, isolation, and competition and diversity. *Cracking the Corporate Code* provides inspirational guidance for young African Americans considering a corporate career.

Cross, Elsie Y. (2000). *Managing diversity: the courage to lead.* Westport, CT: Quorum Books.

Drawing on her African American background, Elsie Y. Cross provides the practical assistance today's organizational leaders need. She demonstrates how oppression functions at individual, group, and system levels. She makes clear that if executives are to solve such problems, they must confront their own emotional and psychological barriers. This knowledgeable book is a major contribution to the understanding of gender and cultural problems, as well as a sign of hope that both can be solved.

Iwata, Kay. (2004). *the power of diversity: 5 essential competencies for leading a diverse workforce.* Petaluma, CA: Global Insights.

Offering specific guidelines and tools to increase competency at managing and leading a diverse workforce, *The Power of Diversity* draws from a field study of sixteen companies. This book allows the reader to assess his or her level of diversity competence, while activities provide an opportunity to sharpen skills and abilities.

Lieberman, S. ;Simons G. & Berardo, K. (2003). *Putting diversity to work: how to successfully lead a diverse workforce.* Canada: Crisp Publications, Inc.

Employing people from different backgrounds can give organizations an edge, both internally and externally. This book will help managers integrate diversity management into their search for highly skilled, multitalented employees. It shows how to recruit the best people and build a creative, flexible, inclusive workforce. Additionally, effective communication skills, rapport building, and management-conflict resolution are included in this book on diversity.

Sonnenschein, W. (1997). *The practical executive and workforce diversity.* New York: McGraw-Hill.

The Practical Executive and Workforce Diversity will help every manager translate the potential benefits of modern diverse workforces into tangible, productive workplace gains. This book contains practical guidance for improving team-building relationships and more.

Srivastva, S. & Cooperrider, D.L. (1999). *Appreciative management and leadership: the power of positive thought and action in organization.* Brunswick, OH: Crown Custom Publishing.

Organizations in the twenty-first century look very different from those in the past. Faced with an environment of unpredictable demands and a workforce of great cultural and ethnic diversity, organizations will have to find new ways of engaging their members in a spirit of common purpose. This book offers a new perspective on management that allows executives to unlock their organizations' potential for creativity, innovation, and collaboration.

Gauging the Degrees of Separation between Global Diversity and Diversity Management

Deresky, H. (1999). *International management: managing across borders and cultures*, 3rd ed. Upper Saddle River, NJ: Prentice Hall.

This book covers the most current research and trends in international management. It offers comprehensive and integrative cases illustrating actual behaviors and functions that are required for successful cross-cultural management at both the strategic and interpersonal levels. *International Management* is a great resource for international business professionals.

Dowling, P.J., Welch, D.E., & Schuler, R.S. (1999). *International human resource management: managing people in a multinational context*. Cincinnati, OH: South Western College Publishing.

While covering key topics on international human-resource management, this book also makes reference to the emerging theory and issues related to such management.

Elliott, C. (1999). *Locating the energy for change: an introduction to appreciative inquiry*. New York: International Institute for Sustainable Development.

The main purpose of this book is for readers to understand what appreciative inquiry is and how it can be utilized to change organizations. Charles Elliott speaks of how feeling is just as important as understanding and that appreciative inquiry takes the energy from the positive present and uses it to build a vision of a positive, desired future that is grounded in reality.

Gardenswartz, L., Rowe, A., Digh, P., & Bennett, M.F. (2003). *The global diversity desk reference: managing an international workforce.* San Francisco: Pfeiffer.

This book provides readers with conceptual models, practical guides, and training tools to lead, manage, facilitate, and coach a diverse workforce. It equips intellectuals to reach higher creativity and performance in global business. This is a highly recommended book for professionals in global diversity.

Granrose, C.S., & Oskamp, S. (1997). *Cross-cultural work groups.* Thousand Oaks, CA: Sage Publications.

This book pulls together findings from several disciplines and presents the most current research available on cross-cultural work groups. It explores issues that are often present when different cultural groups are brought together, as well as issues of prejudice, discrimination, ethnocentrism, and intergroup dynamics.

Harris, P.R., Moran, R.T., & Moran, S.V. (2004). *Managing cultural differences: global leadership strategies for the 21st century.* Burlington, MA: Elsevier Butterworth-Heinemann.

The authors of *Managing Cultural Differences* have constructed a valuable network of resources for multicultural managers. They provide new pathways to competence on a global scale grounded in empirical research and illustrated by fascinating stories and examples. Guiding readers toward an accurate awareness of their own cultural identity relative to others, the authors provide meaningful knowledge about the facts and information necessary to comprehend cultural context and take appropriate action in making decisions that will benefit all parties.

Morosini, P. (1998). *Managing.* New York: Pergamon. *cultural differences: effective strategy and execution across cultures in global corporate alliances*

Managing Cultural Differences examines the complexities of cultural and organizational differences that arise during mergers and acquisitions, joint ventures, and alliances. According to the book, more than 50 percent of all corporate alliances fail, and those across cultural divides are even less likely to succeed. Such failures can be attributed to executives concentrating on the financial aspects of a deal rather than, and at the expense of, cultural, organizational, and execution aspects.

Tayeb, M.H. (1996). *Management of a multicultural workforce.* New York: Wiley.

The existence of a multicultural workforce has important implications for human-resource management policies. This book takes a systematic approach to relating organizational features and activities to specific national cultures. This book will be of interest to managers, as well as researchers and MBA students.

Leveraging Employee Resource Groups, Diversity Councils, and High-Performance Teams To Enhance Organizational Performance

Gardenswartz, L. & Rowe, A. (1995). *Diverse teams at work: capitalizing on the power of diversity.* Chicago: Irwin Professional Pub.

Making differences in the workplace an asset rather than a liability can be accomplished through strategies provided in *Diverse Teams at Work.* This practical guide gives team members ways to understand and make the most of their differences while overcoming barriers to achievement—barriers that are often the result of diversity. The book also provides work sheets, processes, guidance, and tools to learn how to diversify groups while building relationships. An annotated list of resources is also provided.

Jackson, S.E., & Ruderman, M.N. (1995). *Diversity in work teams: research paradigms for a changing workplace,* 5th ed. Washington, DC: American Psychological Association.

This book explores how diversity affects one of the most popular management strategies employed by business leaders today. That popular strategy is the formation of employee work teams. Organizations must learn to understand and adjust to workplace diversity, as many of the specific assets and liabilities of work teams arise directly from the diverse talents and perspectives inherent in them.

Karp, H. (2002). *Bridging the boomer–xer gap: creating authentic teams for high performance at work.* Mountain View, CA: Davies-Black Publishing.

It seems the stereotypical notion that Generation Xers are more individualistic than baby boomers does not hold true, at least in the research conducted by Hank Karp. In fact, Generation Xers are real team players, perhaps even more so than boomers. There are only subtle differences that separate the boomers and Xers when it comes to working on teams. This book is recommended for those who are pursuing solid, general team-management guidance, as well as a way to manage cross-generational workers.

Considering Diversity Management as a Force of Organizational Change

Kossek, E.E., & Lobel, S.A. (1996). *Managing diversity: human resource strategies for transforming the workplace.* Cambridge, MA: Blackwell Business.

This book considers the implications of workforce diversity for the development and synthesis of specific human-resource policies. Contributors provide a range of perspectives on significance of workforce diversity as it relates to human resources, as well as the workplace in general. Additionally, the degrees to which current theory and practice have incorporated issues of diversity management are discussed.

Leach, J., G., Bette, J., & Labelle, A. (1995). *A practical guide to working with diversity: the process, the tools, and the resources.* New York: AMACOM.

There has been much inspirational talk about diversity and the importance of managing it properly. Working with differences and not against them is very important when dealing with diversity issues. This book is a pragmatic guide that gives readers everything they need to know in order to implement an effective diversity-management plan within their organization.

Lebo, F. (1996). *Mastering the diversity challenge: easy on-the-job applications for measurable results.* Delray Beach, FL: St. Lucie Press.

Mastering the Diversity Challenge is an easy-to-use guidebook that goes beyond the basic requirements for mastering diversity. It gives important reasons on why managing diversity is good for overall business success.

Wilson, Trevor. (1998). *Diversity at work: the business case for equity.* Ontario: John Wiley & Sons.

Diversity at Work is a hands-on, practical guide to the why and how to strive for diversity and equality in the workplace. It guides managers in creating a fair employment system for all employees, accommodating and valuing differences, hiring and retaining the best-qualified people for jobs, and overcoming backlash associated with controversial affirmative-action and employment legislation, plus many more issues. It is a must-have for managing professionals.

Creating Inclusive Work Environments

Bucher, R., & Bucher, P. (2003). *Diversity Consciousness: Opening Our Minds to People, Cultures, and Opportunities.* New York: Prentice Hall.

The ability to understand, respect, and value diversity is an empowering personal attribute. This book demonstrates how opening one's mind to views of other peoples and cultures is central to quality education and a successful career. *Diversity Consciousness* provides a variety of real-life experiences and perspectives throughout the book. It discusses topics in a style that promotes self-reflection and dialogue, while using an approach to diversity that is balanced, comprehensive, well-integrated, and relevant to achieving one's life goals.

Chemers, M., Oskamp, S., & Constanzo, M. (Ed.). (1995). *Diversity in organizations: new perspectives for a changing workplace.* Thousand Oaks, CA: Sage Publications, Inc.

The largest percentage of new workers in the coming decades will be those considered nontraditional employees. Such new workforce diversity presents both challenges and opportunities to individuals and organizations alike. Benefits include a broader talent pool and development of potential. However, new perspectives can create tension, misunderstanding, and even hostility. *Diversity in Organizations* helps readers come to grips with new diversity issues by applying varied perspectives and approaches in a scholarly manner that is both contemporary and insightful.

Cobbs, P.M., and Turnock, J.L. (2000). *Cracking the corporate code: from survival to mastery.* Washington, DC: Executive Leadership Council

Although written from a uniquely African American perspective, this book speaks to the human experience, making it relevant for anyone seeking advice and inspiration to succeed in a diverse workforce. It offers informative and inspirational self-help career development via career stories and success strategies of thirty-two senior-level African American executives in Fortune 500 companies.

Hanamura, S. (2000). *In Search of Vision: Finding Significance Through Difference.* Petaluma, CA: Global Insights.

This thought-provoking, motivational, and inspirational book integrates Steve Hanamura's life experiences into applications from both home and business. It weaves together all aspects of his life as a single parent, a Christian, a blind person, a child of a blended family, and a corporate consultant to teach breakthrough concepts about the process of living and working together. He demonstrates how his own life has been affected through understanding the importance of humility and surrendering his life to accomplish a purpose God has intended for him.

Harvey, C., and Allard, M. J. (2002). *Understanding and managing diversity: readings, cases, and exercises.* Upper Saddle River, NJ: Prentice Hall.

This book provides cases and exercises organized in terms of three perspectives: individual, social-group identity, and organizational diversity. It also includes classic diversity-management contributions by well-known authors such as Peggy McIntosh, Milton Bennett, David Thomas, and more. Difficult-to-find original teaching material topics such as the business case for diversity, ethics, and board diversity are also included in this edition. Coverage of multiple aspects of workforce diversity beyond race, gender, and ethnicity are also discussed, along with features such as assessment assignments and web-based exercises.

Lecca, Pedro J. (1998). Cultural Competency in Health, Social & Human Services: Directions for the 21st Century. Dallas: Garland.

As thousands of people come to the United States each year, cultural competency is an issue that is becoming increasingly more important. Health-care professionals are finding it difficult to communicate effectively with the members of diverse racial and ethnic backgrounds who come to them for help. This book presents the latest information and techniques for improving cultural competency in health, social, and human services to those individuals of ethnic and racial minorities. Anyone who comes into contact with ethnic and racial minorities will benefit from such information and techniques.

Norton, J. Renae, and Fox, Ronald E. (1997). *change equation: capitalizing on diversity for effective organizational change.* Washington, DC: American Psychological Association.

Showing how to tap into the power of existing diversity within an organization, this book demonstrates how managers can turn such diverse environments into pluralistic workplaces where change is something to embrace, not something to resist. Organizational-change agents, business leaders, human-resource managers, and anyone wanting to make his or her organization stronger and more competitive will find in this book a wealth of practical solutions to advance their organizations.

Prasad, P.M., Albert J., Elmes, M., & Prasad, A. (1997). *Managing the organizational melting pot: dilemmas of workplace diversity.* Thousand Oaks, CA: Sage Publications, Inc.

Managing the Organizational Melting Pot covers key issues related to diversity, such as individual and institutional resistance, performance of diversity-change efforts, and exclusion and discrimination issues— issues that most management literature glosses over. The contributors to this collection adopt an array of theoretical frameworks in order to assist readers in understanding some of diversity's dilemmas. A departure from the more traditional and functional perspective on diversity, this book employs a variety of theoretical perspectives, such as intergroup-relations theory, critical theory, and postmodernism, just to name a few. All in all, this book is beneficial to managers as well as researchers dealing with issues of diversity.

Rodgers, J.O., and Hunter, M. (2004). *Managing differently: getting 100% from 100% of your people 100% of the time.* Winchester, VA: Oakhill Press.

This handbook for leaders is a great tool in the ever-changing diverse workplace. *Managing Differently* begins with the notion that diversity-management initiatives should focus on managers and their leadership capabilities. This practical approach makes it possible to improve communications in an organization as well as improve performance. Everyone in an organization wants to feel valued, and it is the manager's responsibility to create an environment where everyone feels valued and employee engagement is natural.

Sonnenschein, W. (1999). *The diversity toolkit: how you can build and benefit from a diverse workforce.* Lincolnwood, IL: Contemporary Books.

With help from this book, managers of all levels can learn to adapt and be sensitive to new workforce realities. *The Diversity Toolkit* features easy-to-use tips for improving communication skills, practical guidance for perfecting team relationships, and helpful suggestions for using disability metaphors to teach leadership principles that supplement best practices in business as well as in transformational thinking, and ideas and strategies for creating a positive workplace environment.

Defining Diversity and Other Terms Used in the Field of Diversity Management

Pringle, J., Konrad, A.M. & Prasad, P. (2006). *Handbook of Workplace Diversity.* Thousand Oaks, CA: SAGE.

By assembling an international cast of contributors from all walks of research life, Professors Prasad, Pringle and Konrad successfully broaden the scope of scholarly discourse on workplace diversity. This stimulating volume considers how to define this fuzzy construct, what differences are more important than others, and how to make best use of alternative research methods at different levels of analysis. It reviews what we have learned about workplace diversity along several important dimensions (e.g., gender, race, ethnicity, weight, sexual orientation, disabilities, class), and it offers useful recommendations for how to conduct future research that will expand our knowledge of the implications of diversity for individuals, marginalized groups, work organizations, and societies.

In this much-needed Handbook, an international collection of first-rate scholars deals incisively and perceptively with the problems of diversity, difference, inclusion, and cultural pluralism in organizations. This Handbook will be invaluable for researchers and advanced students - one of those books that stays on the top of the desk, covered with bookmarks. Globalization and its melting pot of different nationalities, ethnicities and cultures is attracting research that is gathering in substance and theory. A dynamic new field that represents a significant focus within management and organization studies is emerging.

This Handbook showcases the scope of international perspectives that exist on workplace diversity and is the first to define this hotly contested field. Part I of the Handbook dissects the theoretical reasons and shows how the study of workplace diversity follows different directions. Part II critiques quantitative and qualitative research methods within the field, while Part III investigates the parallels and distinctions between different workplace groups. Key issues are drawn together in an insightful introduction from the editors, and future directions for research are proposed in the conclusion.

The Handbook of Workforce Diversity is an indispensable resource for students and academics of human resource management, organizational behavior, organizational psychology and organization studies. The Handbook of Workforce Diversity served as the definitive source for terms found in Appendix B of this book.

APPENDIX B

SELECTED TERMS AND DEFINITIONS

acculturation – The process of addressing cultural differences, cultural change, and adaptation between groups.

affinity groups – Voluntary employee associations organized around a common dimension of diversity that are created by employees who want to raise awareness in the company to ensure all employees are respected, valued, and productive. Affinity groups support diversity and business objectives by coordinating activities that promote networking, mentoring, peer coaching, and community outreach. Also known as *employee resource groups and business resource groups*.

affirmative action – Specific actions in recruiting, hiring, promoting, and eliminating the present effects of past discrimination, or to prevent discrimination.

affirmative-action plan – The written document through which management assures that all persons have equal opportunities in recruitment, selection, appointment, promotion, training, discipline, and related employment areas. The plan is tailored to the employer's workforce and the skills available in the labor force. It prescribes specific actions, goals, timetables, and responsibilities, and describes resources to meet identified needs. The plan is a comprehensive, results-oriented program designed to achieve equal-employment opportunity rather than merely to assure nondiscrimination.

American Indian (Native American) or Alaska Native – A person having origin in any of the original peoples of North America and who maintains cultural identification through tribal affiliation or community recognition.

Asian or Pacific Islander – A person having origin in any of the original peoples of the Far East, Southeast Asia, the Indian Subcontinent, or the Pacific Islands. This area includes, for example, China, Japan, Korea, the Philippine Islands, and Samoa.

bias – A subjective opinion, preference, or prejudice without reasonable justification that is detrimental to a group's or an individual's ability to treat ideas or people objectively.

bigot – An obstinate and intolerant believer in a religion, political theory, and so on.

black – A person not of Hispanic origin who has origin in any of the black racial groups of the original peoples of Africa.

civil rights – Personal rights guaranteed and protected by the Constitution, e.g., freedom of speech and press, and freedom from discrimination.

cross-cultural – Refers to cultures around the world. There is no universally agreed-upon distinction between diversity management and cross-cultural work, although *cross-cultural* sometimes refers only to country or regional cultures rather than a broader definition of culture.

cultural competency – A set of interpersonal skills that allow individuals to increase their understanding, sensitivity, appreciation, and responsiveness to cultural differences and the interactions resulting from them. The particulars of acquiring cultural competency vary among different groups, and they involve an ongoing relational process tending to inclusion and trust building. Cultural competence refers to an ability to interact effectively with people of different cultures. Cultural competence comprises four components: (1) awareness of one's own cultural worldview, (2) attitude toward cultural differences, (3) knowledge of different cultural practices and worldviews, and (4) cross-cultural skills. Developing cultural competence results in an ability to understand, communicate with, and effectively interact with people across cultures. Cultural competence is a developmental process that evolves over an extended period.

culture – A pattern of thinking, feeling, and acting learned early in one's life. A set of values that create rituals, symbols, heroes, and so on. Culture is learned, very often hard to articulate, and derived from one's social environment.

differential consequences – Outcomes that are applied to different groups exhibiting identical behaviors, yet one group's behavior is valued and the other is devalued.

differential validation – Validation of tests at different score levels for different classes of people. This is tantamount to lowering standards for one or more groups to favor them over others. Differential validation occurs only where lower test scores by one class actually do predict a level of job performance equivalent to that predicted by the higher scores of another class.

disability – A physical, mental, or cognitive impairment or condition that qualifies under federal and state disability nondiscrimination laws for special accommodations to ensure programmatic and physical access.

discrimination – Acting or behaving based on prejudices when dealing with others.

diverse supplier – A comprehensive term that includes small, small disadvantaged, small woman-owned, small veteran-owned, small service-disabled veteran-owned, HUB Zone, Alaska Native, and Indian tribe business concerns.

diversity – The full range of human and/or organizational differences and similarities. This includes, in part, dimensions such as age, culture, education, ethnicity, geography, gender, job level, job function, language, marital status, national origin, political affiliation, race, religion, sexual orientation, job skills, thought process, and years of service. Diversity is generally defined as acknowledging, understanding, accepting, valuing, and celebrating differences among people with respect to age, class, ethnicity, gender, physical and mental ability, race, sexual orientation, spiritual practice, and public-assistance status.

diversity climate – The degree to which an organization implements fair human-resource policies and socially integrates underrepresented employees. Diversity climate is a function of individual-level factors involving the extent of prejudice and stereotyping in organizations, group-intergroup factors referring to the degree of conflict between various groups within an organization, and organizational-level factors regarding such domains as organizational culture. Diversity climate is also the degree that underrepresented personnel are integrated into higher-level positions and within an organization's social networks, and whether institutional bias prevails in an organization's human-resource systems such as recruiting, hiring, training, developing, promoting, and compensating employees.

diversity communication – The process of providing information to employees and managers regarding diversity-management strategy and progress. Activities include conveying information via employee newsletters, closed-circuit television, employee focus groups, town-hall meetings, organization websites, and social media.

diversity competency – A process of learning that leads to an ability to effectively respond to the challenges and opportunities posed by the presence of social-cultural diversity in a defined social system.

diversity councils – Voluntary employee associations organized around a department, organization, function, line of business, or business unit. They are created by the organization to raise diversity awareness in the organization and to ensure all employees are respected, valued, and productive. They support the company's diversity and business objectives by coordinating activities that promote networking, mentoring, peer coaching, and community outreach.

diversity management – A strategically driven process whose emphasis is on building skills, making quality decisions that bring out the best in every employee, and assessing organizational mixtures and tensions as a result of changing workforce and customer demographics.

diversity-management initiatives – Proactive and intentional actions to get the best from the mix of employees, customers, suppliers, and other stakeholders in order to achieve organizational objectives. Actions often include efforts to improve human-resource processes and enhance organizational culture such as how the organization recruits, hires, trains, mentors, promotes, develops, and integrates employees.

diversity-management training – Intentional actions to educate a culturally diverse workforce and to sensitize employees and managers to differences in the organization such as gender, race, and generation in an attempt to maximize the potential productivity of all employees. Numerous organizations with these goals in mind have developed training-program titles such as "Managing Diversity," "Valuing Differences," and "Leading Diverse Work Teams."

diversity metrics – The process of quantitatively and qualitatively measuring the impact of the organization's diversity strategy.

diversity practitioner or professional – Individual responsible for managing the diversity-management initiatives, or the chief diversity officer in an organization. This person has expertise in diversity management but may or may not be a full-time diversity professional.

dominant culture – The most powerful cultural grouping. For example, in most parts of the United States, the dominant culture is composed of white, English-speaking, middle- to upper-income Christians.

duty to accommodate – The obligation of an employer, service provider, or union to take steps to eliminate disadvantage to employees, prospective employees, or clients resulting from a rule, practice, or physical barrier that has or may have an adverse impact on individuals or groups protected under state or federal law.

employee resource groups – Voluntary employee associations organized around a common dimension of diversity that are created by employees who want to raise awareness in the company to ensure all employees are respected, valued, and productive. Employee resource groups support diversity and business objectives by coordinating activities that promote networking, mentoring, peer coaching, and community outreach. Also known as *affinity groups* or *business resource groups*.

equal access – Absence of barriers to admittance, such as those motivated by cultural or racial discrimination, to the institutions of a society. This includes access to services, programs, and employment. To facilitate equal access, an outreach program is often needed to inform people that the program is available.

equal employment opportunity (EEO) – The process of administering human-resource activities to ensure equal access in all phases of the employment process. Employment decisions are based solely on the individual merit and fitness of applicants and employees related to specific jobs, without regard to race, color, religion, sex, age, national origin, handicapping conditions, marital status, or criminal record.

Equal Employment Opportunity Commission (EEOC) – The federal government agency mandated to enforce Title VII of the Civil Rights Act of 1964, as amended. The commission has five members, each appointed to a five-year term by the president of the United States with the advice and consent of Congress. The federal Equal Employment Opportunity Commission has the power to bring suits, subpoena witnesses, issue guidelines that have the force of law, render decisions, provide legal assistance to complainants, and so on, in regard to fair employment.

equal pay – As required by the Equal Pay Act of 1963 for employers subject to the Fair Labor Standards Act, businesses must provide equal pay for men and women performing the same or substantially similar jobs in the same establishment. For example, in a department store, a female salesperson in the ladies' shoe department must receive pay equal to that of a male salesperson in the men's shoe department.

equity – Equity is the principle of fair treatment, access, opportunity, and advancement for all employees, while at the same time striving to identify and eliminate barriers that have prevented the full participation of some groups. The principle of equity acknowledges that there are historically underserved and underrepresented populations and that fairness regarding these unbalanced conditions is needed to assist equality in the provision of effective opportunities to all groups.

ethnic – An adjective used to describe groups that share a common language, race, customs, lifestyle, social view, or religion. Everyone belongs to an ethnic group. The term is often confused with nonwhite. *Ethnic*, however, refers to those traits that originate from racial, linguistic, and cultural ties with a specific group.

ethnocentrism – Characterized by, or based on, the attitude that one's own group is superior. Ethnocentric habitual disposition is to judge foreign peoples or groups by the standards or practices of one's own culture or ethnic group.

Eurocentrism – Reflecting a tendency to interpret the world in terms of Western, and especially European, values and experiences.

gender – Gender is a socially constructed system of classification that ascribes qualities of masculinity and femininity to people. Gender characteristics can change over time and are different between cultures. Words that refer to gender include man, woman, transgender, masculine, feminine, and genderqueer. Gender also refers to one's sense of self as masculine or feminine, regardless of external genitalia. Gender is often conflated with sex; however, this is inaccurate, because *sex* refers to bodies and *gender* refers to personality characteristics.

Hispanic – A person, regardless of race, who is of Spanish culture or origin. This includes, for example, persons from Mexico, Central or South America, Puerto Rico, the Dominican Republic, and Cuba.

homophobia – The hatred or fear of homosexuals. It is characterized by negative attitudes and behaviors toward gays and lesbians, and is expressed in a variety of ways, from insulting remarks and humor that reinforce stereotypes, to discrimination and violent behavior.

human rights – Freedoms that are enjoyed by all people, simply because they are human. Human rights are supposed to apply equally to all people regardless of characteristics such as age, race, or gender. The Universal Declaration of Human Rights extends these rights to all people around the world.

immigrant – The word, technically, means people who have moved to a country with the intention of settling. This meaning would exclude refugees.

inclusion – The act of creating environments in which any individual or group can be and feel welcomed, respected, supported, and valued to fully participate. An inclusive and welcoming climate embraces differences and offers respect in words and actions for all people. Inclusion integrates the fact of diversity and embeds it into the core mission and institutional functioning. It is the active, intentional, and ongoing engagement with diversity.

inclusive leadership – The ability of managers (regardless of their human dimension of diversity) to get all the human and organizational mixes of an organization working better together for higher business and human outcomes.

individual racism – Learned behavior taught through socialization, manifested in attitudes, beliefs, and behaviors.

institutional racism – Conscious or unconscious exercise of notions of racial superiority by social institutions through policies, practices, procedures, organizational culture, and organizational values.

multicultural education – A long-term life commitment and dynamic process; it is for all people, it is inclusive, and it is the beginning of self-respect and respect of other cultures. It is building awareness, respect, interest, and appreciation of the cultures of a variety of racial, ethnic, and social groups and a willingness to create policies, programming, and practices that encourage the expression, exchange of information, and inclusion of differing cultural perspectives.

multiculturalism – Multiculturalism is an acknowledgment that, as people, we are culturally diverse and multifaceted, and a process through which the sharing and transforming of cultural experiences allows us to rearticulate and redefine new spaces, possibilities, and positions for ourselves and others. There are many different—and sometimes conflicting—ideas around the highly contested term of *multiculturalism*. While more-mainstream discourses around diversity and multiculturalism have become abundant, such definitions— particularly when historical and asocial in their grounding—tend to miss parts of the picture, and may thus unproductively disguise, and even reproduce (perhaps unintentionally), forms of injustice and oppression still prevalent in our society.

nonwhite – A protected group or protected classes that have been historically underrepresented in organizations or who have been oppressed or ignored in society, whether or not legislation exists to protect these groups. For equal-employment opportunity official reporting purposes, and for purposes of the workforce analysis required in Revised Executive Order No. 4, the term *nonwhite* includes blacks, Hispanics, Alaskan Natives or American Indians, and Asian or Pacific Islanders.

nonwhite recruitment – Special recruitment efforts undertaken to assure that qualified protected class members are well-represented in the applicant pools for positions from or in which they have been excluded or substantially underutilized. Such efforts may include contacting organizations and media with known protected-class constituencies. Open job posting and advertising and equal-opportunity employer statements necessary in many situations are matters of nondiscrimination rather than measures of affirmative-action recruitment.

organizational climate – A measure (real or perceived) of the organization's work environment as it relates to interpersonal professional interactions. Climate refers to the experience of individuals and groups in an organization, and the quality and extent of the interaction between those various groups and individuals. Diversity and inclusion efforts are not complete unless they also address climate. In a healthy climate, individuals and groups generally feel welcomed, respected, and valued by the organization. A healthy climate is grounded in respect for others, nurtured by dialogue between those of differing perspectives, and is evidenced by a pattern of civil interactions among community members. Not all aspects of a healthy climate necessarily feel positive—indeed, uncomfortable or challenging situations can lead to increased awareness, understanding, and appreciation. Tension, while not always positive, can be healthy when handled appropriately. Conversely, in an unhealthy climate, individuals or groups often feel isolated, marginalized, and even unsafe.

organizational culture – A set of values within an organization that become practices. The rules of how things get done here can be both spoken and unspoken. The values of an organization are often based on the values of the company founders.

organizational preference or tradition – Refers to the thinking or practices that are sometimes confused with requirements. An example of an organizational preference is a company almost always hiring employees with degrees from certain schools or universities, even though other schools offer comparable degrees.

overt racism – Racism that is frank and open, including graffiti, intimidation, or physical violence, and that legitimates negative racial stereotypes. Racial and ethnic slurs or so-called jokes are other examples of obvious racial discrimination. People often ignore racism because they do not know how to deal with it.

people of color – A term defined by race or color only, not citizenship, place of birth, religion, language, or cultural background. The term applies to people who are black, aboriginal, Chinese, South Asian, Southeast Asian, Filipino and to Hispanic American, and others. These terms are generally regarded as positive identities as opposed to *nonwhites, minorities, visible minorities*, or *ethnics*. Also known as *racially visible people*.

person with a disability – A person who has a physical or mental impairment that substantially limits one or more of such person's major life activities, has a record of such impairment, or is regarded as having such an impairment. Also called *physically challenged person*. See *physically challenged person* for further definitions as to the meaning of disability.

physically challenged person – A person who has a physical or mental impairment that substantially limits one or more of such person's major life activities, has a record of such impairment, or is regarded as having such an impairment. Also known as *person with a disability*.

The following are general definitions as to the meaning of disability: *Physical or mental impairment* means: 1) any physiological disorder or condition, cosmetic disfigurement, or anatomical loss affecting one or more of the following body systems: neurological, musculoskeletal, special sense organs, respiratory (including speech organs), cardiovascular, reproductive, digestive, genitourinary, hemic and lymphatic, skin, and endocrine; or 2) any mental or psychological disorder such as mental retardation, organic brain syndrome, emotional or mental illness, and specific learning disabilities. The term *physical or mental impairment* includes, but is not limited to, such diseases and conditions as orthopedic, visual, speech and hearing impairments, cerebral palsy, epilepsy, muscular dystrophy, multiple sclerosis, cancer, heart disease, diabetes, mental retardation, emotional illness, drug addiction, and alcoholism.

Major life activities means functions such as caring for oneself, performing manual tasks, walking, seeing, hearing, speaking, breathing, learning, and working.

Has a record of such impairment means has a history of a mental or physical impairment that substantially limits one or more life activities.

Is regarded as having an impairment means: 1) has a physical or mental impairment that does not substantially limit major life activities but that is treated by an agency as constituting such a limitation, 2) has a physical or mental impairment that substantially limits major life activities only as a result of the attitudes of others toward such impairment, or 3) has none of the impairments defined above but is treated by an agency as having such an impairment.

Substantially limits refers to the degree to which the impairment affects employability. A handicapped individual who is likely to experience difficulty in securing, retaining, or advancing in employment will be considered substantially limited.

pluralism – A state of society in which members of diverse ethnic, racial, religious, or social groups maintain an autonomous participation in and development of their traditional culture or special interest within the confines of a common civilization.

power – Access to resources, position, status, wealth, or personal strength of character that gives a person or a group or a system the ability to influence others. Power can be used to affect others positively or negatively.

prejudice – Prejudging another person, place, or thing that is not backed with facts to substantiate the attitude or feeling; to prejudge a person or group negatively, usually without adequate evidence or information to substantiate the position. Frequently, prejudices are not recognized as false or unsound assumptions. Through repetition, they come to be accepted as commonsense notions, and when backed up with power, result in acts of discrimination and oppression.

privilege – A special advantage, immunity, or benefit not enjoyed by all and possibly not recognized by an individual or class of individuals.

protected classes – Groups identified in Executive Order No. 6 (nonwhites, women, disabled persons, and Vietnam-era veterans) that are specifically protected against employment discrimination.

quotas – In employment law, court-ordered or -approved hiring and/ or promoting of specified numbers or ratios of nonwhites or women in positions from which a court has found they have been excluded as a result of unlawful discrimination. Quotas are not the same as goals and timetables.

race – A social category used to classify humankind according to common ancestry or descent and reliant upon differentiation by general physical characteristics such as color of skin and eyes, hair type, stature, and facial features.

race relations – Interaction between diverse racial groups within one society.

racial/ethnic groups – The four racial/ethnic groups protected by federal equal-employment opportunity laws are blacks, Hispanics, Asians or Pacific Islanders, and American Indians or Alaska Natives. Racial/ethnic groups are defined by the federal government as follows:

- **white** (not of Hispanic origin): Persons having origins in any of the original peoples of Europe, North Africa, or the Middle East.
- **black** (not of Hispanic origin): Persons having origins in any of the black racialgroups of Africa.
- **Hispanic**: Persons of Mexican, Puerto Rican, Cuban, Central or South American, or other Spanish culture or origin, regardless of race.
- **Asian or Pacific Islander**: Persons having origins in any of the original peoples of the Far East, Southeast Asia, the Indian Subcontinent, or the Pacific Islands. This area includes, for example, China, Japan, Korea, the Philippine Islands, and Samoa.
- **American Indian or Alaska Native**: Persons having origins in any of the original peoples of North America and who maintain cultural identification through tribal affiliation or community recognition.

racially visible people – A term defined by race or color only, not citizenship, place of birth, religion, language, or cultural background. The term applies to people who are black, aboriginal, Chinese, South Asian, Southeast Asian, Filipino and Latin American Canadian, and others. These terms are generally regarded as positive identities as opposed to *nonwhites, minorities, visible minorities,* or *ethnics.* Also known as *people of color.*

representation – The results of intentional efforts to achieve a balanced workforce. It refers to an area of emphasis in diversity management where the goal is to ensure that people are hired based on their qualifications, thereby making the various business units, departments, teams, and functions equitable regarding the various dimensions of diversity and/or making those dimensions mirror the labor market or customer base.

selective perception – A subconscious process of noticing a specific behavior by one group while not noticing or dismissing the same behavior on the part of another group.

senior-management team – Describes the team or individuals who have the responsibility for showing leadership to accomplish the organization's vision and goals.

sexism – Stems from a set of implicit or explicit beliefs, erroneous assumptions, and actions based upon an ideology of inherent superiority of one gender over another, and is evident within organizational or institutional structures and programs, as well as within individual thought or behavior patterns. Sexism, like racism, is a discriminatory act backed by power. Sexism is any act or institutional practice backed by institutional power that subordinates people because of gender.

sexual harassment – Interference, intimidation, or other offensive behavior from one work associate to another and based in part on the gender of the workers involved. The intent is to exert power over another.

sexual orientation – Sexual orientation is the deep-seated direction of one's sexual (erotic) attraction toward the same gender, opposite gender, or other genders. It is on a continuum and not a set of absolute categories.

social class – The hierarchical order of a society based on such indicators of social rank as income, occupation, education, ownership of property, family, religion, and political relationships.

social justice – This refers to the concept of a society that gives individuals and groups fair treatment and an equitable share of the benefits of society.

stereotyping – An extension of prejudice by labeling others based solely on their membership in a group and then labeling others like them in one broad characteristic, as if they have the same characteristic; also, false generalizations of a group of people that result in an unconscious or conscious categorization of members of that group. Stereotypes may be based upon misconceptions about ethnic, linguistic, geographical, religious, and physical or mental attributes, as well as race, age, marital status, and gender. Stereotyping is the tendency to lump together members of a group and to think of them as types rather than as individuals. All members of the group are falsely assumed to be alike, with exceptions being ignored or their existence denied. It is to generalize when we have an unpleasant experience with an individual belonging to a particular group. The resulting feelings of aversion and hostility, which may or may not be justified, are sometimes irrationally generalized to include all members of that group.

supplier diversity professional – A person, typically with a procurement or supply-chain background, charged with designing a supplier-diversity program that reflects a commitment to diversity and inclusion of diverse suppliers in its procurement process. This individual also oversees and drives internal diversity-knowledge and awareness initiatives, including training and communication efforts that emphasize the corporation's strong commitment to diversity. Additional responsibility includes strengthening relationships between the organization and community organizations that align and share a diversity commitment.

supplier-diversity program – A diversity-management initiative that encompasses due diligence efforts to include diverse suppliers in all bid opportunities by seeking them out, assisting in their development, and encouraging joint ventures. In order to provide the maximum practicable opportunity (MPO) as required by the federal government's *Small Business Liaison Office Handbook, 2005*, prime contractors are encouraged to advertise subcontracting opportunities, break large requirements into smaller packages, keep the playing field level, mentor/develop small businesses, and allow adequate time for firms to offer proposals and submit bids.

systemic discrimination – A general condition, practice, or approach that applies equally to the majority, but negatively affects opportunities or results for specific groups of people.

underrepresented – Refers to groups that have been denied access and/or suffered past institutional discrimination in the United States, and according to the census and other federal measuring tools, includes African Americans, Asian Americans, Hispanics or Latinos, and Native Americans. This is revealed by an imbalance in the representation of different groups in common pursuits such as education, jobs, housing, and so on, resulting in marginalization for some groups and individuals and not for others relative to the number of individuals who are members of the population involved. Other groups in the United States have been marginalized and are currently underrepresented. These groups may include, but are not limited to, other ethnicities; adult learners; veterans; people with disabilities; lesbian, gay, bisexual, and transgender individuals; people from different religious groups; and people from different economic backgrounds.

underserved – Underserved populations are ones that are disadvantaged in relation to other groups because of structural or societal obstacles and disparities.

United States Commission on Civil Rights – An independent, bipartisan agency established by Congress in 1957 and directed to: 1) Investigate complaints alleging that citizens are being deprived of their right to vote by reason of their race, color, religion, sex, age, handicap, or national origin, or by reason of fraudulent practices; 2) Study and collect information concerning legal developments constituting discrimination or a denial of equal protection of the laws under the Constitution because of race, color, religion, sex, age, handicap, or national origin, or in the administration of justice; 3) Appraise federal laws and policies with respect to discrimination or denial of equal protection of the laws because of race, color, religion, sex, age, handicap, or national origin, or in the administration of justice; 4) Serve as a national clearinghouse for information in respect to discrimination or denial of equal protection of the laws because of race, color, religion, sex, age, handicap, or national origin; and 5) Submit reports, findings, and recommendations to the president and Congress.

values – General guiding principles that are to govern all activities; the manner in which people should behave and the principles that should govern behavior.

valuing diversity – The recognition that it is not only ethical and fair to make one's organization accessible to all people, but that their differences in identity, perspective, background, and style are, in fact, valuable qualities and human resources that can significantly enrich and strengthen the organization and its capacity to achieve excellence.

visually impaired – A phrase used to describe people who can only see very little. They see better with the assistance of technical aids such as magnifiers, telescopes, special glasses, and computers with special features such as large print.

workforce diversity – Refers to ways in which people in a workforce are similar and different from one another. In addition to the characteristics protected by law, other similarities and differences commonly cited include background, education, language skills, personality, sexual orientation, and work role.

workforce profile – An organizational snapshot illustrating the dispersion of race, national origin, gender, and/or disability groups within specified employment categories.

xenophobia – Xenophobia is hatred, resistance, and negative prejudice against foreign people and everything that is foreign.

APPENDIX C

REFERENCES

Acker, J. (2000). Gendered contradictions in organizational equity projects, *organization*, vol. 7, no. 4, pp. 625–32.

Acosta, A. S. (2004). A diversity perspective on organizational learning and learning perspective on organizational diversity, *Academy of Management Best Conference Paper*, CMS: D1–D6.

Addleson, M. (2000). What is good organization? learning organizations, community and the rhetoric of the bottom line, *European Journal of Work and Organizational Psychology*, vol. 9, no. 2, pp. 233–52.

Adler, N. J. (1986). *International Dimensions of Organizational Behavior*. Boston: Kent Publishing Company.

Adler, N. J., and Ghadar, F. (1990). Strategic human resource management: a global perspective. In R. Pieper (Ed.), *Human Resource Management: An International Comparison* (pp. 235–60). Berlin, New York: Walter de Gruyter.

Aguilera, R. V., and Jackson, G. (2003). the cross-national diversity of corporate governance: dimensions and determinants, *Academy of Management Review*, vol. 28, pp. 447–65.

Ahmed, P. K. (1998). Culture and climate for innovation, *European Journal of Innovation Management*, vol. 1, pp. 30–43.

Ahmed, P. K., and Zairi, M. (1999). Benchmarking for brand innovation, *European Journal of Innovation Management*, vol. 2, 36–48.

Alderfer, C. P., (1992). Changing race relations embedded in organizations: report on a long-term project with the xyz company, in S. E. Jackson (Ed.), *Diversity in the Workplace: Human Resources Initiatives.* New York: Guilford.

Alderfer, C. P., and Smith, K. K. (1982). Studying intergroup relations embedded in organizations, *Administrative Science Quarterly*, vol. 27, pp. 35–65.

Alderfer, C. P., and Thomas, D. A. (1988). The significance of race and ethnicity for understanding organizational behavior, *International Review of Industrial and Organizational Psychology*, pp. 1–42.

Allard, M. J. (2002). Theoretical underpinnings of diversity, in C. Harvey and M. J. Allard (eds.), *Understanding and Managing Diversity.* New Jersey: Prentice-Hall, pp. 3–27.

American Management Association (1995). *AMA Survey on Managing Cultural Diversity.* New York: American Management Association.

Ancona, D. G., and Caldwell, D. F. (1998). Rethinking team composition from the outside in, in D. Greenfield (ed.), *Research on Managing Groups and Teams.* Stamford, CT: JAI Press.

Andrialopolos, C. (2001). Determinants of organizational creativity: a literature review, *Management Decision*, vol. 39, pp. 834–40.

Appelbaum, S. H., and Fewster, B. M. (2002). Global aviation human resource management: contemporary recruitment and selection and diversity and equal opportunity practices, *Equal Opportunities International*, vol. 21, pp. 66–80.

Archer, M. (1995). *Realist Social Theory: The Morphogenetic Approach*. Cambridge: Cambridge University Press.

Argos, C. (1997). Institutionalized resistance to organizational change: denial, inaction, and repression, *Journal of Business Ethics*, vol. 16, pp. 917–31.

Argos, C., and Burr, C. (1996). Employment equity, affirmative action, managing diversity: assessing the differences, *International Journal of Manpower*, vol. 17, pp. 30–45.

Argyris, C., and Schön, D. A. (1978). *Organizational Learning: A Theory in Action Perspective*. Reading, MA: Addison-Wesley.

Arredondo, P. (1996). *Successful Diversity Management Initiatives: A Blueprint for Planning and Implementation*. Thousand Oaks, CA: Sage.

Arts Council England. (2005). *Children, Young People and the Arts: London Regional Strategy*,www.artscouncil.org.uk.

Ashkanasy, N. M., Hartel, C. E. J., and Daus, C. S. (2002). Diversity and emotion: the new frontiers in organizational behavior research, *Journal of Management*, vol. 28, no. 3, pp. 307–38.

Ashworth, P., and Saxton, J. (1992). *Managing Work Experience*. Routledge: London.

Atkinson, J. (1985). *Flexibility, Uncertainty and Manpower Management*. Brighton: Institute of Manpower Studies.

Auyero, J. (2002). The judge, the cop, and the queen of carnival: ethnography, storytelling, and the (contested) meanings of protest, *Theory and Society*, vol. 31, pp. 151–87.

Avery, D. R., and Thomas, K. M. (2004). Blending content and contract: the roles of diversity curriculum and campus heterogeneity fostering diversity management competency, *Academy of Management & Learning*, vol. 3, pp. 380–96.

Bacharach, S. B., Bamberger, P. A., and Vashdi, D. (2005). Diversity and homophily at work: supportive relations among white and african-american peers, *Academy of Management Journal*, vol. 48, pp. 619–44.

Bachman, A. (2006). melting pot or tossed salad? implications for designing effective multicultural workgroups, *management International Review, 46* (6), 721–747.

Bantel, K. A., and Jackson, S. E. (1989). Top Management and innovation in banking: does the composition of the top team make a difference? *Strategic Management Journal*, vol. 10, pp. 107–24.

Barak, M. E. M. (2000). The Inclusive workplace: an ecosystems approach to diversity management, *Social Work*, vol. 45, no. 4, pp. 339–52.

Barkema, H. G., Baum, J. A. C., and Mannix, E. A. (2002). Management challenges in a new time, *Academy of Management Journal*, vol. 45, no. 5, pp. 916–30.

Barkema, H. G., and Vermeulen, F. (1998). International expansion through start-up or acquisition: a learning perspective, *Academy of Management Journal*, vol. 41, pp. 7–26.

Barmes, L., and Ashtiany, S. (2003). The diversity approach to achieving equality: potential and pitfalls, *The Industrial Law Journal*, vol. 32, pp. 274–96.

Barone, T. E. (1992). Beyond theory and method: a case of critical storytelling, *theory into practice*, vol. 31, no. 2, pp. 142–46.

Barrett, R. S. (1967). Guide to using psychological tests, in E. A. Fleishman (ed.), *Studies in Personnel and Industrial Psychology*. Chicago: Dorsey Press.

Barrick, M. R., Bradley, B. H., and Colbert, A. E. (2007). The moderating role of top management team interdependence: implications for real teams and working groups, *Academy of Management Journal, 50* (3), 544–557.

Barrick, M., Stewart, G., Neubert, M., and Mount, M. (1998). Relating member ability and personality to work-team processes and team effectiveness, *Journal of Applied Psychology*, 83(3): 377–391.

Barry, B., and Bateman, T. S. (1996) A social trap analysis of the management of diversity, *Academy of Management Review*, vol. 21, pp. 757–90.

Barsade, S., Ward, A., Turner, J., and Sonnenfeld, J. (2000). To your heart's content: a model of affective diversity in top management teams, *Administrative Science Quarterly*, 45: 802–836.

Barthorpe, S., and Hall, M. (2000). A collaborative approach to placement preparation and career planning for university students:

a case study, *Journal of Vocational Education and Training*, vol. 52, no. 2, pp. 165–75.

Bartol, K. M., Evans, C. L., and Stith, M. T. (1978). Black versus white leaders: a comparative review of the literature, *Academy of Management Review*, April, pp. 293–304.

Bartram, D. (2004). Assessment in Organizations, *Applied Psychology: An International Review*, vol. 53, no. 2, pp. 237–59.

Bartunek, J. M., Bobko, P., and Venkatraman, N. (1993). Toward innovation and diversity in management research methods, *Academy of Management Journal*, vol. 36, pp. 1362–73.

Bass, B. M. (1995). From transactional to transformational leadership: learning to share vision, *Organizational Dynamics*, vol. 18, no. 3, pp. 19–31.

Battu, H., Seaman, P., and Zenou, Y. (2004). Job contact networks and the ethnic minorities, *Working Paper no. 628*. New York: The Research Institute of Industrial Economics.

Baugh, S., and Graen, G. (1997). Effects of team gender and racial composition on perceptions of team performance in cross-functional teams. *Group & Organizational Management*, 22: 366–384.

Becker, G. S. (1975). *Human Capital*. Chicago: University of Chicago Press.

Beckhard, R. (1969). *Organizational Development: Strategies and Methods*. Reading, CA: Addison-Wesley.

Bedeian, A. G., and Mossholder, K. W. (2000). On the use of the coefficient of variation as a measure of diversity, *Organizational Research*, vol. 3: 285–297.

Beer, M., and Nobria, N. (2000). Cracking the code of change, *Harvard Business Review*, May–June, pp. 133–41.

Bell M.P., Harrison D.A., McLaughlin M.E. (1992). Asian American attitudes toward affirmative action in employment. *Journal of Applied Behavioral Science*, 33, 356-377.

Bell, E. L. J., and Nkomo, S. M. (2001). *Our separate ways: black and white women and the struggle for professional identity*. Boston, MA: Harvard Business School Press.

Benschop, Y. (2001). Pride, prejudice and performance: relations between HRM diversity and performance, *International Journal of Human Resources Management*, vol. 12, pp. 1166–81.

Bergen, C. W. V., Soper, B., and Foster, T. (2002). Unintended negative effects of diversity management, *Public Personnel Management*, vol. 31, pp. 239–51.

Beynon, H. (1973). *Working for Ford*. London: Allen Lane, Penguin Books.

Bezrukova, K., and Jehn, K. A. (2001). *The effects of diversity training programs*. Unpublished manuscript, Solomon Asch Center for the Study of Ethnopolitical Conflict, University of Pennsylvania, Philadelphia.

Bhadury, J., Mighty, E. J., & Damar, H. (2000). Maximizing workforce diversity in project teams: a network flow approach, *The International Journal of Management Science*, vol. 28, pp. 143–153.

Bhawuk, D. (1994). *Bridging the gap between theory and practice: a comparative study of current diversity programs*. Champaign: University of Illinois Center for Human Resource Management.

Bhimani, A. (1999). Mapping methodological frontiers in cross-national management control research, *Accounting, Organizational and Society*, vol. 24, pp. 413–440.

Biech, E. (2003). Executive Commentary, *Academy of Management Executive*, vol. 17, pp. 92–93.

Bigley, A. G., & Pearce, J. L. (1998). Straining for shared meaning in organization science: problems of trust and distrust, *Academy of Management Review*, vol. 23, pp. 405–421.

Blake, S. (2005). Managing cultural diversity: implications for organizational competitiveness, *Academy of Management Executive*, 5, 45–56.

Blalock, H. M. (1967). *Toward a Theory of Group Relations*. Wiley, New York.

Blankfield, S. (2001). Think, problematic and costly? the dyslexic student on work placement, *SKILL Journal*, vol. 70, pp. 23–26, July.

Blau, F. (1977). *Equal pay in the office*. Lexington: MA, Lexington Books.

Blazevic, V., & Lievens, A. (2002). Learning during the new financial service innovation process: antecedents and performance effects, *Journal of Business Research*, vol. 57, no. 4, pp. 374–391.

Bleise, P. D., & Halverson, R. R. (1998). Group consensus and psychological well-being: a large field study, *Journal of Applied Social Psychology,* vol. 28, pp. 563–580.

Blyler, M., & Coff, R. W. (2003). Dynamic capabilities, social capital, and rent appropriation: ties that split pies, *Strategic Management Journal,* vol. 24, no. 7, pp. 677–686.

Boeker, W. (1997). Strategic change: the influence of managerial characteristics and organizational growth, *Academy of Management Journal,* vol. 40, pp. 152–170.

Boje, D. M. (1991a). Consulting and change in the storytelling organization, *Journal of Organizational Change Management,* vol. 4, no. 3, pp. 7–17.

Boje, D. M. (1991b). The storytelling organization: a study of story performance in an office supply firm, *Administrative Science Quarterly,* vol. 36, pp. 106–126.

Boje, D. M. (1995). Stories of the storytelling organization: a postmodern analysis of Disney as "tamara-land," *Academy of Management Journal,* vol. 38, no. 4, pp. 997–1035.

Boje, D. M., & Winsor, R. D. (1993). The resurrection of Taylorism: total quality management's hidden agenda, *Journal of Organizational Change Management,* vol. 6, no. 4, pp. 57–70.

Boone, C., & Hendricks, W. (2009). Top management team diversity and firm performance: moderators of functional-background and locus-of-control *Diversity, 55* (2), 165–180.

Bourdieu, P. (1977). *Outline of theory of practice.* Cambridge: Cambridge University Press.

Bourdieu, P. (1984). *Distinction: a social critique of the judgment of taste*. London: Routledge.

Bourdieu, P. (1990). *The logic of practice*. Stanford, CA: Stanford University Press.

Bourdieu, P. (1998). *Practical reason: on the theory of action*. Cambridge: Polity Press.

Bourdieu, P., & Wacquant, L. (1992). *An invitation to reflexive sociology*. Cambridge: Polity Press.

Bouty, I. (2000). Interpersonal and interaction influences on informal resource exchanges between R&D researchers across organizational boundaries, *Academy of Management Journal*, vol. 43, no. 1, pp. 50–65.

Boxall, P., & Purcell, J. (2003). *Strategy and human resource management*. New York: Palgrave Macmillan.

Boyce, M. E. (1995). Collective centering and collective sense-making in the stories and storytelling of one organization, *Organization Studies*, 1995, vol. 16, no. 1, pp. 107–137.

Boyce, M. E. (1996). Organizational story and storytelling: a critical review, *Journal of Organizational Change Management*, vol. 9, no. 5, pp. 5–26.

Brewer, M. (1995). The role of social identities, in S. J. Ruderman, *Diversity in Work Teams: Research Paradigms for a Changing Workplace* (pp. 47–68). Washington, DC: American Psychological Association.

Brickson, S. (2000). The impact of identity orientation on individual and organizational outcomes in demographically diverse settings, *Academy of Management Review*, vol. 25, pp. 82–101.

Brief, A. (2000). Establishing a climate for diversity: the inhibition of prejudiced reactions in the workplace. in G. Ferris, *Research in Personnel and Human Resource Management*, vol. 19, pp. 91–129. New York: Elsevier.

Brief, A. P. (2004) Editor's Comments: AMR—It is about diversity, *Academy of Management Review*, vol. 29, p. 7.

Brimm, L., & Arora, M. (2001). Diversity management at Hewlett-Packard, Europe, in M. A. Albrecht (ed.), *International HRM: Managing Diversity in the Workplace*. Oxford: Blackwell, pp. 108–124.

Bronstein, A. S. (1991). Temporary work in western Europe: threat or complement to permanent employment? *International Labor Review*, vol. 130, no. 3, pp. 291–311.

Brooks, W., & Trompenaars, F. (1995). Global diversity begins at home, *People Management*, vol. 1, pp. 16–18.

Brown, K. G., Kozlowski, S. W. J., & Hattrup, K. (1996). *Theory, issues, and recommendations in conceptualizing agreement as a construct in organizational research: the search for consensus regarding consensus*. National Academy of Management, Cincinnati, OH.

Buchanan, D. & Boddy, D. (1992). *The expertise of the change agent*. London: Prentice Hall.

Bunderson, J. S. & Sutcliffe, K. M. (2002). Comparing alternative conceptualizations of functional diversity in management teams:

process and performance effects, *Academy of Management Journal*, vol. 45, pp. 875–893.

Burke, W. W. (1998). From the Editor, *Academy of Management Executive*, August, p. 184.

Burton, D. (2000). Ethnicity, identity and marketing: a critical review, *Journal of Marketing Management*, vol. 16, pp. 853–877.

Butler, J. (1997). *Excitable speech: a politics of the performativity*. New York: Routledge.

Butler, J. (1999). Performativity's Social Magic, in R. Schusterman (ed.), *Bourdieu: A Critical Reader*. Oxford: Blackwell, pp. 113–128.

Canen, A. G., & Canen, A. (1999). Logistic and cultural diversity: hand in hand for organizational success, *Cross Cultural Management*, vol. 6, pp. 3–10.

Cannella, A. P. (2008). Top management team functional background diversity and firm performance: examining the roles of team member colocation and enviromental uncertainty, *Academy of Management Journal, 51* (4), 768–784.

Cao, G., Clarke, S., & Lehaney, B. (2003). Diversity management in organizational change: towards a systematic framework, *Systems Research and Behavioral Science*, vol. 20, pp. 231–242.

Carpenter, M. (2002). The implications of strategy and social context for the relationship between top management team heterogeneity and firm performance, *Strategic Management Journal, 23*, 275–284.

Carr, C. (1993). Diversity and performance: a shotgun marriage? *Performance Improvement Quarterly, 6*, 115–126.

Carrell, M. (1995). Defining workforce diversity in publc sector organizations, *Public Personnel Management, 24* (1), 99–117.

Carrell, M. M. (2006). Defining worforce diversity programs and practices in organizations: A Longitudinal Study, *Labor Law Journal, 57* (1), 5–12.

Carroll, G. R., & Hannan, M. T. (2000). Why Corporate Demography Matters: Policy Implications of Organizational Diversity, *California Management Review*, vol. 42, pp. 148–163.

Carter, D., Simkins, B., and Simpson, W. (2003). Corporate governance, board diversity, and firm value. *The Financial Review* 38 (1), 33-53

Cartwright, S., & Gale, A. (1995). Project management: different gender, different culture? part 2, *Leadership & Organizational Development Journal*, vol. 16, pp. 12–16.

Cassell, C., & Biswas, R. (2000). Managing diversity in the new millennium, *Personnel Review*, vol. 29, pp. 268–273.

Caudron, S. (2000). Are diversity programs benefitting african-americans? *Black Enterprise, 27* (7), 12–18.

Cavanaugh, J. M. (1997) (In)corporating the other? managing the politics of workplace difference, in P. Prasad, A. J. Mills, M. Elmes, and A. Prasad (eds.), *Managing the Organizational Melting Pot: Dilemmas of Workforce Diversity*. Thousand Oaks, CA: Sage, pp. 31–53.

Certo, S. L. (2006). Top management teams, strategy and financial performance: a meta analytic examination, *Journal of Management Studies, 43* (4), 813–839.

Chaharbaghi, K., & Lynch, R. (1999). Sustainable competitive advantage: towards a dynamic resource-based strategy, *Management Decisions*, vol. 37, pp. 45–50.

Chakravarthy, B. S. (1990). management systems for innovation and productivity, *European Journal of Operational Research*, vol. 47, pp. 203–213.

Charmaz, C. (2000). Grounded theory: objectivist and constructivist methods, in Denzin, N. and Lincoln, Y. (eds.), *Handbook of Qualitative Research*, 2nd ed. London: Sage.

Chatman, J. A., & O'Reilly, C. A. (2004). Asymmetric reactions to work group sex diversity among men and women, *Academy of Management Journal*, vol. 47, pp. 193–208.

Chatman, J. A., Polzer, J. T., Barsade, S. G., & Neale, M. A. (1995). Being different yet feeling similar: the influence of demographic composition and organizational culture on work processes and outcomes, *Administrative Science Quarterly*, vol. 43, no. 4, pp. 749–780.

Cheng, C. (1997). A review essay on the books of bell hooks: organizational diversity lessons from a thoughtful race and gender heretic, *Academy of Management Review*, vol. 22, pp. 553–574.

Chevrier, S. (2003). Cross-cultural management in multinational project groups, *Journal of World Business*, vol. 38, pp. 141–149.

Clair, J. A., Beatty, J. E., & Maclean, T. L. (2005). Out of sight but not out of mind: managing invisible social identities in the workplace, *Academy of Management Review*, vol. 30, pp. 78–95.

Cockburn, C. (1989). Equal opportunities: the short and long agenda, *Industrial Relations Journal*, vol. 20, no. 4, pp. 213–225.

Cockburn, C. (1991). *In the Way of Women: Men's Resistance of Sex Equality in Organizations.* London: Macmillan.

Cohen, C. F., Baskin, O. W., & Harlow, D. N. (1982). the effects of manager's sex and attitudes toward women, *Academy of Management Proceedings*, August, pp. 395–3988.

Coll, R. K., & Eames, R. (2000). The role of the placement coordinator: an alternative model, *Asia-Pacific Journal of Cooperative Education*, vol. 1, no. 1, pp. 9–14.

Collins S.M. (1996). Black mobility in white corporations: Up the ladder but out on a limb. *Social Forces*, 44, 55-67.

Collinson, D. L., & Hearn, J. (eds.). (1996). *Men as Managers, Managers as Men: Critical Perspectives on Men, Masculinities and Managements.* London: Sage.

Collinson, D. L., Knights, D., & Collison, M. (1990). *Managing to Discriminate.* London and New York: Routledge.

Colson, H. (1990). Citation rankings of public administration journals, *Administration and Society, 21* (4), 452–471.

Commission Communication of 12 April 2005. *Integrated Guidelines for Growth and Jobs (2005–2008).* COM (2005), 141 (final).

Contu, A., & Willmott, H. (2003). Re-embedding situatedness: the importance of power relations in learning theory, *Organization Science*, vol. 14, no. 3, pp. 283–296.

Cope, P., Cuthbertson, P., & Stoddart, B. (2000). Situated learning in the practice placement, *Journal of Advanced Nursing*, vol. 31, no. 4, pp. 850–856.

Cordero, R., Ditomaso, N., & Farris, G. F. (1997). Gender ethnic composition of technical work groups: relationship to creative productivity and race/morale, *Journal of Engineering and Technology Management*, vol. 13, pp. 205–221.

Covin, J. (1989). Strategic management of small firms in hostile and benign environments, *Strategic Management Journal, 10* (1), 75–87.

Cox, T. H. (1991a). The multicultural organization, *Academy of Management Executive*, vol. 5, no. 2, pp. 34–47.

Cox, T. H. (1991b). Effects of ethnic and group cultural differences on cooperative and competitive behavior on a group task, *Academy of Management Journal, 34* (4), 827–847.

Cox, T. H. (1991c). The multicultural organization, *Academy of Management Executive*, 33–47.

Cox, T. H. (1993). *Cultural Diversity in Organizations: Theory, Research and Practice*. San Francisco: Berrett-Koehler.

Cox, T. H. (1994). A diversity framework, in S. O. Martin M. Cmerers, *Diversity in Organizations* (pp. 246–260). Thousand Oaks, CA: Sage Publications.

Cox, T. H., & Blake, B. (1991). Managing cultural diversity: implications for organizational competitiveness, *Academy of Management Executive*, vol. 5, no. 3, pp. 45–56.

Crebert, G., Bates, M., Bell, B., Patrick, C., & Cragnolini, V. (2004). Developing generic skills at university, during work placement and in employment: graduates' perceptions, *Higher Education Research and Development*, vol. 23, no. 2, pp. 147–165.

Crompton, R., & Mann, M. (1994). *Gender and Stratification*. Oxford: Polity Press.

Cui, G., & Choudhury, P. (2002). Marketplace Diversity and Cost-effective Marketing Strategies, *Journal of Consumer Marketing*, vol. 19, pp. 54–73.

Cummings, J. N. (2004). Work groups, structural diversity and knowledge sharing in a global organization, *Management Science*, vol. 50, pp. 352–364.

Cutcher-Gershenfeld, J., Nitta, M., Barrett, B., Belhedi, N., Bullard, J., Couthcie, C., Inaba, T., Ishino, I., Lee, S., Lin, W. J., Mothersell, W., Rabine, S., Ramanand, S., Strolle, M., and Wheaton, A. (1994). Japanese teamwork-based work systems in north America: explaining diversity, *California Management Review*, vol. 37, no. 1, pp. 842–864.

D'Netto, B., & Sohal, M. S. (1999). Human resources practices and workforce diversity: an empirical assessment, *International Journal of Manpower*, vol. 20, pp. 530–547.

Dadfar, H., & Gustavsson, P. (1992). Competition by effective management of cultural diversity, *International Studies of Management and Organization*, vol. 22, pp. 81–92.

Dale, A., & Bamford, C. (1988). Temporary workers: cause for concern or complacency? *Work, Employment and Society*, vol. 2, no. 2, pp. 191–209.

Daley, D. (1998). Gender differences and managerial competencies, *Review of Public Personnel Administration*, 18 (2), 41–56.

Dansky, K. H., Weech-Maldonado, R., De Souza, G., & Dreachslin, J. L. (2003). Organizational strategy and diversity management:

diversity-sensitive orientation as a moderating influence, *Health Care Management Review*, vol. 28, no. 3, pp. 243–253.

Darton, D., & Hurrell, K. (2005). *People Working Part-time Below Their Potential*. Manchester: Equal Opportunities Commission.

Dass, P., & Parker, B. (1999) Strategies for managing human diversity: from resistance to learning, *Academy of Management Executive*, vol. 13, pp. 68–80.

Dawson, P. (1994). *Organizational Change: A Procession Approach*. London: Paul Chapman Publishing.

Dawson, P. (2003). *Understanding Organizational Change: The Contemporary Experience of People at Work*. London: Sage.

Deshpande, R. (1999). What are the contributions of marketing to the organizational performance and the societal welfare, *Journal of Marketing Management*, vol. 63, pp. 164–167.

Desrochers, P. (2003). Local diversity, human creativity, and technological innovation, *Growth and Change*, vol. 32, pp. 369–394.

De Valk, S. (1993). Holding up a mirror to diversity issues, *Training & Development*, July, pp. 11–12.

Dickens, L. (1999). Beyond the business case: a three-pronged approach to equality Action, *Human Resource Management Journal*, vol. 9, no. 1, pp. 9–19.

Digh, P. (1997). Well-managed employee networks and business value, *HR Magazine*, 67–72.

Digh, P. (1999). Getting people in the pool: diversity recruitment that works, *HR Magazine, 44* (10), 94–99.

DiTomaso, N., Cordero, R., & Farris, G. F. (1996). Effects of Group Diversity on Perceptions of Group and Self Among Scientists and Engineers, in M. N. Ruderman, M. W. Hughes-James, and S. E. Jackson (eds.), *Selected research on work team diversity.* Washington, DC: APA and Center for Creative Leadership, pp. 99–119.

DiTomaso, N., Farris, G. F., & Cordero, R. (1993). Diversity in the technical workforce: rethinking the management of scientists and engineers, *Journal of Engineering and Technology Management,* vol. 10, pp. 101–127.

DiTomaso, N., & Hooijberg, R. (1996) Diversity and the demand of leadership, *Leadership Quarterly,* vol. 7, no. 2, pp. 163–187.

Dobbs, M. F. (1996). Managing diversity: lessons from the private sector, *Public Personnel Management,* vol. 25, no. 3, pp. 351–367.

Dodgson, M. (1993). Organizational learning: a review of some literatures, *Organization Studies,* vol. 14, no. 3, pp. 375–394.

Doherty, L. (2004). Work-Life Balance Initiatives: Implications for Women, *Employee Relations,* vol. 26, pp. 433–452.

Doktor, R., Tung, R. L., Fraser, S., & Von Glinow, M. A. (1991). future directions for management theory development, *Academy of Management Review,* vol. 16, pp. 362–365.

Doney, P. M., Cannon, J. P., & Muller, M. R. (1998). Understanding the influence of national culture on the development of trust, *Academy of Management Review,* vol. 23, pp. 601–620.

Drach-Zahavy, A., & Somech, A. (2002). Team heterogeneity and its relationship with team support and team effectiveness, *Journal of Educational Administration*, vol. 40, pp. 44–66.

Druker, J., & Stanworth, C. (2001). Partnerships and the private recruitment industry, *Human Resource Management Journal*, vol. 11, no. 2, pp. 73–89.

Duignan, J. (2002). Undergraduate work placement and academic performance: failing by doing, *HERDSA*, pp. 214–221.

Dunphy, D,. & Stace, D. (1993). The strategic management of corporate change, *Human Relations*, vol. 46, no. 8, pp. 905–918.

Durgee, J. F. (1988). On Cezanne, hot buttons, and interpreting consumer storytelling, *The Journal of Consumer Marketing*, vol. 5, no. 4, pp. 47–51.

Dutton, J. E., & Ashford, S. J. (1993). Selling issues to top management, *Academy of Management Review*, vol. 18, no. 3, pp. 397–428.

Dwyer, S., Richard, O. C., and Chadwick, K. (2003). Gender diversity in management and firm performance: the influence of growth orientation and organizational culture, *Journal of Business Research*, vol. 56, no. 12, pp. 1009–1019.

Dyer, J. H., & Nobeoka, K. (2000). Creating and managing a high-performance knowledge-sharing network: the Toyota case, *Strategic Management Journal*, vol. 21, pp. 345–367.

Echeverri-Carroll, E. L. (1999). Knowledge Flows in Innovation Networks: A comparative analysis of Japanese and U.S. high-technology firms, *Journal of Knowledge Management*, vol. 3, pp. 296–303.

Egan, M. L., & Bendick, Jr., M. (2003). Workforce diversity initiatives of u. s. multinational corporations in Europe, *Thunderbird International Business Review*, vol. 46, pp. 701–728.

Elmes, M., & Connelley, D. L. (1997). dreams of diversity and realities of intergroup relations in organizations, in P. Prasad, A. J. Mills, M. Elmes and A. Prasad (eds.), *Managing the Organizational Melting Pot: Dilemmas of Workplace Diversity*. Thousand Oaks, CA: Sage, pp. 148–167.

Elsass, P. M., & Graves, L. M. (1997). demographic diversity in decision-making groups: the experiences of women and people of color, *Academy of Management Review*, vol. 22, pp. 946–73.

Elsbach, K. D., Sutton, R. I., & Whetten, D. A. (1999). Perspectives on developing management theory, circa 1999: moving from shrill monologues to (relatively) lame dialogues, *Academy of Management Review*, vol. 24, pp. 627–633.

Ely, R. (1991). The effects of organizational demographics and social identity on relationships among professional women, *Administrative Science Quarterly*, vol. 39, pp. 203–238.

Ely, R. (1995). The power in demography: women's social constructions of gender identity at Work, *Academy of Management Journal*, vol. 38, pp. 589–631.

Eron Vann, M. (1995). Ways to assess diversity success, *HR Magazine*, *40* (8), 51–52.

Eisinger, P. K. (1982a). Black employment in municipal jobs: The impact of black political power. *American Political Science Review*, *76*, 380-392.

Eisinger, P. K. (1982b). The economic conditions of black employment in municipal bureaucracies. *American Journal of Political Science, 26,* 754-771.

Ettore, B., & Capowski, G. (1997). Value-added HR: people, performance and the bottom line, *HR Focus,* July, pp. 9–11.

Eveline, J., & Todd, P. (2002). Teaching managing diversity via feminist theory, *International Journal of Inclusive Education,* vol. 6, pp. 33–46.

Evenden, R. (1993). The strategic management of recruitment and selection, in R. Harrison (ed.), *Human Resource Management: Issues and Strategies.* Wokingham: Addison-Wesley Publishing Company, pp. 219–246.

Everett, J. (2002). Organizational research and the praxeology of Pierre Bourdieu, *Organizational Research Methods,* vol. 5, no. 1, pp. 56–80.

Fagenson, E. A., & Mason, G. (1993). Is what's good for the goose also good for the gander? on being white and men on a diverse workforce, *Academy of Management Executive,* vol. 7, pp. 80–1.

Faludi, S. (1991). *Backlash: The Undeclared War Against American Women.* New York: Crown.

Fernandez, J. P. (1999). *Managing a Diverse Work Force.* Lexington: Lexington Books.

Ferris, G. R., Arthur, M. M., Berkson, H. M., Kaplan, D. M., Harrell-Cook, G., & Frink, D. D. (1998). Toward a social context theory of human resources management-organizational effectiveness relationship, *Human Resource Management Review,* vol. 8, pp. 235–264.

Festinger, L. (1951). A theory of social comparison processes, *Human Relations,* vol. 7, pp.117–140.

Fine, M. G. (2003). Building successful multicultural organizations: challenges and opportunities, in R. J. Ely, E. G. Foldy, M. A. Scully and the Centre for Gender in Organizations Simmons School of Management (eds.), *Reader in Gender, Work and Organization.* Oxford: Blackwell, pp. 308–317.

Fink, J. S., Pastore, D. L., & Riemer, H. A. (2001). Do differences make a difference? managing diversity in division in-a intercollegiate athletics, *Journal of Sport Management,* vol. 15, pp. 10–50.

Finn, C., & Chattopadhyay, P. (2000). Managing emotions in diverse work teams: an effective events perspective, *Academy of Management Proceedings,* MOC: D1–D6.

Fish, A. (1999). Cultural diversity: challenges facing the management of cross-border business careers, *Career Development International,* vol. 4, pp. 96–205.

Flood, R. L., & Romm, R. A. N. (1996). Contours diversity management and triple loop learning, *Kybernetes,* vol. 25, pp. 154–164.

Forbes, L. H. (2002). Improving quality through diversity—more critical now more than ever before, *Leadership and Management in Engineering,* October, pp. 49–52.

Ford, L. (2000). Diversity: from cartoons to confrontations, *Training & Development,* Media Reviews, August 2000.

Forsyth, D. R. (1990). *Group Dynamics.* Brooks/Cole Publishing, Pacific Grove, CA.

Foster, C., & Harris, L. (2005). Easy to say, difficult to do: diversity management in retail, *Human Resource Management Journal*, vol. 15, pp. 4–17.

Fox, T. L., & Spence, J. W. (1999). An examination of the decision styles of project managers: evidence of significant diversity, *Information & Management*, vol. 36, pp. 313–320.

Frasse-Blunt, M. (2003). Thwarting the diversity backlash: develop an inclusive plan that highlights the bottom-line effect and benefits to all employees, *HR Magazine, 48* (6), 37–42.

Freeman-Evans, T. (1994). Benefiting from multiculturalism, *Association Management*, February, 52–56.

Gammie, E., Gammie, B., & Duncan F. (2002). Operating a distance learning module within an undergraduate work placement: some reflections, *Education and Training*, vol. 44, no. 1, pp. 11–22.

Gardenswartz, I. (1993). *Managing Diversity:A Complete Desk Reference and Planning Guide.* New York: Irwin.

Garrick, J., & Clegg, S. (2001). Stressed-out knowledge workers in performative times: a postmodern take on project-based learning, *Management Learning*, vol. 32, no. 1, pp. 119–134.

Gatley, S. & Lessem, R. (1995). Enhancing the competitive advantage of transcultural businesses, *Journal of European Industrial Training*, vol. 19, pp. 3–11.

Geppert, M., Matten, D., and Williams, K. (2003). Change management in multinational corporations: How global convergence intertwines with national diversities, *Human Relations*, vol. 56,pp. 807–39.

Gershon, N., & Page, W. (2002). What storytelling can do for information visualization, *Communications of the ACM*, vol. 44, no. 8, pp. 31–37.

Giddens, A. (1984). *The Constitution of Society: Outline of the Theory of Structuration*. Cambridge: Polity Press.

Gilbert, J. A., & Ivancevich, J. M. (2000). Valuing Diversity: A Tale of Two Organizations, *Academy of Management Executive*, vol. 14, no. 1, pp. 93–105.

Gilbert, J. A., & Stead, B. A. (1999). Stigmatization revisited: does diversity management make a difference in applicant success, *Group and Organization Management*, vol. 24, pp. 239–256.

Gilbert, J. A., Stead, B. A., & Ivancevich, J. M. (1999). diversity management: a new organizational paradigm, *Journal of Business Ethics*, vol. 21, pp. 61–76.

Glassner, A. (1999). Active Storytelling, *Eurographics*, vol. 18, no. 3, pp. 1–4.

Glover, J., Rainwater, K., Jones, G., & Friedman, H. (2002). Adaptive Leadership (part two): Four Principles for Being Adaptive, *Organization Development Journal*, vol. 20, pp. 18–38.

Golembiewski, R. T. (1995). *Managing Diversity in Organizations*, Tuscaloosa, London: University of Alabama Press.

Goll, I., & Rasheed, A. A. (2005). The relationship between two top management demographic characteristics, rational decision making, environmental munificence, and firm performance, *Organization Studies*, vol. 26, no. 7, pp. 999–1023.

Gomez-Mejia, L. and Palich, L. (1999). A theory of global strategy and firm efficiencies: Considering the effects of cultural diversity. *Journal of Management*. Vol. 25 (4), 587-606.

Goode, S. J., & Baldwin, J. N. (2005). Predictors of african-american representation in municipal government, *Review of Public Personnel Administration*, vol. 25, no. 1, pp. 29–55.

Goodman, P. S., Lawrence, B. S., Ancona, D. G., & Tushman, M. L. (2001). Introduction, *Academy of Management Review*, vol. 26, pp. 507–11.

Gooley, T. B. (2000). A world of difference: special report, *Logistics*, June, pp. 51–54.

Gottfried, H. (1992). In the margins: flexibility as a mode of regulation in the temporary help industry, *Work, Employment and Society*, vol. 6, no. 3, pp. 443–460.

Govindarajan, V., & Gupta, A. K. (2001). Building an effective global business team, *MIT Sloan Management Review*, vol. 42, pp. 63–72.

Granovetter, M. (1985). Economic action and social structure: the problem of embeddedness, *American Journal of Sociology*, vol. 91, no. 3, pp. 481–510.

Greene, A. (2002). Variety may not always be the spice of life, *People Management*, May, p. 50.

Griggs, L. B., & Louw, L. (eds.). (1995). *Valuing Diversity: New Tools for a New Reality*. New York: McGraw-Hill.

Grisham, T. (2006). Metaphor, poetry, storytelling and cross-cultural leadership, *Management Decision*, vol. 44, no. 4, pp. 486–503.

Groschi, S., & Doherty, L. (1999). Diversity management in practice, *International Journal of Contemporary Hospitality Management*, vol. 11, pp. 262–268.

Gunn, B., & Gullickson, R. (2003). Performativity, *Strategic Finance*, vol. 85, no. 6, pp. 9–10.

Hall, L., Harris, J., Bakewell, C., & Graham, P. (2000). Supporting placement-based learning using networked technologies, *The International Journal of Educational Management*, vol. 14, no. 4, pp. 175–179.

Hambrick, D. C., Cho, T., & Chen, M. (1996). The influence of top management team heterogeneity on firms' competitive moves, *Administrative Science Quarterly*, vol. 41, pp. 659–684.

Hamilton, R. D., & Zimmerman, M. A. (1995). Lessons learned: getting your board to initiate change, *Academy of Management Executive*, vol. 9, pp. 67–68.

Hannabus, S. (2000). Narrative knowledge: eliciting organizational knowledge from storytelling, *Aslib Proceedings*, vol. 52, no. 10, pp. 402–413.

Hansen, F. (2003). Diversity's business case doesn't add up. *Workforce*, pp. 28-32.

Hardy, C., Palmer, I., & Phillips, N. (2000). Discourse as a strategic resource, *Human Relations*, vol. 53, no. 9, pp. 1227–1248.

Harris, E. W., & Tanner, J. R. (1996). Employment of recent university graduates: do age, gender and non-white status make a difference? *Journal of Employment Counseling*, vol. 33, pp. 121–129.

Harrison, D. A., Price, K. H., & Bell, M. P. (1998). Beyond relational demography: time and the effects of the surface- and deep-level diversity on work group cohesion, *Academy of Management Journal*, vol. 41, pp. 96–107.

Harrison, D. A., Price, K. H., & Gavin, J. H. (2000). Time, teams and task performance: a longitudinal study of changing effects of diversity on group functioning, *Academy of Management Proceedings*, GDO: C1–C6.

Harrison, D. A., Price, K. H., & Gavin, J. H. (2002). Time, teams and task performance: changing effects of the surface- and deep-level diversity on group functioning, *Academy of Management Journal*, vol. 45, pp. 1029–1045.

Harung, H. S., & Harung, L. M. (1995). Enhancing the organizational performance by strengthening diversity and unity, *The Learning Organization*, vol. 2, pp. 9–21.

Harvey, M. G., & Buckley, M. R. (1997). Managing inpatriates: building a global core competency, *Journal of World Business*, vol. 32, no. 1, pp. 35–53.

Harzing, A.W., (2009). *Journal Quality List*, 34th Edition, University of Melbourne, Parkville, Australia.

Hayghe, V. H., & Bianchi, S. (1994). Married mothers' work patterns: the job-family compromise, *Monthly Labor Review*, June: pp. 24–30.

Hays-Thomas, R. (2003). Why Now? The contemporary focus on managing diversity, in M. S. Stockdale and F. J. Crosby (eds.), *The Psychology and Management of Workplace Diversity*. Malden: Blackwell, pp. 1–30.

Heilman, M. K. (1993). When similarity is a liability: effects of sex-based preferential selection on reactions to like-sex and different-sex others, *Journal of Applied Psychology, 78*, 912–927.

Henley, A. B., & Price, K. H. (2002). Want a better team? foster a climate of fairness: research briefs, *Academy of Management Executive*, August, pp. 153–154.

Heugens, P. P. (2002). Managing public affairs through storytelling, *Journal of Public Affairs*, vol. 2, no. 2, pp. 57–70.

Hill, W. H., & Fox, W. M. (1973). Black and white marine squad leaders' perceptions of racially mixed squads, *Academy of Management Journal*, vol. 16, pp. 680–686.

Hofmann D.A., Gavin M.B. (1985). Centering decisions in hierarchical linear models: Implications for research in organizations. Journal of Management, 5, 623-641 .

Hoffman, L. R. (1978). Group problem solving, in L. Berkowitz (ed.), *Group Processes*. New York: Academic Press.

Holladay, C. (2003). The influence of framing on attitudes toward diversity training, *Human Resource Development Quarterly, 14* (3), 245–263.

Hon, N. C., & Brunner, B. (2000). Diversity issues and public relations, *Journal of Public Relations Research*, vol. 12, no. 4, pp. 309–340.

Hopkins, W. E., & Hopkins, S. A. (2002). Effects of cultural recomposition on group interaction processes, *Academy of Management Review*, vol. 27, pp. 541–53.

Hordes, M. W., Clancy, J. A., & Baddaley, J. (1995). A Primer for global start-ups, *Academy of Management Executive*, vol. 9, no. 2, pp. 7–11.

Horwitz, S.K. & Horwitz, I.B,. (2005). the effects of team diversity on team outcomes: a meta-analytic review of team demography, *Journal of Management*, Vol. 33, No.6, pp. 987-1015.

Howard-Grenville, J. A., & Hoffman, A. J. (2003). The importance of cultural framing to the success of social initiatives in business, *Academy of Management Executive*, vol. 17, pp. 70–84.

Howarth, C. (1999). *Monitoring Poverty and Social Exclusion*. York, PA: Joseph Rowntree Foundation.

Huckle, P. (1984). A decade's difference: Mid-level managers and affirmative action. Public *Personnel Management Journal*, 249-257.

Humphries, M., & Grice, S. (1995). Equal employment opportunity and the management of diversity, *Journal of Organizational Change*, vol. 8, pp. 17–32.

Huntington, S., Stephen, J., & Oldfield, B. M. (1999). Formal assessment of student placement within a retail sandwich degree, *Industrial and Commercial Training*, vol. 31, no. 3, pp. 10–11.

Huy, Q. N. (2001). Time, temporal capability and planned change, *Academy of Management Review*, vol. 26, no. 4, pp. 601–623.

Ibarra, H. (1995). Race, opportunity and diversity of social circles in managerial networks, *Academy of Management Journal*, vol. 38, pp. 673–703.

Iles, P. (1995). Learning to Work With Differences, *Personnel Review*, vol. 24, pp. 44–60.

Iles, P., & Hayers, P. K. (1997). Managing diversity in transnational project teams: a tentative model and case study, *Journal of Managerial Psychology*, vol. 12, pp. 95–117.

Itzin, C. (1995). Crafting strategy to create women-friendly work, in C. Itzin and J. Newman (eds.), *Gender Culture and Organizational Change: Putting Theory Into Practice*. London and New York: Routledge, pp. 127–151.

Ivancevich, J. M., & Gilbert, J. A. (2000). Diversity management: time for a new approach, *Public Personnel Management*, vol. 29, pp. 75–92.

Ivancevich, J., & Gilbert, J. A. (2001). Diversity management: time for a new approach, *Public Personnel Management, 29*, 75–92.

Iverson, K. (2000). Managing for effective workforce diversity, *Cornell Hotel and Management Administration Quarterly*, April, pp. 31–38.

Jackson, S. E., & Joshi, A. (2004). Diversity in social context: A multi-attribute, multilevel analysis of team diversity and sales performance. *Journal of Organizational Behavior, 25*, 675–702.

Jackson, S. E., Joshi, A., & Erhardt, N. L. (2003). Recent research on team and organizational diversity: SWOT analysis and implications. *Journal of Management, 29*, 801–830.

James, E. H., & Wooten, L. P. (2001). Managing diversity, *Executive Excellence*, August, pp. 17–18.

James, K., Lovato, C., & Khoo, G. (1991). Social identity correlates of non-white workers' Health, *Academy of Management Journal*, vol. 37, p. 383–393.

Jayne, M.E. A. & Dipboye, R.L., (2004). Leveraging diversity to improve business performance: research findings and recommendations for organizations, *Human Resource Management*, Vol. 43, No.4, pp. 409-424,2004.

Jehn, K. A., Northcraft, G. B., & Neale, M. A. (1999). Why differences make a difference: a field study of diversity, conflict and performance in work groups, *Administrative Science Quarterly*, vol. 44, no. 4, pp. 741–763.

Jenkins, R. (1992). *Pierre Bourdieu*. New York: Routledge.

Jenner, L. (1994). Diversity management: what does it mean? *HR Focus*, vol. 71, pp. 11–15.

Jewson, N., & Mason, D. (1986). The theory and practice of equal opportunity policies: liberal and radical approaches, *Sociological Review*, vol. 34, no. 2, pp. 307–329.

Johnson, B. M. (1995). Comparison of three major meta-analytic approaches, *Journal of Applied Psychology, 80* (1), 94–116.

Johnston, W. B., & Packer, A. H. (1997). *Workforce 2000: Work and Workers for the 21st Century*. Washington, DC: Hudson Institute.

Jones, R. T., Jerich, B., Copeland, L., & Boyle, M. (1989). Four by four: how do you manage a diverse workforce, *Training and Development Journal*, vol. 43, no. 2, pp. 13–21.

Joplin, J. R. W., & Daus, C. S. (1997). Challenges of leading a diverse workforce, *Academy of Management Executive*, vol. 11, pp. 32–47.

Joshi, A. Hui, L. & Jackson, S.E., (2006) Cross-level effects of workplace diversity on sales performance and pay, *Academy o/Management Journal*, Vol. 49, No.3, pp. 459-481.

Joshi, A. & Roh, H., (2009) The role of context in work team diversity research: a meta-analytic review, *Academy of Management Journal*, Vol. 52, No.3, pp. 599-627.

Kahan, S. (2006). The power of storytelling to jumpstart collaboration, *The Journal for Quality and Participation*, Spring: 23–25.

Kanter, R. M. (1977). Some effects of proportions on group life: skewed sex ratios and reactions to token women, *American Journal of Sociology*, vol. 82, pp. 965–990.

Kanter, R. M. (1983). *Men and Women of the Corporation*. Basic Books, New York, NY.

Kanter, R. M. (1984). *The Change Masters*. London: Allen & Unwin.

Kanter, R. M. (1999). *Leading Change*. London: Simon & Schuster.

Kaplan, R., & Norton, D. (1996). *The Balanced Scorecard: Translating Strategy Into Action*. Boston: Harvard Business School Press.

Kaplan, S., & Norton, D. P. (2001). Transforming the balanced scorecard from performance measurement to strategic management: Part I, *Accounting Horizons*, vol. 15, pp. 87–104.

Katz, D., & Kahn, R. L. (1978). *The Social Psychology of Organizations*, 2nd ed. New York: Wiley.

Keller, R. T. (2001). Cross-functional project groups in research and new product development: diversity, communications, job stress and outcomes, *Academy of Management Journal*, vol. 44, pp. 547–555.

Kellough, J. E., & Naff, K. (2004). Responding to a wake-up call: an examination of federal agency diversity management programs, *Administration & Society*, 36 (1), 62–90.

Kersten, A. (2000). Diversity management, dialogue, dialects and diversion, *Journal of Organizational Change Management*, vol. 13, pp. 235–248.

Kidder, D. L., Lankau M. J., Chrobot-Mason, D., Mollica, K. A., & Friedman, R. A. (2004). Backlash toward diversity initiatives: examining the impact of diversity program justification, personal and group outcomes, *International Journal of Conflict Management*, vol. 15, pp. 77–102.

Kirby, S. L. (1996). An Investigation of Workforce diversity programmes: a multiple perspective approach, *Equal Opportunities International*, 15 (6/7), 17–26.

Kirby, S. L., & Richard, O. C. (2000). Impact of marketing workplace diversity on employee job involvement and organizational commitment, *The Journal of Social Psychology*, vol. 140, no. 3, pp. 367–377.

Kirchmeyer, C., & McLellan, J. (1991). Capitalizing on ethnic diversity: an approach to managing the diversity work groups in the 1990s, *RCSA/Canadian Journal of Administrative Sciences*, vol. 8, no. 2, pp. 72–79.

Kirkpatrick, S. A., & Locke, E. A. (1991). Leadership: do traits matter? *Academy of Management Executive*, vol. 5, no. 2, pp. 48–60.

Kirton, G., & Greene, A. (2000). *The Dynamics of Managing Diversity: A Critical Approach*. Oxford: Butterworth-Heinemann.

Kirton, G., Greene, A. M., & Dean, D. (2007). British diversity professionals as change agents—radicals, tempered radicals or liberal reformers? *International Journal of Human Resource Management*, vol. 18, pp. 1979–94.

Kluge, H. (1997). Reflections on Diversity, *Vital Speeches of the Day*, vol. 63, pp. 171–176.

Knouse, S. B., & Dansby, M. R. (2000). Recent diversity research at the defense equal opportunity management institute (DEOMI): 1991–1996, *International Journal of Intercultural Relations*, vol. 24, pp. 203–225.

Kochan, T., Bezrukova, K. Ely, R. Jackson, S., Joshi, A., Jehn, K. et. al. (2003). The effects of diversity on business performance. Report of the diversity research network. *Human Resource Management*, 42, 3-21.

Kodama, M. (2003). Strategic innovation in traditional big business: case study of two Japanese companies, *Organization Studies*, vol. 24, no. 2, pp. 235–268.

Kossek, E. E., & Lobel, S. A. (1996). Introduction: transforming human resource systems to manage diversity, in *Managing Diversity: Human Resource Strategies for Transforming the Workplace*, Blackwell, Oxford, pp. 1–19.

Kossek, E. E., & Lobel, S. A. (eds.). (1996). *Managing Diversity: Human Resources Strategies for Transforming the Workplace*. Cambridge: Blackwell.

Kossek, E. E., & Zonia, S. C. (1993). Assessing diversity climate: a field study of reactions to employer effort to promote diversity, *Journal of Organizational Behavior*, vol. 14, pp. 61–81.

Kravitz, D. A., & Klineberg, S. L. (2002). Affirmative action attitudes: effects on respondent ethnicity, AAP strength, and anticipated impacts, *Academy of Management Proceedings*, GDO: C1–C6.

Kumar, R., & Andersen, P. H. (2000). Inter-firm diversity and the management of meaning in international strategic alliances, *International Business Review*, vol. 9, pp. 237–252.

Kurowski, L. L. (2002). cloaked culture and veiled diversity: why theorists ignored early u. s. workforce diversity, *Journal of Academic History*, vol. 40, pp. 183–191.

Kusku, F., Özbilgin, M. F., & Özkale, L. (2007). Against the tide: gendered prejudice and disadvantage, in engineering study from a comparative perspective, *Gender, Work and Organization*, vol. 14, no. 2, pp. 109–129.

Lampel, J. (2001). The core competencies of project execution: the challenge of diversity, *International Journal of Project Management*, vol. 19, pp. 471–483.

Lang, J. C. (2000). Managing in knowledge-based competition, *Journal of Organizational Change Management*, vol. 14, no. 6, pp. 539–553.

Larkey, L. K. (1996). Toward a theory of communicative interactions in culturally diverse workgroups, *Academy of Management Review*, vol. 21, pp. 463–491.

Lau, D. C. & Murnighan, J. K. (1998). Demographic diversity and fault lines: the compositional dynamics of organizational groups, *Academy of Management Review*, vol. 23, pp. 325–340.

Lau, D.C. and Murnighan, K., (2005). Interactions within groups and subgroups: the effects of demographic faultlines, *Academy of Management Journal*, Vol. 48, No.4, pp. 645-659.

Lawrence, E. (2000). Equal opportunities officers and managing equality changes, *Personnel Review*, vol. 29, no. 3, pp. 381–401.

Layder, D. (1993). *New Strategies in Social Research*. Cambridge: Polity Press.

Ledwith, S., & Colgan, F. (eds.). (1996a). *Women and Organizations: Challenging Gender Politics*. London: Macmillan.

Ledwith, S., & Colgan, F. (1996b). Women as organizational change agents, in S. Ledwith and F. Colgan (eds.), *Women and Organizations: Challenging Gender Politics*. London: Macmillan, pp. 1–43.

Lee, H. (2001). Paternalistic human resources practices: their emergence and characteristics, *Journal of Economic Issues*, vol. 35, pp. 841–869.

Leonard, B. (2002). Ways to tell if a diversity program is measuring up, *HR Magazine*, July, p. 21-25.

Lerner, G. H. (1992). Assisted Storytelling: Deploying Shared Knowledge as a Practical Matter, *Qualitative Sociology*, vol. 15, no. 3, pp. 247–271.

Leslie, D. (1994). TQM and student work experience (SWE), *Quality Assurance in Education*, vol. 2, no. 3, pp. 26–32.

Levy, B. (2002). The competitiveness of multinational corporations in a globalized and regionalized economy: the war for talent and the role of women executives, *Management International*, vol. 7, pp. 103–111.

Lewan, L. (1990). Diversity in the Workplace, *Human Resource Magazine, 3*, 42–45.

Lewin, K. (1951). *Field Theory in Social Science*. New York: Harper & Row.

Lewis, G. B., & Nice, D. (1994). Race, sex, and occupational segregation in state and local government. *American Review of Public Administration, 24*(4), 393-413.

Liff, S. (1996). Two routes to managing diversity: individual differences or social group characteristics, *Employee Relations*, vol. 19, no. 1, pp. 11–26.

Lim, G. S. (2003). Compositional dynamics and interviewer judgments in the panel employment interview, *Academy of Management Best Conference Paper*, OB: N1–N6.

Lindell, M. K., & Brandt, C. J. (2000). Climate quality and climate consensus as mediators of the relationship between organizational antecedents and outcomes, *Journal of Applied Psychology*, vol. 85, pp. 331–348.

Lindsay, C. (1993). Paradoxes of organizational diversity: living within the paradoxes, *Academy of Management Proceedings*, pp. 374–379.

Linnehan, F., Chrobot-Mason, D., & Conrad, A. M. (2002). The importance of ethnic identity to attitudes, norms, and behavioral intentions, toward diversity, *Academy of Management Proceedings*, GDO: D1–D6.

Llewellyn, N. (2001). The role of storytelling and narrative in a modernization initiative, *Local Government Studies*, vol. 27, no. 4, pp. 35–58.

Locke, D. C. (1992). *Increasing Multicultural Understanding*. Newbury Park, CA: Sage.

Lorbiecki, A. (2001). Changing views on diversity management: the rise of learning perspective and the need to recognize social and political contradictions, *Management Learning*, vol. 32, no. 3, pp. 345–361.

Lorde, A. (2003). The transformation of silence into language and action, in R. J. Ely, E. G. Foldy, M. A. Scully, and the Centre for Gender in Organizations, Simmons School of Management (eds.), *Reader in Gender, Work and Organization*. Oxford: Blackwell, pp. 273–276.

Loudin, A. (2000). A diversity management program should be part of every company's basic training, *warehousing management*, April, pp. 31–3.

Lunt, P. (1994). Should you do diversity training? *ABA Banking Journal*, August, pp. 53–54.

Mahar, C., Harker, R., & Wilkes, C. (1990). The basic theoretical position, in R. Harker, C. Wilkes, and C. Mahar (eds.), *An Introduction to the Work of Pierre Bourdieu: The Practice of Theory*. London: Macmillan, pp. 1–25.

Mannix, E. (2003). Editor's comments: conflict and conflict resolution—a return to theorizing, *Academy of Management Review*, vol. 28, pp. 543–546.

Marable, M. (2000). We need a new and critical study of race and ethnicity, *The Chronicle of Higher Education*, vol. 25, pp. B4–7.

Mason, R. M. (2003). Culture-free or culture-bound? a boundary-spanning perspective on learning knowledge management systems, *journal of Global Information Management*, vol. 11, no. 4, pp. 20–36.

Mathiasen, D. G. (1999). The new public management and its critics, *International Public Management Journal*, vol. 2, no. 1, pp. 90–111.

Mayrhofer, W. (1997). Warning: flexibility can damage your organizational health, *Employee Relations*, vol. 19, pp. 519–534.

McClain, P. D. (1993). Changing dynamics of urban politics: Black and Hispanic municipal employment-is there competition? *The Journal of Politics, 55*(2), 399-414.

McDougall, M. (1996). Equal opportunities versus managing diversity: another challenge for public sector management? *International Journal of Public Sector Management*, vol. 9, no. 5/6, pp. 62–72.

McEnrue, M. P. (1993). Managing diversity: los Angeles before and after the riots, *Organizational Dynamics*, vol. 21, no. 3, pp. 18–29.

McFadzean, E. (2000). What can we learn from creative people? the story of brain Eno, *Management Decision*, vol. 38, pp. 51–56.

McGrath, J. E., Berdahl, L., & Arrow, H. (1995). traits, expectations, culture, and clout: the dynamics of diversity in work groups, in Jackson, S. E., and Ruderman, M. N. (eds.), *Diversity in Work Teams: Research Paradigms for a Changing Workplace*. American Psychological Association, Washington, DC.

McKay, P. F., & Avery, D. R. (2005). What has race got to do with it? Unraveling the role of racio-ethnicity in job seekers reactions to site visits. Personnel Psychology, 59, 395–429.

McKay, P. F., Avery, D. R., Tonidandel, S., Morris, M. A., Hernandez, M., & Hebl, M. R. (2007). Racial differences employee retention: Are diversity climate perceptions the key? *Personnel Psychology*, 60, 35–62.

McLellan, H. (2006). Corporate storytelling perspectives, *The Journal for Quality and Participation*, Spring, pp. 17–20.

McMahan, G. C., Bell, M. P. & Virick, M. (1998). Strategic human resource management: employee involvement, diversity and international issues, *Human Resource Management Review*, vol. 8, pp. 193–214.

McMahon, A. (2010). Does workplace diversity matter? a survey of empirical studies on diversity and firm performance 2000–2009, *Journal of Diversity Management*, 5 (2), 37–48.

McMahon, U., & Quinn, U. (1995). Maximizing the hospitality management student work placement experience: a case study, *Education and Training*, vol. 37, no. 4, pp. 13–17.

McNerney, D. (1994). Competitive advantage: diverse customers and stakeholders, *HR Focus*, June, pp. 9–10.

McWilliams, A., Siegel, D. & Van Fleet, D.D. (2005). Scholarly journals as producers of knowledge: theory and empirical evidence based on data envelopment analysis, Organizational *Research Methods*, Vol. 8, No.2, pp. 185-201.

Meier, K. J., & Smith, K. B. (1994). Representative democracy and representative bureaucracy: Examining the top-down and bottom-up linkages. *Social Science Quarterly, 75(4)*, 790-803.

Metzler, C. (2003). Ten reasons why diversity initiatives fail, *the Diversity Factor, 11* (2), 1–20.

Meyer, S. (1981). *The Five Dollar Day: Labor Management and Social Control in the Ford Motor Company, 1908–1921.* Albany: State University of New York Press.

Meyerson, D. E. (2001a). *Tempered Radicals: How People Use Difference to Inspire Change at Work.* Boston, MA: Harvard Business School Press.

Meyerson, D. E. (2001b). Radical change, the quiet way, *Harvard Business Review*, October, pp. 92–100.

Meyerson, D. E.,& Fletcher, J. K. (2003). A modest manifesto for shattering the glass ceiling, in R. J. Ely, E. G. Foldy, M. A. Scully, and the Centre for Gender in Organizations Simmons School of Management (eds.), *Reader in Gender, Work and Organization.* Oxford: Blackwell, pp. 230–241.

Meyerson, D. E., & Scully, M. A. (1995). Tempered radicalism and the politics of ambivalence and change, *Organization Science*, vol. 6, no. 5, pp. 585–600.

Michielsens, E., Shackleton, L., & Urwin, P. (2000). PPPs and the jobless: can private employment agencies help deliver the new deals? *New Economy*, vol. 7, pp. 168–171.

Mighty, E. J. (1991). Valuing workforce diversity: a model of organizational change, *Canadian Journal of Administrative Sciences*, vol. 8, no. 2, pp. 64–71.

Miller, L., & Neathey, F. (2004). *Advancing Women in the Workplace: Case Studies*. Equal Opportunities Commission Working Paper Series no. 13, Manchester: EOC.

Milliken, F. J., & Martins, L. L. (1996). Searching for common threads: understanding the multiple effects of diversity in organizational groups, *Academy of Management Review*, vol. 21, pp. 402–433.

Millward, N., Bryson, A., and Forth, J. (2000). *All Change at Work?* London: Routledge.

Milton, L. P., & Westphal, J. D. (2005). Identity confirmation networks and cooperation in work groups, *Academy of Management Journal*, vol. 48, pp. 191–212.

Mitchell, S. A. (2000). *Relationality: From Attachment to Intersubjectivity*. Hillsdale, NJ: The Analytic Press.

Mohammed, S., & Ringseis, E. (2001). cognitive diversity and consensus in group decision making: the role of inputs, processes and outcomes, *Organizational Behavior and Human Decision Processes*, vol. 85, pp. 310–335.

Moore, S. (1999). Understanding and managing diversity among groups at work: key issues for organizational training and development, *Journal of European Industrial Training*, vol. 23, pp. 208–217.

Mor Barak, M. E. (2000). The inclusive workplace: an ecosystems approach to diversity management, *Social Work*, vol. 45, pp. 339–3252.

Morgan, A., & Turner, D. (2000). Adding value to the work placement: working towards a professional qualification in an undergraduate degree program, *Education and Training*, vol. 42, no. 8, pp. 453–60.

Morgan, S., & Dennehy, R. F. (1997). The power of organizational storytelling: a management development perspective, *Journal of Management Development*, vol. 16, no. 7, pp. 494–501.

Morrell, J., Boyland, M., Munns, G., & Astbury, L. (2001). *Gender Equality in Pay Practices*. EOC Research Discussion Series, Equal Opportunities Commission.

Morris, L. (1995). Research Capsules: Why Don't We Change? *Training and Development*, October, pp. 59–61.

Morrison, A. M. (1992). *The New Leader: Guidelines on Leadership Diversity in America*. San Francisco, CA: Jossey-Bass.

Muir, C. (1996). Workplace Readiness for Communicating Diversity, *The Journal of Business Communication*, vol. 33, no. 4, pp. 475–486.

Mulholland G. Özbilgin, M., & Worman, D. (2005). Managing diversity: linking theory and practice to business performance. London: CIPD Publications.

Munduate, L., & Gravenhorst, K. M. B. (2003). Power dynamics and organizational change: an introduction, *Applied Psychology: An International Review*, vol. 52, no. 1, pp. 1–13.

Nadler, D. A., & Tushman, M. L. (1990). Beyond the charismatic leader: leadership and organizational change, *California Management Review*, Winter: pp. 77–97.

Nash, R. (2003). Social explanation and socialization: on Bourdieu and the structure, disposition, practice scheme, *The Sociological Review*, vol. 51, pp. 43–62.

Naylor, D. M. (2000). Should western managers be encouraged to adopt JMPS? *Employee Relations*, vol. 22, no. 2, pp. 160–178.

Neathey, F., Dench, S., & Thomson, L. (2003). *Monitoring Progress Towards Pay Equality*. EOC Research Discussion Series, Equal Opportunities Commission.

Neathey, F., Willison, R., Akroyd, K., Regan, J., & Hill, D. (2005). *Equal Pay Reviews in Practice*. EOC Working Paper Series no. 33, Equal Opportunities Commission.

Neck, C. P., Smith, W. J. & Godwin, J. L. (1997). thought self-leadership: a self-regulatory approach to diversity management, *Journal of Managerial Psychology*, vol. 12, pp. 190–203.

Neill, A. N., Mulholland, G. A., Ross, A. V,. & Leckey, A. J. (2004). The influence of part-time work on student placement, *Journal of Further and Higher Education*, vol. 28, no. 2, pp. 123–137.

Neill, N. T., & Mulholland, G. E. (2003). Student placement: structure, skills and support, *Education and Training*, vol. 45, no. 2, pp. 89–99.

Nemeth, C. J. (1986). Differential contributions of majority and non-white influence, *Psychological Review*, vol. 93, pp. 23–32.

Nemetz, P. L., & Christensen, S. L. (1996). The challenge of cultural diversity: harnessing a diversity of views to understand multiculturalism, *Academy Management Review*, vol. 21, pp. 434–462.

Newman, J. (1995). Making connections: frameworks for change, in C. Itzin and J. Newman (eds.), *Gender Culture and Organizational Change: Putting Theory Into Practice*. London and New York: Routledge, pp. 273–286.

Nishii, L. & Özbilgin, M. F. (2007). Global diversity management: towards a conceptual framework, *International Journal of Human Resource Management*, vol. 18, no. 11, pp. 1883–1894.

O'Brien, M., & Shemilt, I. (2003). *Working fathers: earning and caring*. Equal Opportunities Commission Research Discussion Series. Manchester: EOC.

O'Hara, S. U. (1995). Valuing socio-diversity, *International Journal of Social Economics*, vol. 22, pp. 31–49.

O'Mara, J.& Richter, A, (2011). Global diversity inclusion benchmarks: standards for organizations around The World, pp. 1–32.

O'Reilly, C. A., Caldwell, D. F., & Barnett, W. P. (1989). work group demography, social integration, and turnover, *Administrative Science Quarterly*, vol. 34, pp. 21–28.

Orlitzky, M. F., & Benjamin, J. D. (2003). The effects of sex composition on small-group performance in business school case competition, *Academy of Management Learning and Education*, vol. 2, pp. 128–138.

Parker, C. (1999). How to win hearts and minds: corporate compliance policies for sexual harassment, *Law and Policy*, vol. 21, no. 1, pp. 21–48.

Parkin, M. (2004). *Tales for Change: Using Storytelling to Develop People and Organizations*. London: Kogan Page.

Payne, R. L., & Pugh, D. S. (1976). Organizational structure and climate, in Dunnette, MD. (ed.), *Handbook of Industrial and Organizational Psychology*. Rand McNally, Chicago, IL, pp.1125–1173.

Pedler, P., Burgoyne, J., & Boydell, T. (1991). *The learning company: a strategy for sustainable development*. London: McGraw-Hill.

Pelled, L. H., & Xin, K. R. (2000). Relational demography and relationship quality between two cultures, *Organization Studies*, vol. 21, pp. 1077–1094.

Peng, M. W., & Heath, P. S. (1996). The growth of the firm in planned economies in transition: institutions, organizations and strategic choice, *Academy of Management Review*, vol. 21, pp. 492–525.

Pfeffer, J. (1993). Barriers to the advance of organizational science: paradigm development as a dependent variable, *Academy of Management Review*, vol. 18, pp. 599–620.

Piercy, N. F. (1995). Marketing and strategy fit together (in spite of what some management educators seem to think!), *Management Decision*, vol. 33, pp. 42–47.

Polzer, J. T., Milton, P., & Swann, Jr. W. B. (2001). Capitalizing on diversity: interpersonal congruence in small work groups, *Academy of Management Proceedings*, pp. h1–h6.

Powell, G. N. (1987). The effects of sex and gender on recruitment, *Academy of Management Review*, vol. 12, pp. 731–743.

Prasad, P., & Mills, A. J. (1997). From showcase to shadow: understanding the dilemmas of managing workplace diversity, in P. Prasad, A. J. Mills, M. Elmes, and A.

Prasad (eds.), *Managing the Organizational Melting Pot: Dilemmas of Workplace Diversity*. Thousand Oaks, CA: Sage, pp. 3–27.

Pratt, G. M., & Foreman, P. O. (2000). the beauty of and barriers to organizational theories of identity, *Academy of Management Review*, vol. 25, pp. 141–52.

Procter, S., & Mueller, F. (eds.) (2000). *Team working*. Basingstoke: Palgrave Macmillan.

Puffer, S. M. (2004). Introduction: Rosabeth Moss Kanter's Men and Women of The Corporation and the Change Masters, *Academy of Management Executive*, vol. 18, pp. 92–95.

Raatikainen, P. (2002). Contributions of multiculturalism to the competitive advantage of an organization, *Singapore Management Review*, vol. 24, pp. 81–88.

Ragins, B. R. (1997). Diversified mentoring relationships in organizations: a power perspective, *Academy of Management Review*, vol. 22, pp. 482–521.

Randel, A. E. (2000). How do members of groups diverse on multiple dimensions conceptualize one another? social contextual triggers and work group conflict implications of identity salience, *Academy of Management Proceedings*, GDO: A1–A6.

Randel, A. E., & Jaussi, K. S. (2003). Functional background identity, diversity, and individual performance in cross-functional teams, *Academy of Management Journal*, vol. 46, pp. 763–774.

Rapper, B., Webster, A., & Charles, D. (1999). Making sense of diversity and reluctance: academic-industrial relations and intellectual property, *Research Policy*, vol. 28, pp. 873–890.

Rausseau, R. (1997). Employing the New America, *R&I Exclusive*, March, pp. 40–52.

Ready, D. A. (2002). How storytelling builds next-generation leaders, *MIT Sloan Management Review*, Summer, pp. 63–69.

Reinmoeller, P., & N. Van Baardwijk, (2005). The link between diversity and resilience, *MIT Slogan Management Review*, vol. 46, pp. 61–65.

Riccucci, N. M. (1997). Cultural diversity program to prepare for work force 2000: what's gone wrong? *Public Personnel Management*, 26 (1), 35–41.

Richard, O. C. (2000). Racial diversity, business strategy, and firm performance: a resource-based view, *Academy of Management Journal*, vol. 43, pp. 164–177.

Richard, O. C., Barnett, T., Dwyer, S., & Chadwick, K. (2003). cultural diversity in management, firm performance, and the moderating role of entrepreneurial orientation dimensions, *Academy of Management Review*, vol. 47, pp. 255–266.

Richard, O. C., & Murthi, B. P. S. (2004). Does race matter within a multicultural context? alternate modes of theorizing and theory testing, *Academy of Management Best Conference Paper*, GDO: C1–C6.

Richard, O.C., McMillan, A., Chadwick, K., Dwyer, S. (2003) Employing an innovation strategy in racially diverse workforce. *Group & Organization Management*, 28 (1), 107-126.

Robbins, S. (2001). *Organizational Behavior*. New Jersey: Prentice-Hall.

Roberson, L., Kulik, C.T. & Pepper, M.B. (2003). Using needs assessment to resolve controversies in diversity training design. *Group & Organization Management*, 28(1), 148-174.

Roberson, Q. M., & Park, H. M. (2004). Diversity reputation and leadership diversity as a source of competitive advantage in organizations, *Academy of Management Best Conference Paper*, GDO: F1–F6.

Roberson, Q. M., & Park, H. J. (2007). Examining the link between diversity and firm performance: The effects of diversity reputation and leader racial diversity. *Group & Organizational Management*, 32, 548–569.

Robinson, G., & Decant, K. (1997). Building a business case for diversity, *Academy of Management Executive*, vol. 11, pp. 21–31.

Rodgers, J. O. (2002). Diversity management strategies bring rewards, www.elp.com, November, p. 8.

Rolfe, H., & Nadeem, S. (2006). *Opening up opportunities through advice and guidance*. Equal Opportunities Commission Working Paper Series no. x, Manchester: EOC.

Roper, A., Brookes, M., & Hampton, A. (1997). The multi-national management of international hotel groups, *International Journal of Hospitality Management*, vol. 16, pp. 147–159.

Rynes, S. (1995). A field survey of factors affecting the adoption and perceived success of diversity training, *Personnel Psychology*, 48 (2), 247–270.

Sacco, J.M. & Schmitt, N.W. (2003). The relationship between demographic diversity and profitability: A longitudinal study.

Paper presented at 18th Annual Conference of Society for Industrial Organizational Psychology, Orlando, FL.

Saltzstein, G. H. (1986). Female mayors and women in municipal jobs. <u>American Journal of</u> Political Science, 30, 140-164.

Sanches-Burks, J., Nisbett, R. E., & Ybarra, O. (2000). Cultural styles, relational schemas and prejudice against out-groups, *Academy of Management Proceedings*, OB: pp. G1–G6.

Sanchez, J. I., & Brock, P. (1996). Outcomes of perceived discrimination among Hispanic employees: is diversity management a luxury or necessity? *Academy of Management Journal*, vol. 39, pp. 704–719.

Schneider, S. K., & Northcraft, G. B. (1999). Three Social Dilemmas of Workforce Diversity in Organizations: A Social Identity Perspective, *Human Relations,* vol. 52, pp. 1445–1467.

Schoenberger, E. (1997). *The Cultural Crisis of the Firm.* Oxford: Blackwell.

Schuler, R. S., & Jackson, S. E. (1987). Linking competitive strategies with human resource management practices, *Academy of Management Executive,* vol. 1, pp. 207–219.

Senge, P. (1990). *The Fifth Discipline.* New York: Doubleday Press.

Shapiro, G. (2000). Employee involvement: opening the diversity Pandora's box? *Personnel Review,* vol. 29, pp. 304–323.

Shaw, M. (1993). Achieving equality of treatment and opportunity in the workplace, in R. Harrison (ed.), *Human Resource Management: Issues and Strategies.* Wokingham: Addison-Wesley Publishing Company.

Simmons, J. C. (2001). Addressing diversity in the health care setting to achieve quality care, *The Quality Letter*, December, pp. 2–9.

Simons, T., Pelled, H., & Smith K. A. (1999). Making use of difference: diversity, debate and decision comprehensiveness in top management teams, *Academy of Management Journal*, vol. 42, pp. 662–673.

Simpson, P., French, R., & Harvey, C. E. (2002). Leadership and negative capability, *Human Relations*, vol. 55, no. 10, pp. 1209–1226.

Skinner, D. (1999). The reality of equal opportunities: the expectations and the experiences of part-time staff and their managers, *Personnel Review*, vol. 28, pp. 425–438.

Slack, J. (1997). From Affirmative action to full spectrum diversity in the american workplace, *Review of Public Personnel Administration, 17*, 75–87.

Smith, J., & Barnes, M. (2000). Developing primary care groups in the new NHS: towards diversity or uniformity? *Public, Money and Management*, vol. 20, no. 1, pp. 45–52.

Smith, K. G., Smith, K. A., Olian, J. D., Sims, H. P., O'Bannon, D. P., & Scully, J. A. (1994). Top management team demography and process: the role of social integration and communication, *Administrative Science Quarterly*, vol. 39, pp. 412–438.

Smith, W. J., Wokutch, R. E., Harrington, K. V., & Dennis, B. S. (2004). organizational attractiveness and corporate social orientation: do our values influence our preference for affirmative action and managing diversity? *Business and Society*, vol. 43, pp. 69–96.

Solorzano, D. G., & Yosso, T. J. (2002). Critical race methodology: counter-storytelling as an analytical framework for education research, *Qualitative Inquiry*, vol. 8, no. 1, pp. 23–44.

Somers, M. R. (1998). We're no angels: realism, rational choice, and rationality in social science, *American Journal of Sociology*, vol. 104, no. 3, pp. 722–784.

Soni, V. (2000). A twenty-first century reception for diversity in the public sector: a case study, *Public Administration Review*, vol. 60, pp. 395–408.

Spender, J. C. (1989). *Industrial recipes: the nature and sources of managerial judgment*. Oxford: Blackwell.

Spich, S. (1995). Globalization Folklore: problems of myth and ideology in the discourse of globalization, *Journal of Organizational Change Management*, vol. 8, pp. 6–29.

Srinivas, K. M. (1995). Globalization of business and the third world: challenge of expanding the mindsets, *Journal of Management Development*, vol. 14, pp. 26–49.

Stedham, Y. E., & Yamamura, J. H. (2004). Measuring national culture: does gender matter? *Women in Management Review*, vol. 19, pp. 233–243.

Steingard, D. S., & Fitzgibbons, D. E. (1995). Challenging the juggernaut of globalization: a manifesto for academic praxis, *Journal of Organizational Change Management*, vol. 8, pp. 30–54.

Steward, R., & Barsoux, J. (1994). *The Diversity of management: twelve managers talking*. Basingstoke: Macmillan.

Stoner, C. R., & Russell-Chapin, A. (1997). Creating a culture of diversity management: moving from awareness to action, *Business Forum*, Spring/Fall, pp. 6–12.

Straw, J. (1990). *Equal opportunities.* Manchester: Equal Opportunities Commission.

Streufert, S., Pogash, R., Piasecki, M., & Post, G. M. (1990). Age and management: team performance, *Psychology and Aging*, vol. 5, pp. 551–559.

Stumpf, S. A., Watson, M. A., & Rustogi, H. (1994). Leadership in a global village: creating practice fields to develop learning organizations, *Journal of Management Development*, vol. 13, pp. 16–25.

Svyantek, D. J., Mahoney, K. T., & Brown, L. L. (2002). Diversity and effectiveness in the roman and Persian empires, *International Journal of Organizational Analysis*, vol. 10, pp. 260–283.

Swan, J., Newell, S., Scarbrough, H., & Hislop, D. (1999). Knowledge management and innovation: networks and networking, *Journal of Knowledge Management*, vol. 3, pp. 262–275.

Swann Jr., W. B., Polzer, J. T., Seyle, D. C., & Ko, S. J. (2004). Finding value in diversity: verification of personal and social self-views in diverse groups, *Academy of Management Review*, vol. 29, pp. 9–27.

Swap, W., Leonard, D., Shields, M., & Abrams, L. (2001). Using mentoring and storytelling to transfer knowledge in the workplace, *Journal of Management Information Systems*, vol. 18, no. 1, pp. 95–114.

Taylor, L. (2001). Melee Law, *People Management*, September, p. 55.

Thomas, D.A. (2004). Diversity as a strategy, *Harvard Business Review*, September, pp. 98–108.

Thomas, D. A., & Ely, R. J. (1996). Making Differences Matter: a new paradigm for managing diversity, *Harvard Business Review*, vol. 74, no. 5, pp. 79–90.

Thomas, R. R. (1990). From affirmative action to affirming diversity, *Harvard Business Review*, vol. 68, no. 2, pp. 107–117.

Thomas Jr., R. R. (1991). *Beyond race and gender: unleashing the power of your total workforce by managing diversity*. New York: AMACOM.

Thomas Jr., R. R. (1996). Redefining diversity, *HR Focus*, April, pp. 6–7.

Thomas Jr., R. R. (1999). Diversity management, *Executive Excellence*, vol. 16, pp. 8–9.

Thompson, F. J. (1991). Equal employment opportunity and representation. In F. J. Thompson (Ed.), *Classics of public personnel policy* (2nd ed., pp 227-235). Pacific Grove, CA: Brooks-Cole Publishing Co.

Thorne, D., & Davig, W. (1999). toppling disciplinary silos: one suggestion for accounting and management, *Journal of Education for Business*, November/December, pp. 99–103.

Tichy, N. M. (1974). Agents of planned social change: congruence of values, cognitions and actions, *administrative science quarterly*, vol. 19, no. 2, pp. 164–182.

Todd, S. (2002). Stakeholder perspectives: a personal account of an equality and diversity practitioner's intervention experience, in N. Cornelius (ed.), *Building Workplace Equality: Ethics, Diversity and Inclusion*. London: Thomson, pp. 265–95.

Triandis, H. C., Krowski, L. L., & Gelfand, M. J. (1994). Workplace diversity, in Triandis, H. C. & Dunnette, M. D. (eds.), *Handbook of Industrial and Organizational Psychology*. Consulting Psychologists Press, Palo Alto, CA, vol. 4, pp. 769–827.

Triandis, H. K. (1992). Workplace diversity. In M. D. H. C. Triandis, *Handbook of Industrial and Organizational Psychology* (pp. 770–827). Palo Alto, CA: Consulting Psychologists Press.

Tsui, A. S. (1992). Being different: relational demography and organizational attachment. *Administrative Sceince Quarterly, 37*, 549–579.

Tsui, A. S., & Ashford, S. J. (1991). Reactions to demographic diversity: similarity-attraction or self-regulation, *Academy of Management Proceedings*, pp. 240–244.

Tsui, A. S., Egan, T. D. & O'Reilly, C. A., III (1992). Being Different: Relational Demography and Organizational Attachment, *Administrative Science Quarterly*, vol. 37, pp. 549–79.

Tsui, A. S., & Gutek, B. (1999). *Demographic differences in organizations: current research & future directions*, Lexington Books, New York.

Tyson, S. (1995). *Human resource strategy: towards a general theory of human resource management*. London: Pitman Publishing.

Uran, C. (2005). Assimilation and exoticisms: the dialectic of diversity management, *American Quarterly*, June, pp. 583–592.

Vance, C. M. (1991). Formalizing storytelling in organizations: a key agenda for the design of training, *Journal of Organizational Change Management*, vol. 4, no. 3, pp. 52–58.

Van Der Vegt, G. S., & Bunderson, J. S. (2005). Learning and performance in multidisciplinary teams: the importance of collective team identification, *Academy of Management Journal*, vol. 48, pp. 532–547.

Van Der Vegt, G. S., & Janssen, O. (2001). The joint effects of psychological diversity and interdependence on individual performance, *Academy of Management Proceedings*, OB: pp. J1–J5.

Vechio, R. P., & Bullis, R. C. (2001). Moderators of the influence of supervisor-subordinate similarity on subordinate outcomes, *Academy of Management Proceedings*, GDO: pp. B1–B6.

Verloo, M., & Benschop, Y. (2002). Shifting responsibilities: the position of equal agencies in gender mainstreaming, *Management International*, vol. 7, pp. 93–101.

Volberda, H. W. (1998). *Building the flexible firm: how to remain competitive*. Oxford: Oxford University Press.

Wacquant, L. (2006). *Body and soul: notebooks of an apprentice boxer*. Oxford: Oxford University Press.

Walters, F. M. (1995). Successfully managing diversity, *Vital Speeches of the Day*, vol. 61, pp. 496–501.

Wanous, J. P., & Youtz, M. A. (1986). Solution diversity and the quality of group decision, *Academy of Management Journal*, March, pp. 149–158.

Ward, J., & Winstanley, D. (2004). Sexuality and the city: exploring the experience of non-white sexual identity through storytelling, *Culture and Organization*, vol. 10, no. 3, pp. 219–236.

Watson, W. E., Kumar, K., & Michaelsen, L. K. (1993). Cultural diversity's impact on interaction process and performance: comparing homogenous and diverse task groups, *Academy of Management Journal*, vol. 36, pp. 590–602.

Watts, A. G. (1996). Careers guidance and public policy, in A. G. Watts, B. Law, J. Killeen, J. M. Kidd, and R. Hawthorn (eds.), *Rethinking Careers Education and Guidance: Theory, Policy and Practice*. London: Routledge, pp. 380–91.

Webber, S.S. & Donahue, L.M. (2001). Impact of highly and less job-related diversity on work group cohesion and performance: A meta-analysis. *Journal of Management*, 27 (2), 141-162.

Weech-Maldo, R. (2002). Racial/ethnic diversity management and cultural competency: the case of Pennsylvania hospitals, *Journal of Healthcare Management*, vol. 47, pp. 111–24.

Weick, K. E. (1984). Small wins: redefining the scale of social problems, *American Psychologist*, vol. 39, pp. 40–49.

Weick, K. E. (1998). Theory construction as disciplined imagination, *Academy of Management Review*, vol. 14, pp. 516–31.

Weick, K. E., & Quinn, R. E. (1999). organizational change and development, *Annual Review of Psychology*, vol. 50, pp. 361–86.

Welch, D., & Welch, L. (1997). Being flexible and accommodating diversity: the challenge for multinational management, *European Management Journal*, vol. 15, pp. 677–685.

Wentling, R. R. (1998). Current status and future trends of diversity initiatives in the workplace: diversity experts perspective. *Human Resource Development Quarterly*, (3), 235–252.

Westley, F., & Mintzberg, H. (1989). Visionary leadership and strategic management, *Strategic Management Journal*, vol. 10, pp. 17–32.

Wharton, A. (1992). The social construction of gender and race in organizations: a social identity and group mobilization perspective, in Tolbert, P. T., and Bacharach, S. B. (eds.), *Research in the Sociology of Organizations*. JAR Press, Greenwich, CT, vol. 10, pp. 55–84.

Wharton, A. S., & Baron, J. N. (1987). So happy together? the impact of gender segregation on men at work, *American Sociological Review*, vol. 52, pp. 574–587.

Wheeler, R. D. (1997). Managing workforce diversity, *Tax Executive*, vol. 49, pp. 493–496.

Whiteley, J. (2004). Creating behavioral change in leaders, *Industrial and Commercial Training*, vol. 36, pp. 162–165.

Williams, K . Y., & O'Reilly, C. A . (1 998) . Demography and diversity in organizations: A review of 40 years of research. *Research in Organizational Behavior*, 20, 7 7- 1 40.

Wilson, E. M., & Iles, P. A. (1999). Managing Diversity—An Employment and Service Delivery Challenge, *The International Journal of Public Sector Management*, vol. 12, pp. 27–48.

Wise, L. R. (2000). Examining empirical evidence on diversity effects: how useful is diversity research for public-sector managers. *Public Administration Review, 60* (5), 386–402.

Wise, L.R. (1997). *Diversity research: a meta-analysis*. Stockholm, Sweden: Institute for Future Studies.

Wise, L. R., Tschirhart, M., Hosinski, D.K. and Bandy, L., (1997). *Diversity research: a meta-analysis.* Stockholm, Sweden: Institute for Future Studies.

Wise, L.R. and Tschirhart, M., (1999). *Can managing for diversity the public sector be informed by the empirical literature on diversity? An assessment and agenda.* Paper presented at: the Fifth National Public Management Research Conference, Texas A&M University, December 5.

Wiseman, J., & Dent, R. (2005). *Satisfaction levels amongst temporary agency workers.* research by BMG Research for the REC's Industry Research Unit, November. New York: NY

Woods, R. H., & Scidrini, M. P. (1995). Diversity programs in chain restaurants, *Cornell Hotel and Restaurant Administration Quarterly,* June, pp. 18–23.

Worman, D. (2001). Press home the advantage, *People Management,* November, p. 25.

Wright, P., Perris, S. P., Hiller, J. S., & Kroll, M. (1995). Competitiveness through management of diversity: effects on stock price valuation, *Academy of Management Journal,* vol. 38, pp. 272–287.

Yin, R. K. (2002). *Case study research: design and methods,* 3rd ed. Applied Social Research Methods Series, London: Sage.

Zander, A. (1994). *Making groups effective,* Jossey-Bass, San Francisco, CA.

Zanoni, P., & Janssens, M. (2003). Deconstructing the differences: the rhetoric of human resources managers' diversity discourse, *Organization Studies,* vol. 25, no. 1, pp. 55–74.

ABOUT THE AUTHOR

Dr. Shelton Goode is a diversity leader with over twenty years of human resource and business experience. He has held executive HR positions for companies ranging in size from $300M to $11B+ and has developed or implemented talent-management programs, performance-management systems, sales-incentive plans, labor-relations strategies, and large-scale culture-change initiatives. As a result, he has earned a reputation as a strategic, yet results-oriented, HR and business leader.

Dr. Goode learned the value of diversity management firsthand by rolling up his sleeves and providing CEOs and senior executives with counsel, insight, resources, tools, and innovative ideas that helped advance their companies' strategic business goals. For the last ten years, he has leveraged seasoned leadership and consulting skills to help companies implement diversity-management initiatives that enhanced their talent-acquisition, employee-retention, and employee-engagement strategies.

Dr. Goode has also used his knowledge and experience to teach and mentor others. In 1993, he was awarded the first-ever African American Doctoral Fellowship by Troy University and began teaching at the university in 1996. Since that time, he has been dedicated to helping adult learners achieve their educational goals. For example, as an adjunct professor at Troy University, Dr. Goode taught thousands of students in the school's Masters in Public Administration program. His teaching excellence was recognized when he received the school's prestigious Faculty Member of the Year Award in 2005. Dr. Goode leveraged his extensive teaching experience to publish his first book, *So You Think You Can Teach: A Guide for the New College Professor in*

Teaching Adult Learners. He is also the founder and CEO of My ABD Network, an organization that helps students succeed in doctoral education programs.

Dr. Goode, a highly decorated Air Force veteran, has not only served the country in time of war, but also consistently served his community in time of need. In July 2011, the Supreme Court of Georgia appointed him to the State Bar Ethics Investigative Panel. He was one of only three nonlawyers serving on this prestigious panel. He co-chaired the Conference Board Diversity and Inclusion Leadership Council and has served on the board of numerous professional organizations, such as the Atlanta Compliance and Ethics Roundtable, American Association National of Blacks in Energy, Society for Human Resource Management, and the Atlanta and Diversity Management Advocacy Group. The National Association of African Americans in Human Resources awarded him their HR Trailblazer Award in 2005 and 2012—he was the only person selected for the award twice. In April 2013, the Technology Association of Georgia presented him with the organization's first Lifetime Achievement Award for his body of work in diversity management and human resources.

Dr. Goode received his bachelor's degree from Southwest Texas State University (now Texas State University) and his master's degree in Human Resource Management from Troy University. He obtained his doctorate in Public Administration from the University of Alabama. Dr. Shelton Goode speaks nationally on a variety of human resource management and diversity topics.

INDEX

CPSIA information can be obtained at www.ICGtesting.com
Printed in the USA
BVOW05s1718250214

345951BV00006B/16/P